Longman sociology of education

Social Psychology: Theories and discussions

Longman sociology of education

Social Psychology:
Theories and discussions

W. T. Edwards

Longman

LONGMAN GROUP LIMITED
London

*Associated companies, branches and
representatives throughout the world*

First published 1974
ISBN 0 582 32455 6 *cased edition*
ISBN 0 582 32456 4 *paper edition*

*Printed in Great Britain by
Lowe & Brydone (Printers) Ltd., Thetford, Norfolk*

Contents

Part 1

Social influences on the individual

In this first part, we consider the individual as the focus of influences emanating from society in general, from face-to-face groups such as the family, and from other individuals. We shall see that the transaction between individual and society is marked by the conferring of social advantages in return for conformity to group norms.

1

Society and self

Without society, man would not be human (G. H. Mead)

In our society and time, much discussion, especially among younger people, seems to revolve around the idea of conflict between society and the individual. Society and the individual are seen as protagonists in a never-ending battle, with society being cast in the role of a policeman or oppressor trying to force a straightjacket on to an individual who is struggling to 'be himself'. There is, of course, some truth in this picture; there *is* friction between these two. Such friction may, however, be analogous to what happens in a transaction between buyer and seller in a marketplace. The fact that each may be very dependent on the other does not prevent haggling over the price. In a similar way, a satisfactory balance must be achieved between the individual and the others who form society. Society's constraints on an individual may be less important than society's contribution to the making of that individual.

In our making, each one of us receives a unique genetic endowment, although we should avoid being so entranced by the differences between people that we forget their remarkable basic similarity. This genetic endowment is only a part, however, of what becomes our personality. Much of what we become results from development or learning taking place in social contexts, in interactions with others. Of these social interactions, the ones which are most fundamental to our development are those which occur in what Cooley called 'primary groups'. These are the small groups, such as the family, in which each member can interact face-to-face with each other member and in which influence is mutual. We shall have more to say later about these groups. They certainly exact much from the individual, especially in the way of conformity to the group norm, but the relationship is one of reciprocal benefit. 'There is no natural opposition of man and society' (Lindesmith and Strauss, 1968).

In return for the price of conformity, the individual receives the numerous benefits which accrue from group membership. Man would not be human but for the influence of these primary groups. They are, in the words of Cooley (1902), 'the great incubators of human character'.

The point about reciprocity becomes clearer if we consider what another social psychologist, Abram Maslow (1943), called 'the ladder of wants, from the belly to the brain'. These wants, needs or basic goals he saw as being characteristic of all the many different Western societies which he had studied. They were needs for:

(*a*) physiological satisfaction
(*b*) safety, both physical and psychological
(*c*) belongingness, love and affection
(*d*) self-esteem, status, respect
(*e*) self-actualization.

Maslow arranged them in this ladder because, he said, 'the appearance of one need usually rests on the prior satisfaction of another, more pre-potent need'. Teachers have long been forced to acknowledge the validity of this point. Between the wars it was all too evident that many children could not learn on empty bellies, whereas now that most children in this country are adequately fed, emphasis has moved to the next rung, to the well fed pupil whose attention is concentrated more on his problems of psychological insecurity than on his lessons. In fact, sociologists have recently paid increasing attention to the upper rungs of the ladder, emphasizing the failure of our schools system to satisfy the self-esteem and self-actualization needs of sizeable numbers of their pupils. Schools are, of course, particularly concerned with self-actualization but this is of little use until the more prepotent needs have been satisfied. It is an interesting exercise to determine the part played in the satisfaction of needs (*a*) to (*e*) by the family, peer groups and school.

The other point stressed by Maslow was that it is characteristic of humans to go on climbing this ladder, to be continually revising their aims in an upward direction. 'It is quite true that man lives by bread alone—when there is no bread. But what happens to man's desires when there *is* plenty of bread and when his belly is chronically filled? At once other (and higher) needs emerge and these, rather than physiological hungers, dominate the organism. . . . What a man *can* be, he *must* be'. What becomes clear from a consideration of Maslow's list is that as humans develop so they generate new wants, wants which are linked with the emergence of what is called a 'self-concept'. In the next chapter we will attempt to show how this self-concept plays a crucial part in human behaviour and learning but before we do so we must, in this chapter, discuss the origins of this self-concept and note, in particular, the contributions made to it by society.

The self-concept

The self-concept is generally thought of as including three elements:

1. The self-image is the impression or picture we have of ourselves.
2. The ideal-self is the image we have of ourselves as we could be, ought to be or would like to be.
3. Self-esteem consists of the feelings we have about the self we see, as might be illustrated when a person says, 'I'm annoyed with myself'.

Let us take these elements in turn.

The self-image

Imagine yourself in a situation where you are confronted by a table on which is a pile of about one hundred cards. The first one you pick up has written on it the words 'I am shy'. The next one you pick up says 'I am optimistic'. Each successive one you pick up has a different adjective, such as 'confused', 'impulsive', 'unreliable', 'worthless', 'poised' or 'tolerant'. You are asked to sort these cards into a number of piles arranged on a continuum from a pile at one end containing those cards most descriptive of you to a pile at the other end containing those cards you think are least descriptive of you. When you have finished, you will have given the tester a fairly accurate picture of what you think you are like. This picture we can call the self-image.

The most commonly used procedure for measuring the self-image is the 'Q-sort test' which we have just described. Another method commonly used would be a self-rating scale where a subject might be asked to respond to perhaps fifty trait-names by ticking each on a five-point scale. Highly structured tests such as Q-sorts and rating scales allow you to choose only from what is provided by the tester and may possibly miss out something fairly significant. They do, however, allow comparisons to be made fairly easily between different people and between an individual's self-image at one time and at another time. An open-ended procedure, such as writing an essay on 'myself', might allow for the unusual but illuminating flash, but is less easy to score and use for comparison.

Obviously there are pitfalls in these processes. We cannot be quite sure that the picture we are given is an accurate representation of the self-image. To give one example; the human being, since he is capable of such internalized interaction as 'I think he thinks this, so I had better...', is liable to distort his answers in order to fit better the picture he thinks the tester will consider desirable. Such answers would be called 'social desirability' responses. Despite such difficulties, there is an increasing use of such self-image measures and the measures themselves are being continually refined. This increase reflects the growing conviction among many psychologists that the information gained is central to the understanding of human behaviour.

The existence of a self-image can be illustrated by a consideration of statements which we must often make to ourselves, statements such as 'I think I know myself quite well', or 'I just cannot understand myself doing such a thing', or 'I think I'm pretty good at . . .'. A curious thing about being human is that one part of oneself, the 'I', is able, as it were, to stand apart and regard the other part of oneself, the 'me', as an object about which the 'I' has knowledge and opinions.

Emergence of the self-image

The crucial ability to regard oneself as an object is not one which the human being possesses at birth. The infant of six months probably has no clear notion of himself as a differentiated entity; at two years the child is still commonly misusing personal pronouns. By about five, however, he has developed a fairly clear picture of himself as a distinct person with his own peculiar pattern of characteristics and it is in terms of himself as a total, unified being that he will tend to react to events and persons that impinge on him. This self-image is one which will go on developing in response to future experience but it will also have a profound effect on the way these experiences are selectively perceived and responded to.

Probably the first part of the self-image to emerge is the body-image. The infant gradually comes to perceive portions of his physique and their allied sensations of pleasure and pain as constant elements in his many different experiences. He also extends this notion of self to those material objects, such as clothing and toys, which are being continually associated with his presence, much as an adult may extend his image of self to include his family or his car.

However, the most important element in ensuring that the self-image emerges with clarity is the development of language in the second and third years. The self-image is essentially the common factor which has been extracted from all one's experiences. In other words, it is formed much like other concepts and would be more difficult to attain without language. The child's own name, for example, is an important label attaching to these abstractions; it serves as 'an anchorage to our self-identity'. Again, the differentiation of 'I' and 'me' depends upon the capacity language gives us to symbolise ourselves and our acts. Statements we make to ourselves and about ourselves are illustrations of the individual's incorporation within his own personality of a social process, conversation.

Not all cultures lay the same degree of emphasis on the uniqueness of the individual and, therefore, on the clarity and strength with which the self-image emerges. It is 'the I of the Western man (which) sticks out like a stubbed thumb' (G. W. Allport, 1961). This reflects different patterns of 'socialization', which is the term used to denote the process by which an individual comes to accept the norms of behaviour and, later, the attitudes and values of his social group. Socialization involves the nudging of the individual, by rewards and punishments, in the direction of the particular ideals of that society. One society may have an image of the ideal person in which cooperation is emphasized; another may emphasize competitiveness. The child comes first to imitate the behaviour it sees and ends, usually, by internalizing the values or ideals of society, which then appear as his own. This process of bringing the individual child to an acceptance of the ways of his society is undertaken mainly by the small, face-to-face groups, especially the family. The family's work is reinforced and extended by institutions such as Cubs, Brownies and, of course, the school, as observation and analysis of an infant school assembly would clearly illustrate. In return for acquiescence in this process, the individual receives from these groups satisfaction of his basic needs. These 'primary' groups also contribute fundamentally to the individual's developing self-image.

According to Cooley's 'looking-glass theory' of the self, our self-image is built up largely from reflections from the minds of others. It is when others treat us as though we were intelligent or friendly or untrustworthy or 'C'-stream that we gradually come to see ourselves as such. To put it more precisely, our self-images are formed largely on the basis of what we *think* others think of us. We may, of course, be misperceiving what these others think, but this is a point we shall leave to chapter 5.

An individual's self-image is not, however, equally influenced by the reflections from all others. Some others, such as parents, friends and (it may be hoped) teachers, are much more significant to us (Manis, 1955; Dornbusch and Miyamoto, 1956); we are usually very concerned with trying to imagine what we look like from their standpoint. As Mead has described it, the individual puts himself into the role of the 'significant other'. Later, the individual develops a synthesis of his interactions with many people over a long time and is able to put himself into the role of the 'generalized other'. 'What would *people* think if I did that?' is a question we often ask ourselves and for which we provide our own generalized answer.

Frequently, we may discriminate among these generalized others by categorizing them. Thus we may ask ourselves what a typical teacher or typical prospective employer would think of our contemplated behaviour; we categorize others and their reactions to us. At the same time, others are categorizing us and indicating to us, by their behaviour towards us, what these categorizations are. When a student perceives teachers and pupils behaving towards him as they would to other teachers, he comes the more readily to accept himself as a teacher. Others' categorizations, as perceived by us, come to be internalized in our self-images.

One view of socialization is that of society providing a range of categories, or positions and roles, for the individual to grow into. Each position and its associated role has attached to it a set of expectations or norms concerning behaviour. To describe a person as a father, teacher and churchwarden would be to describe also much of his likely behaviour. This is not to say that the process is entirely one way; influence is reciprocal. Individuals *can* and do bring some idiosyncrasy into their playing of a role; society *can* gradually change in response to the changing activities of its members. By and large, however, the pressure is great upon the individual to develop roles that are already delineated. The more an individual throws himself into a role and the more totally or 'organismically involved' (Sarbin and Jones, 1956) he becomes in the part, the more likely it is that the role will bite inward on his personality, that the mask will make a more permanent impression upon the face and perhaps, eventually, even become the face. It was Waller, in 1932, who described how the collar and tie donned by the young teacher each morning became, at length, a plaster cast which he could not remove. People tend to become, eventually, what they do.

If roles and personality are intertwined in this way then the positions we occupy and the roles we play in society are an important part of our self-image. They are indications to us of how we are regarded by others. As children grow into adults they tend more and more to describe themselves in terms of such roles. Thus, an analysis of self-descriptions given by over a thousand adults in Iowa (Kuhn, 1960) showed that the most common descriptions of self were in terms of family relationships, especially for women, and occupations, especially for men. At the time of writing there are, unfortunately, many examples before us, among redundant middle-aged executives and unemployed school-leavers, of the undermining effects on the self-concept of being labelled as occupational rejects.

To summarise thus far, we have said that the self-image begins as a body-image and is considerably clarified and strengthened by the use of language. The human being is in this way unique, presumably, among animals. The self-image is to a considerable extent moulded by our perceptions of the reactions to us of 'significant' and 'generalized' others and by our internalisation of many of the norms or expectations which society has organized in the form of roles it provides for us to grow into and play. To Mead, the 'me' represented 'the community in the individual'.

The ideal-self

Imagine once again that you are confronted by the same table and one hundred cards of the kind that we described at the beginning of this chapter. The cards have written on them such descriptions as 'I am curious' or 'I am efficient'. This time you are asked to sort them in the same manner, but not according to how you see yourself but according to how you think you hope to be or could be or should be. This time the Q-sort will be describing not your self-image but your ideal-self image.

This ideal-self image arises largely from the subject's perceptions of the expectations others have for him. Expectations set before us by parents and by social institutions such as church and school become internalized into a conscience which can be viewed as an ideal to which we feel we ought to direct ourselves. Conscience 'becomes a kind of generic self-guidance' (Allport, 1961).

Overlapping with this is the process of modelling ourselves on others. One analysis of compositions on the subject 'The person I would like to be like' showed how the model changed with age (Havighurst *et al*, 1946). Between the ages of six and eight, subjects tended to choose family members; from eight to sixteen they chose glamorous persons such as film stars and athletes; after sixteen, attractive visible adults were the models, but this gave way to a model who was a composite, imaginary person. We should also note the existence of cultural and subcultural (e.g. social-class) stereotypes of the ideal person, the ideal male, the ideal female, and so on. For example, in some subcultures it would be tantamount to social suicide for a boy to express any tender feelings. These stereotypes are, to varying degrees, absorbed into the individual's ideal-self image.

Self-esteem

Whereas self-image refers to how a person sees himself, self-esteem is concerned with his *feelings* towards this self that he sees. In general, he may feel worthy or unworthy as a person. A subject using such a technique as Q-sorting may draw two separate profiles, one for his self-image and one for his ideal-self image. Alternatively, he may tick an adjective-list, once for 'as I am' and once for 'as I would like to be'. Where the gap between the two profiles is small, high self-esteem is indicated, whereas a large discrepancy indicates a state of low self-esteem in which the subject sees himself as falling far short of his own ideals. Correlations have been found between levels of self-esteem and a host of other factors, but before summarizing these findings we should emphasize that to establish a correlation between self-esteem and another factor does not tell us which is cause and which is effect; the two might, in fact, be related only through having some common parent factor.

Very high self-esteem is often regarded with suspicion by psychologists who realise that it may be based on an unrealistic self-appraisal and the denying or suppressing of threatening features (Block and Thomas, 1955). Friedman (1955), for example, found unusually high self-esteem to characterize a group of paranoid schizophrenics. What is generally regarded as healthy is a moderately small discrepancy such as marks most normal persons who set themselves realizable goals and, having attained them, revise them slightly in an upward direction. On the other hand, low self-esteem, as indicated by a large gap between self and ideal-self, is usually seen as 'one of the basic elements of neurosis' (Rosenberg, 1965). Those with low self-esteem have been found by most researchers to be characteristically self-centred, anxious, insecure and easily persuaded; to exhibit inferiority feelings, compensatory behaviour and depression; to set themselves unrealistic goals. Wylie (1961), in her survey of research, found some support for the idea that success in psychotherapy was often related to a lessening of the self/ideal-self gap and the inducing of greater self-acceptance.

That the way a person feels about himself has important consequences for his relationships with others is suggested by the correlation that has been found between self-acceptance and the acceptance of others. Those with lower self-esteem tend to feel more alienated from others, to be 'lone wolves'. According to Rosenberg, the 'egophobe' has low faith in himself and in others and believes that others have a low opinion of him; he therefore avoids groups.

From what we said earlier about the social origins of the self-concept, we might expect a clear correlation between self-esteem and social-class, with the 'lower' classes revealing lower self-esteem. In fact, such correlation as has been found is relatively insignificant, at least in the U.S.A. The explanation is suggested by a consideration of William James's simple formula

$$\text{Self-esteem} = \frac{\text{Success}}{\text{Pretensions}}$$

from which we can see that a middle-class youth with aspirations of becoming a doctor is as likely to feel himself a failure as a working-class youth with aspirations to become a plumber (Knight, 1950). What has to be realized is that although evaluations are partly against the standards of society at large they are even more firmly related to the standards of the primary groups with which the individual interacts in a face-to-face way, his 'effective interpersonal environment'. For instance, Rosenberg (1965) found, in the U.S.A., that self-esteem was based on relative prestige *within* a class or ethnic group rather than *between* groups. But, if a member of a minority group mixes with other groups then he is more likely to feel the low or high status of his group. For example, Catholics raised in non-Catholic neighbourhoods were more likely to have low self-esteem and to report more psychosomatic symptoms than Catholics raised in Catholic neighbourhoods. For the most part, comparisons on which our self-esteem may rest are made with friends, neighbours and colleagues rather than with more distant groups.

Identity and adolescence

What we have said about the self-concept, in its three aspects of self-image, ideal-self and self-esteem, can be illustrated in more detail by reference to the particular stage in development we call adolescence.

By the age of about twelve, most children have attained a relative stability of the self-image, but with adolescence they have to go through much of the process anew. First there comes a spurt in body-growth which not only equals that of early childhood but is also accompanied by sexual maturation. The adolescent now has to accommodate himself or herself to a new body-image. Early and late developers may be particularly self-conscious at this time and it is known that some persons may retain into adulthood the self-image which was suited to their adolescent state. Brookover (1964) quotes a case of a girl who at thirteen was taller than others of her age and who still had this image of herself in adulthood, when it was no longer true.

At the same time, adolescence is often characterized by a lowering of self-esteem, especially among the more intelligent. Katz and Zigler (1967), in a study of 120 children aged 10, 13 and 16, found that the self/ideal-self gap increased with age and I.Q. The more mature and more able a person is, they suggest, the more capacity he has to create problems for himself. Thus, as a concomitant of higher cognitive ability comes a greater capacity for self-derogation, guilt and anxiety. The authors go on to question the implicit assumption that anxiety is essentially a negative agent, but we shall postpone discussion of this point to a later chapter.

Another important change occurring in adolescence is the child's breaking away from the family, a rupturing of the psychological umbilical cord. This is a necessary establishing of independence, but if we remind ourselves that Maslow put 'belongingness' as the third most potent of human wants—we then see how big a step this is. The fundamental need to belong is, however, satisfied by the adolescent peer group, which assumes great importance and acts as a staging point for the individual in the journey from his belongingness in the family in which he was a child to his belongingness in the family which he creates.

Adding to the difficulties these changes engender is the status ambiguity which besets the teenager in our society. People are ambivalent towards him, one moment reminding him that he is not an adult and the next moment expecting him to behave like one. Little wonder that the self-image becomes confused! Some simpler societies, where a brief initiation ceremony ends in full adult recognition, can avoid this particular hazard, but our complex society has been requiring longer apprenticeship in school and

13

college just when physical maturity has been occurring at an earlier age.

One way in which the adolescent may dodge some of the discomfort of this status ambiguity is by spending more time in the company of other adolescents who are his equals or peers. Yet he cannot opt out of his family or school. This concurrent membership of a number of groups may give rise to conflict if these groups entice him towards different stereotypes of ideal-image, or life style, and expose him to different sets of expectations. Choices between staying on at school or early leaving, between the solitariness of homework and the social attraction of the peer group, or between the short-term goal of pocketmoney, fun and belonging, and the long-term goal of academic qualifications and their associated but 'deferred gratifications', are all closely linked with the conflicting expectations of his family, friends and school. In the case of a middle-class child there is probably more chance that at least one of the other two groups is pulling in the same general direction as the school, whereas in the case of many a working-class youngster the school is engaged in a losing tug-of-war against the combined pull of family and peer group.

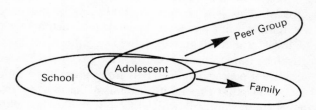

Fig. 1.1

The teacher or parent who realizes that it may be normal in adolescence for the peer group to carry more weight than the family or the school, through its ability to satisfy the basic need of belonging, may be less offended at being relegated to second or third place and may, in fact, more readily look for ways of working with and through a group rather than against it. 'If you can't beat 'em . . .'

Adolescence is also a time when a ripening of physique and

abilities coincides with the appearance on the horizon of the responsibilities of the adult world. In late adolescence the individual begins to give serious consideration to his future roles in marriage and occupation. It is a time for forward projection, for the establishing of a consistent life style and the clarifying of defining objectives. So much is possible, but he must start settling for something. One's identity, one's location in the adult social world, who and what and how valued one is; all these need to be established, and they are established for the individual only insofar as they are constructed in the process of interaction with those around him. Badges have to be negotiated for. Thus, Mr X will indicate to those about him that he is these things: teacher, important person, intelligent, dependable and considerate family man, mushroom-grower, Arsenal fan, worth £x per annum. If those with whom he is interacting open doors for him, direct difficult problems his way, seek his advice on mushrooms, remind him when Arsenal lose and so on, they are acknowledging that he carries those badges. It is, however, adolescence which is the age *par excellence* for such bargaining. In their sometimes crude attempts at impression management (Goffman, 1969), adolescents' changes in dress, hair style, handwriting or form of Christian-name are as common as a politician's pre-election pipe. They indicate the precariousness of the new self-image, as also do the slavish conformity to peer group norms and the avid attention to the reactions of others, albeit hidden by a self-protective shell of 'couldn't care less'. Where adolescence ends and maturity takes over is a matter for some debate, but it probably has as much to do with acceptance of the self, by oneself and by others, as with anything else.

This precariousness of the adolescent self-image was well characterized by Erikson (1965), who saw the adolescent's chief problem to be his need to resolve the conflict between the forces of integration and diffusion, or between identity and role confusion. What he saw as factors contributing to role confusion in the individual were doubts as to sexual identity and, more frequently, the inability to settle on an occupational identity. He argued that those adolescents most affected by this 'crisis of identity' are the ones most likely to be involved in those revolutions of our day that 'attempt to solve and also to exploit the deep need of youth to re-define its identity in an industrialized world'.

Summary

Man shares with the lower animals the basic needs for physiological satisfaction, security and, presumably, belongingness. Where, however, man differs is in the way he develops, particularly through his use of language, a self-concept which generates higher needs for self-esteem and self-actualisation. This means that need-reduction theories which may be sufficient to explain most of the behaviour of rats and pigeons may not be sufficient to explain any but the earlier and simpler manifestations of human learning.

This self-concept, which is so crucial a feature of the human individual, can arise only in social interaction and society can not, therefore, be considered inimical to the development of the indivi- dual. The fact is that only within society and, particularly, its primary groups can the individual find satisfaction of his basic needs and develop and express his most human characteristics. Other persons are fundamental to the emergence of those parts of personality which we label 'self' and 'identity'. This is the broad backcloth against which we can see in perspective such problems as the often-discussed 'alienation' of young people from the society in which they live. What these young people are agitating against is not, presumably, society *per se* but some features of its present systematization. What many are calling for is an 'alternative' society in which some of the wheels of the present system are realigned or rebalanced.

Not only does the self arise out of interactions with others; it also, once formed, has a profound effect in guiding our interaction with others. It is to the effects of the self-concept on behaviour, particularly the sorts of behaviour with which schools are concerned, that we turn in the next chapter.

Discussion and further study

First, see Introduction, page viii.

1. *Maslow*. (i) Do you agree with his arrangement of wants according

to their pre-potency? (ii) Which groups may satisfy these various wants? (iii) How far are needs (*c*), (*d*) and (*e*) satisfied or thwarted by schools you know or have read about? e.g. Lumley Secondary, in Hargreaves (1967).

2. *Socialization*. Observe, analyse and discuss an episode of inter-action between an adult (e.g. teacher, parent, cub-leader) and a young child or group (e.g. infant-school age). Is any pressure exerted? If so, how, and in what directions? Is such socialization un/desirable, un/avoidable or what?

3. *Self-concept*. (i) Read the article by Purkey (see Further reading, below). Assess your self-esteem score on any two of the scales and compare, if possible, with norms and range in your group. (ii) Does a positive correlation between self-esteem and alienation from others (Rosenberg, 1965) tell us anything about cause and effect? (iii) Do you think your own self-esteem is based more on comparisons with those close to you, such as relatives, class-mates or neighbours, than on comparisons with more distant groups?

4. *Roles, group membership and identity*. (i) Consider some role relationships in which you may emphasise different facets of your personality. e.g. with lecturer, peers, pupils, headmaster, colleagues, doctor, bank-manager. Think of, e.g. forms of address, deference, dominance, topics of conversation, appearance.

(ii) How far does the 'self' extend? What insults/compliments to other people or objects might you see as insults/compliments to yourself?

(iii) Allport (1961, p. 401) maintained that 'a proper assessment of personality will without fail include statements regarding: sex; age; occupation; social class; racial, national and regional member-ships; other relevant norms; roles in the principal groups to which the person belongs'. But he also insisted that 'personality is more than the subjective side of culture'. Make lists of memberships and principal roles for yourself and others you know well. How complete are such lists as descriptions of personality?

(iv) Do you agree that a person is, or becomes, what he does?

(v) Is it possible that some pupils may so adapt themselves to labels such as 'dunce', 'clown' or 'awkward' as to feel rewarded when teachers or others refer to them as such?

17

5. *Adolescence*. (i) Erikson's (1965) views were probably influenced by the phenomena of totalitarian youth movements in the 1920s and 30s. Are there modern parallels?

(ii) Adolescence is a time when the education system, with its career-determining examinations, puts a premium on individual or solitary work. Is this desirable? Is it avoidable? Is it true?

Further reading

(Details are given in the Reference section, p. 225).

For Maslow, see his article (1943) or his book *Towards a Psychology of Being*, (1968). A useful introduction to the work of James, Cooley, Mead, Goffman and Merton is ch. 6, 'Role theory', in *Theories in Social Psychology* by Deutsch and Krauss (1965). For Mead and 'symbolic interaction' see Lindesmith and Strauss (1968), also *G. H. Mead on Social Psychology*, Pt IV, 'Self', by A. Strauss (1964); more advanced are units 5 to 8 in the Open University D.283 course. On self-concept, Wylie's book (1961) is comprehensive but difficult to obtain; more easily available is an excellent article by W. W. Purkey, included in the Open University's E.281 course, unit 10, which gives detailed examples of self-concept measures suitable for school-children. Rosenberg (1965) *Society and the Adolescent Self-image* is excellent and readable. Erikson (1964), ch. 7 is worth reading on adolescence, while *Youth and the Social Order* by F. Musgrove (1964) is informative and thought-provoking. Two useful introductions to 'socialization' are Elkin (1960), *The Child and Society*, and units 5 to 9 in the Open University's D.100 course. On 'personality', two classic books are G. W. Allport (1961) and Vernon (1963).

2

Self and learning

A brief look at theory

Self-theory, associated with names such as William James, Cooley and Mead, came into prominence round about the turn of the century. During the first half of this century, however, Behaviourist psychology, deriving from the work of Watson, Pavlov and others, took the lead so that in the 1950s and 60s, under the particular influence of Skinner, it made a successful takeover in courses on psychology of education. Nevertheless, there have, of late, been growing signs of discontent with the limitations of these Stimulus Response learning theories.

If we consider the formulation Stimulus–Organism–Response (S–O–R), we can say that the Behaviourists were busy exploring the connections between the two observable parts (S–R), the ingoing stimulus and the outgoing response. The S–R bonds were regarded as the basic building-bricks of behaviour and it was hoped by some that complex human behaviour could be depicted as an elaboration of these simple bonds. They declined to make inferences about what went on inside the organism (O) as this was largely beyond direct, 'objective' observation. As an example at a simple level, we might observe a consistent link between you raising your hand to hit me (S) and me avoiding you (R). But, as Behaviourists, we would desist from making inferences about what went on inside me (the O), in the way of thoughts or feelings.

The Behaviourists have had considerable success in analysing and controlling the behaviour of animals such as pigeons and rats, but the limited success of their 'hollow-man' approach in adequately describing human behaviour, especially that occurring beyond the first few years, is leading more people to agree with Allport (1961) that 'to leave out this subjective pivot of personality (the sense of self) is to keep the rim but discard the hub of our problem'. Interest in self-theory seems, therefore, to be reviving and there is a slowly growing body of empirical evidence to lend substance to those more speculative ideas of the earlier philosopher-psychologists.

At the end of the nineteenth century, introspection was being enriched by contributions from sociology, clinical psychology and Gestalt psychology. The key ideas to emerge may be summarized as follows. The human animal, particularly through its acquisition of language, is able, as it were, to stand outside itself and regard itself as an object about which it has opinions and feelings. Once the self-concept has emerged, the human animal behaves towards its environment not in terms of discrete bonds between specific stimuli and specific responses but as a unified, organic entity. Hit a Christian and he might turn the other cheek rather than run away or hit you back. This organic unity develops its own pattern of self-direction, its own 'life style' (Adler) or 'theme' (Allport) which is aligned towards the ideal-self image. This organic unity also develops its own ways of perceiving or interpreting events, so that if we wish to understand a person's behaviour we need to see that he is reacting to his own private view of things, to his own 'phenomeno-logical world'. We need to see how things look through his eyes. In the human being, the gap (O) between the Stimulus and the Response is so large and so vital that to bypass its undeniable complexities for the sake of simplicity and objectivity is to seriously limit the relevance of psychology to man.

Once formed, the self-concept has important implications for perception, consistency of behaviour and predictability. It provides an inner frame of reference against which new experiences are measured and choices made. To an extent, it acts as a perceptual filter at an unconscious level, allowing in, or assimilating, those elements which confirm or enhance itself but denying or distorting, rather than accommodating to, those which do not fit. If I see myself as a person who is unprejudiced, I acknowledge confirmatory evidence but may deny, distort or rationalize contrary evidence. In some ways, the framework of the self is analogous to a filing cabinet where we may have categorized early information and allocated a file to each category; this could represent our perception of the 'reality' outside. Further information for which this framework is not prepared is liable to be left in the 'in-tray', or forced into an inappropriate file, or lost, thereby having little influence on our future behaviour. One answer is, of course, to be continually restructuring our filing cabinet to give it a better fit with reality but, as we shall see in the chapter on perception, this is something we tend to avoid doing.

Once we have developed patterns in the way we perceive the world, we have a basis for consistency in that behaviour which is guided by our perceptions. Consistency also follows from the emergence of the ideal-self image which draws so many of our actions into line with a 'lifestyle' or 'theme'. Such consistency is encouraged by pressures from society for predictability in individual behaviour; in fact, we might speculate that we tend to feel threatened by and to dislike those whose behaviour is unpredictable. The individual himself also seems very concerned that his values, opinions and actions should not conflict with one another or be out of line with the self-image. Seeing ourselves as consistent is probably necessary for an adequate sense of identity.

Conflict between self and learning

In the later part of this chapter, we shall deal with ways in which the self-concept can be more profitably harnessed to learning and this will largely centre around *how* we ask the pupil to learn. But first, in this section, we should discuss some of the ways in which conflict may arise from *what* we ask the pupil to learn.

A very important part of our self-concept and identity is tied to the early sex role training we receive. Children go through stages of compliance, identification with and internalization of (see pp. 44-47) the appropriate sex role as a result of picking up cues from significant and generalized others. The effect is often obvious even in our infant schools, where the five-year-old comes in with a developed self-concept which is going to influence his interpretation of experiences and his choice of which experiences to seek and which to avoid.

For instance, we may detect in many infant schools the conflict which occurs for many boys, particularly those from the working-class, between the 'he-man' ideal, which is part of their sex role training at home, and the 'overfeminization' of the teaching, particularly in poetry, drama and reading. One American study found that in the usual classroom conditions, under a female teacher, girls were more successful than boys in learning to read, but that this was reversed when the process was programmed and 'mechanized'. In this overfeminization, both content and manner are involved. The legions of little ducklings which waddle out of our reading-books seem not to have the strength or the skill to pierce that armour-suit of unexpressiveness within which our working-class boys, in particular, have been encased. One wonders also how much these pupils have already rejected of the potentially valuable linguistic experiences which are part of so many of our television productions for preschool children.

If we take as an example from a secondary school curriculum the appealing subject of Cookery, we can see two ways in which the sex role and social class elements within the self-concept may, again, interfere with learning. Firstly, boys generally avoid that applied chemistry which we call Cookery except, perhaps, in such places as seaports, where it can be related to such a manly career as being a ship's cook. Secondly, although girls are usually very keen on the subject, one wonders how many working-class girls, when asked to plan and cook an 'after-theatre supper' or a 'coffee-morning spread', will think 'this is not me' and begin to dissociate themselves from the subject.

Some American studies (summarized in Backman and Secord, 1968, pp. 42-3) have separated out an 'academic self-concept' and have found that for girls at the age of twelve it is correlated with performance in social studies only, whereas for twelve-year-old boys this 'academic self-concept' was not only more important than for girls but was correlated with performance in mathematics and science as well as social studies. Evidence is very sparse for any attempt to explain this difference by genetic factors so that one is forced to conclude that these boys and girls seem to have learned to evaluate their academic powers in terms of the expectations of their elders.

When that which we are asked to learn in school conflicts with the self-concept, tension results which can impede learning. Direct evidence on this is not plentiful, since experimenting with human subjects is not easy, but we may use one such experiment to illustrate the point (Cowen *et al*, 1955). The experimenters asked their subjects to give 'self' and 'ideal-self' responses to a list of adjectives. They then selected, for each subject separately, those adjectives which showed the least and those which showed the greatest discrepancy between the self and ideal-self responses. These adjectives were then paired with nonsense syllables and the subjects were asked to learn these pairs. It was found that the subjects had significantly greater difficulty in learning those pairs where the adjective had a greater 'conflictual' element, i.e. where it had been very differently scored for self and ideal-self. We must guess that these conflictual items divert our energies and attention or bring into action ego-defensive mechanisms which impede learning.

Ego-defence

What the psychoanalysts have chosen to call ego-defensive strategies, those which protect the self-image from deflation, include repression, denial, rationalization, projection and so on. We shall have more to say of them later, as in the chapter on attitudes.

The mechanisms of ego-defense (Freud's term) are sly devices by which we try to circumvent discomfort and anxiety. These self-protective strategies are common, but they do not by any means constitute the normal person's entire repertoire of adjustive actions. Often he faces up to his weaknesses and failings, and proceeds to cope with them realistically. He meets his guilt, his fears, his blunders head on, and works out a way of life that fully and consciously takes them into account and makes of them building blocks for a more integrated personal edifice. The opposite of defense, then, is coping. The neurotic shows much defense, less coping. In the healthy personality coping ordinarily predominates (G. W. Allport, 1961, p. 155).

Most persons are willing to devote much energy and ingenuity to the protection of their self-esteem and the avoidance of failure. In schools, as in our society in general, one of the commonest causes of a feeling of failure, as subjectively experienced, is the

23

competitive rank-ordering which has been our mainstay in seeking to keep children at their school work. In such a system, success for some is emphasized at the expense of emphasizing failure for others. The effect upon the self-esteem of those at the bottom end of a rank order is fairly obvious. What may be less obvious are the possible effects on some of those near the top. Remembering William James's point that self-esteem is a matter of success measured against one's own private aspirations, we can agree with him that the world's second best boxer could die of shame. One way of protecting one's ego in such a situation is to opt out. 'With no attempt, there can be no failure', (Knight, 1950). It is not only the second-ranked pupil who may opt out; so might the first-ranked, in anticipation of a possible dethronement.

One example of opting out of failure situations is provided by the spectacle of many intelligent adults trying hard to avoid situations where arithmetical computations are required, computations which should be easy enough for them. It may be that for many of these persons the trouble started in their primary schools when, for any number of relatively trivial reasons, they might have missed one key step and then internalized into their self-concept the failure reflected to them from the 'significant other' in a prompt and unambiguous rash of red crosses. One can think of few other instances where the processes of reinforcement theory and self-concept formation combine so effectively to polarise the 'good' and the 'bad'. Of course, once formed, the self-concept tends to sustain itself.

So adept does the individual become at the art of ego defence that it is sometimes difficult to distinguish its effects from those of 'real' physical or intellectual difficulties. An adult may go to such lengths as pretending defective eyesight to hide the fact that he cannot read or write. A pupil may successfully persuade a teacher to direct his energies to the solution of 'rational' difficulties which are merely decoys to divert attention away from the more sensitive areas of the self. He might, for example, prefer to explain his omission of homework by claiming lack of understanding rather than by an admission of a breakdown of relationships in the home. How often are we, as teachers, diverted into frontal attacks upon a shield in the deluded belief that it constitutes the real target?

That a person may wish to protect himself from failure may be easy enough to comprehend. What is more puzzling is the way in which some pupils seem to protect themselves from success. These cases are relatively rare but they tax the teacher's resources of understanding and technique to the limit. What does one do with a pupil who will not accept praise? How does one begin to understand such behaviour? The answer may lie in the self-sustaining character of the self-concept, as illustrated in the following experiment.

The experimenter, Silverman (1964), first of all obtained descriptions of self and ideal-self from his subjects and sorted them into those with high, moderate and low self-esteem. He then rigged a test situation in which he led half the subjects to believe that their results were better than average and the other half to believe that their results were worse than average. He found those subjects with high self-esteem to be more receptive to evidence of success than to evidence of failure, while those with low self-esteem were more receptive to evidence of failure than to evidence of success. He concluded, on the basis of this and other experiments, that there is a tendency for all subjects, whether they have high or low self-esteem, to allow in from the environment only that information which fits the self-concept. He contended that those with low self-esteem have adjusted themselves to this unfavourable picture of themselves in such a way that they are rewarded by its maintenance. Perhaps it serves as a justification for dependent behaviour; perhaps they have learned from past experience to lessen the anxiety of expected failure by not allowing their expectations to rise. If you expect to fall you will not easily be tempted to climb. Silverman's evidence was that by such unconscious ego defence mechanisms as avoidance, denial, projection and distortion of incoming information, his subjects were able to sustain their existing self-concept. You can learn to live with and to protect even an unfavourable self-concept.

It is worth mentioning another related suggestion that has been made by other experimenters (Jacobs *et al*, 1971). It is that individuals with low self-esteem are unusually receptive to affection when they realize it is being offered but that it is most difficult for them to recognize affectionate overtures when they occur. This might apply to children who have been exposed to rather violent swings of acceptance and rejection from parents and others.

This filtering of experience through the selective screen of the self-concept probably plays an important part in some of our most refractory educational problems. Many of the educational and social failures of our system are notoriously impervious even to the best-intentioned attempts to improve their self-esteem; they seem to develop a perverse pride in their perceived rejection by significant others such as parents, to the point of denying that their parents are significant to them. Their perceived rejection by generalized others such as 'school' or 'society' brings a similar defensive reaction.

Working with the self-concept

Let us return for a moment to Maslow, whom we discussed in the first chapter (pp. 4-5). Schools are concerned particularly with what Maslow (1943) called self-actualization, but the individual, although having a characteristic urge to get on with the development of his potentialities, has more prepotent needs which must be satisfied first. The problems we have been discussing in the previous section arise largely from the individual's preoccupation with these prior needs for belonging and self-esteem. Only when these are satisfied is he able to emerge from his ego-defensive shell and direct his own development with confidence. The two key words for those teachers who wish to assist in this process by working with, rather than against, the current of a life style are (i) acceptance and (ii) self-direction.

It is worth digressing here to look at some points from a field which has some similarities with teaching, namely, psychotherapy. Psychotherapy is particularly concerned with the needs for belonging and self-esteem, and with bringing the patient back into the open and into touch with experiences with which he can cope and through which he can develop. A psychotherapist who has much to say with regard to acceptance and self-direction is Carl Rogers, whose approach is variously labelled as Client-centred or Self-Directive. Rogers (1965) argued that personality change in the client or patient in psychotherapy came about not because of the professional qualifications and training of the therapist, not because of his special medical or psychological knowledge, not because of his ideological orientations to psychotherapy—psychoanalytic, Jungian, client-centred, Adlerian, Gestalt, etc., not because of his techniques in the interview, not because of his skill in making interpretations, but primarily or solely because of certain attitudinal characteristics in the relationship . . . These attitudes are: congruence or genuineness in the relationship; acceptance or prizing of the client; an accurate empathic understanding of the client's phenomenological world.

Of course, there are a number of important differences of milieu, practice and objectives between psychotherapy and teaching. Perhaps the most obvious is that the psychotherapist usually has one client at a time, whereas the teacher has a class of about thirty. Yet, both are concerned with change and learning. Rogers argues that a person will emerge from his shell into contact with educative experience only when he is assured that he will not be threatened or ridiculed as a person. He will put his foot forward only when he realizes that it will not be stamped upon.

If we attempt to translate Rogers's ideas on the training of therapists to the training of teachers, we should advocate more concern with the cultivation of empathy. We would select for training those who 'already possess a high degree of the qualities I have described . . . people who are warm, spontaneous, real and understanding . . . the essential elements appear to be not technical knowledge nor ideological sophistication, but human qualities'. He goes on to say that 'most of our professional training programmes make it *more* difficult for the individual to be himself, and more likely that he will play a professional role'.

There is insufficient space here to follow the argument about the applicability of Rogers's ideas to teaching. Different pupils in a class will have different levels of need and unless a much more individualized, one-to-one relationship between teacher and pupil becomes possible, perhaps the best that the teacher can do is to play a dual role as suggested later, in the chapter on leadership styles (pp. 135-40). Probably no one will deny the value of Rogers's emphasis on the teacher's acceptance of the pupil as a person, although much elucidation and discussion would be called for on how one can be unconditionally accepting and yet be, as Rogers advocates, oneself.

Perhaps it is safer to stay nearer the present and to quote a finding of Rosenberg's (1965) that suggests that satisfying a child's basic wants need not mean a complete acceptance of that child's whims and fancies. Where Rosenberg divided parents into three categories, 'punitive only', 'supportive only' and 'punitive and supportive', it was the last-named category whose children had the highest self-esteem. These children would be the ones to recognize most clearly that their parents were not indifferent to them, that they mattered to the significant others in their lives.

Earlier in this chapter we discussed the possible damaging effects of rank-ordering upon self-esteem and upon subsequent learning. Some teachers and schools have made efforts to reduce this damage by de-emphasizing competition between pupil and pupil and encouraging competition between a pupil and his own self-chosen target. Most children would naturally, as Maslow has said, continually revise their targets upward. However, we should be aware of the difficulties or limitations. Firstly, it is doubtful if in our present society, or perhaps in any society, we can eliminate competition, though we may reduce it. Secondly, though an individual might reduce his feelings of failure by measuring success against his own private system of values, he cannot detach himself entirely from the values of the society which has helped to make him. 'Self-values are not infinitely malleable and subservient to the demands of psychological comfort' (Rosenberg, 1965).

Having swung from what some people would regard as fantasy to pessimism, perhaps we should end this chapter on a note of reasonable optimism by referring to a recent and very interesting study carried out in four Somerset village schools. It concerned the effects of counselling on retarded readers. The experimenter (Lawrence, 1971) begins his article thus:

'Educational failure is personal failure' (NFER, 1968). The retarded reader sees himself not only as an inferior reader but as an inferior person. Since reading is a skill which adults around him regard as important, failure in this area tends to invade the whole personality. The result is a child who has

28

come to accept failure as inevitable and whose natural curiosity and enthusiasm for learning remain inhibited. . . . It is suggested . . . that in the treatment of retarded readers more attention should be paid to the child's emotional life. The usual system is to focus primarily on cognitive factors.

As subjects, Lawrence chose four groups of eight-year-old children all of whom were about two years retarded in reading age. Each group was matched for sex (8 boys and 4 girls), age, mental age and reading attainment. Over a period of six months, one group was a control group, (C), one received remedial reading, (R), one received remedial reading and counselling, (R+Co), and the fourth received counselling only, (Co). In the case of counselling only, each child was seen individually for twenty minutes each week.

Over the period of six months, the following were the average gains in reading ages made by each group, expressed in years:

Control	R	R+Co	Co
0·2	0·33	0·49	0·61

In fact, the only group to narrow the gap between reading age and chronological age was the one which experienced the indirect approach through counselling. We must now look at what was meant here by 'counselling'.

'Basically this involved a responsible, sympathetic adult, with status in the eyes of the child, communicating to the child that he enjoyed his company'. The counsellor was uncritical, friendly and totally accepting of the child's personality. Throughout, he was alert for 'opportunities of praising the child's personality (not his skills), and in so doing, building up his self-image'. Areas of the child's life which were covered included relationships with parents, siblings, peers, other relatives, hobbies and interests, aspirations, anxieties, attitude to school and attitude to self.

Among further points made by Lawrence are these: that during the six months, the counselled group showed greater than average improvement in the self-image; that the counselling could have been carried out by any sympathetic, intelligent layman, after brief instruction; that most of the children's problems stemmed from family relationships but that it had not been found necessary to involve parents or tackle home conditions. Interestingly, in view of what we said in chapter 1 about very high self-esteem, the boy who made least progress in reading was one who was 'unusually content'. He might have responded better to a more demanding learning situation than to counselling.

Bearing in mind the danger of generalizing from small samples, we can nevertheless appreciate how studies such as the one we have just described are gradually increasing the credibility of the theoretical points we have made earlier in these two chapters on the Self.

Conclusion

The self is a product of interaction between the individual and society. It emerges strongly in the second and third years, before which, according to Allport (1961), such 'quasi-mechanical principles' as reinforcement, conditioning and repetition can account for much of the learning which occurs. But, he says, this generating of a self-concept marks 'a discontinuity in the learning sequence', with the self becoming 'the principal source of subsequent learning'. It is as though, with the acquisition of language and self, a hitherto land-bound animal has taken wing into a new medium where different rules apply. What we need is a matching shift in our emphasis from 'the pessimistic and limited view of motivation based on the avoidance or relief of tension to the more positive concept of self-actualization and self-fulfilment' (Mouly, 1968). Motive power must come ultimately from the learner himself and this is more likely to be released where he is moving toward the realization of his ideal-self picture, towards goals and by methods which matter to him and which he has had a hand in deciding.

Perhaps, in pushing our pupil too hurriedly up the ladder of wants and in being too impatient to allow him to develop his own direction and motivation, we are making less speed in the long run. Piaget's findings with regard to stages of intellectual development may have certain parallels in the socio-emotional world. Certainly, it seems that the teacher's influence upon the self-actualization process will be greater where he has helped to ensure satisfaction of the basic needs of acceptance, belonging and esteem. This does not mean that we have to accept all the attitudes and behaviours of the pupil, but it is possible to disagree with such of these as we deem necessary without dismissing him as a total person. Once we have put him beyond the pale, we run the risk of having encouraged that stubborn pride in self which will resist any further attempt of ours at influence. This is a topic to which we shall return in the chapter on attitude-changing.

Discussion and further study

1. What are the basic principles involved in these orientations in psychology?

(*a*) Behaviourism: stimulus-response (S-R), conditioning and shaping: important names are Pavlov, Watson, Thorndike, Hull and Skinner.

(*b*) Gestalt ideas on perception and wholism.

(*c*) Piaget: assimilation, accommodation, restructuring.

Give one example for each of (*a*), (*b*) and (*c*) to illustrate their applicability to human learning.

2. What are the chief mechanisms of ego-defence as identified mainly by the psychoanalytic school? Identify examples to illustrate their working.

3. What are some various possible reactions to competitive rank-ordering of those children who come first, second or last? Do the ideas and terminology of ego defence apply here?

4. What various interpretations are possible in the case of a pupil's 'couldn't care less' attitude towards a school subject?

5. Do you agree that in 'traditional' mathematics there was a greater polarization than in other subjects between the better and the worse pupils? If so, do you agree that S–R theories and self-theories can help us understand the situation? Does 'modern' mathematics make such polarization less likely?

6. Consider examples of ways in which subjects or methods in schools may be in conflict with ideal-images based on (*a*) sex-role stereotypes and (*b*) social class stereotypes.

7. Would you agree that the good teacher's central strength lies in his attitudes to and empathy with his pupils? How far is the

31

teacher like the psychotherapist?—how far can he be?—is this the *main* function of all teachers or of any teachers? Are Rogers's views on professional training and roles applicable to teaching? Do his views conflict with those of Rosenberg?

8. Read the article by Lawrence (1971) on 'The effects of Counselling on Retarded Readers'. Can you suggest reasons why this approach *might not* work if it was used with more pupils, different pupils, different adults, or for a longer period of time?

Further reading

The first pages of this chapter touched on various orientations or schools within psychology. This is, of course, a huge field of study, but one comprehensive paperback to start with is Wright *et al,* (1970) *Introducing Psychology—an experimental approach.* See also G. W. Allport (1961) for an assessment of the 'quasi-mechanical' view (ch. 5) and on Gestalt ideas (pp. 538-48), both as applied to personality. On the self-concept in relation to order, values, consistency, stability and change, Kelvin (1969), *The Bases of Social Behaviour,* is very good although difficult in parts. On the mechanisms of ego defence, useful summaries may be found in Allport (1961), or in Adcock (1964), *Fundamentals of Psychology* ch. 17; useful passages on the more general psychoanalytic approach are Brown (1961), *Freud and the Post-Freudians,* ch. 1, and Miller (1966), *Psychology: the science of mental life,* ch. 15. Rogers (1965) contains his approach to psychotherapist–client relationships; for anyone wishing to understand better his contributions to curriculum and method changes in modern education, Rogers (1961), *On Becoming a Person* chs. 13, 14, 15 are seminal and thought-provoking. The article by Lawrence (1971) on the counselling of retarded readers is well worth reading in its entirety.

3

Birth order and sibling effects

In the first chapter we discussed some aspects of the development of personality in the context of social influences, particularly those found in primary groups, and quoted Cooley's view that the family was "the great incubator of human character'. In this chapter we put the family under a stronger lens and look more minutely at the way in which different positions and roles within it can be related to significant differences in personality, academic attainment and the learning of sex roles. In particular, we shall concern ourselves with birth order effects and interaction between siblings, that is, children in the same family.

If it can be demonstrated that there are personality differences between firstborn and secondborn children, it can also be argued that these may be due to factors arising at or before birth. For instance, it has been found that secondborn babies are more active than are firstborn babies (Sutton-Smith and Rosenberg, 1970). It is also possible that birth is more difficult in the case of the firstborn and that this generates greater anxiety in these children. The evidence of relationship between birth order and genetic differences between individuals is, however, very limited, so that if personality differences can in any way be systematically linked with birth order it is very likely that they are attributable to differences in social experiences. What we shall see, in fact, is that any one family cannot provide an identical environment for each of its children.

Important literature on this subject dates back to Adler (1945) who, in the early decades of this century, made some interesting observations about different positions in the 'family constellation' and, particularly, about the effects upon the firstborn child of being 'dethroned' by later arrivals. Interest then waned until the publication of Schachter's (1959) book, *The Psychology of Affiliation*. Since then, empirical studies have multiplied rapidly, the most thorough review of these being in *The Sibling* by Sutton-Smith and Rosenberg (1971). Since so much of what we are going to say in this chapter rests on evidence from such empirical studies, it would be wise to make a few general points regarding them.

One complication which arises when one is attempting to compare different studies arises from the use of differing categorizations. For instance, two studies may be concerned with firstborn children but one may be referring to only children and the other to eldest children. Similarly, where one researcher refers to a category of 'later-born' children another might deal with subdivisions such as 'youngest' and 'middle-born'.

Further difficulty comes in interpreting the findings of empirical studies. Most of the human behaviour in which we are interested is the result of multiple-causation and the interaction of a large number of factors and it is very difficult to control all these factors in experiments and studies. As a result, there may be a number of alternative or overlapping explanations for what is found. As an example, a difference in academic achievement which may be demonstrated between firstborn and later-born may be due to birth order effects but may also be explainable in terms of the higher proportion of later-born children who are from large families which are known to differ from small families in a number of ways which are possibly significant, such as economic status. So, is it birth order, is it size of family or is it an interaction of the two (see Eysenck and Cookson, 1970)?

This complexity of interacting factors may be illustrated by a look at the number of possible positions in a two-child family, according to just the two factors of sex and sibling status. Using the notation of Sutton-Smith and Rosenberg, we have:

M1M	the elder of two brothers
MM2	the younger of two brothers
M1F	a brother with a younger sister
FM2	a brother with an elder sister
F1F	the elder of two sisters
FF2	the younger of two sisters
F1M	a sister with a younger brother
MF2	a sister with an elder brother

In a three-child family the number of possible permutations is twenty four. Fortunately for us, the simpler case of the two-child family is likely to become even more typical as pressures for family limitation increase.

A further point about the empirical studies to which we shall refer is that they have been conducted with due regard to the demands for scientific rigour and usually include detailed statistical analyses. However, the inclusion of even a modest amount of statistical detail in this chapter would make it even less attractive to many readers. We have decided, therefore, to omit most of these details but to include adequate references for the reader to consult. The danger is, of course, that we are depriving the curious reader of information which could help towards his own evaluations. Secondly, we could be making it easier for the injudicious reader to reify into dogmatic generalizations findings that are in most cases tentative, qualified and of relatively low magnitude. The truth is that the correlations found are usually low, but since they are also statistically significant and consistent in general direction they give us hope for the setting-up of more refined and detailed hypotheses which may further sort out the tangled web of factors involved.

We should be very foolish to believe that we could make a reliable prediction of an individual's characteristics on the basis of knowing only his family position. Yet, used with care, the research findings may throw increasing light on the relationships between position, role and personality and help us understand the working of factors which may be contributory to the behaviour of many and central to the behaviour of a few. As a possible instance of the latter, the author can recall two former pupils, in different schools, who had these attributes in common: each was demoted from a grammar to a technical school; each was regarded as bright but inexplicably and immovably idle; each provided schools and teachers with a baffling and, eventually, shelved problem; each, so it was later learned, had an elder brother at university. This last factor, possibly involving sibling rivalry, self-image and ego defence, seemed to make the whole picture more coherent. Of course, one proves nothing from describing the isolated and unprovable example, but the patient work of empirical researchers may serve to reinforce the need for us to become more sensitive to a wider range of possible causal factors in behaviour.

Differences in attainment

Much, though by no meals all, of the evidence for differences in attainment comes from the U.S.A. and relates especially to differences between firstborn and later-born. For instance, first-borns accounted for 35 per cent of the American age group born in the late 1930s but accounted for between one-half and two-thirds of those who were in university twenty years later. Firstborns have also been found to be over represented in such categories as 'eminent Englishmen', 'gifted children', 'American men of science' and among persons featured on the covers of *Time Magazine* (Toman, 1970).

In Britain, a large-scale study was carried out in the early fifties by Lees and Stewart (1957), involving a total of about 9,000 children of secondary school age in the East Midlands. One of their findings was that firstborns showed significantly greater ability in academic work. A more recent British study, by Eysenck and Cookson (1970), involving four thousand boys and girls of about eleven years and taking account of the factor of varying family size, found that firstborns tended to do better at school, especially in English and Mathematics, although they did not differ significantly from others in 'ability' as measured by tests of verbal reasoning.

It is difficult to find any evidence or reason for supposing that firstborns are more highly favoured genetically than are their siblings. What has been established as one reason for their greater academic attainment is that they have a greater drive to achieve. In a study by Sampson and Hancock (1967), achievement-need was measured and found to decrease in the following order of family position:

M1F/M/MM2/M1M/F/F1F/FM2/MF2/F1M/FF2

It will be noted that firstborns (onlys and eldests) gain five of the six highest scores.

A number of studies have suggested that the origins of the greater achievement need of firstborns lie in greater parental pressure and expectation. Rothbart (1971) studied the interactions of mothers and fifty-six five-year-old boys and girls from two-child families. Half the children had a sibling two years older, the other half had a sibling two years younger. Mothers were asked to supervise their children in the performance of five different tasks, two of which involved explanations by the mother. Although the mothers spent the same amount of time interacting with each child, they gave more complex technical instructions to firstborns and also 'exhibited greater pressure for achievement and greater anxious intrusiveness into the performance of the firstborn'.

Higher expectations and pressure may be partly the reason for firstborns walking and talking earlier and for them being subjected to more intensive independence training. Firstborn boys, in particular, are liable to inherit the ambitions of the father, especially where the latter have been frustrated. The higher expectations upon firstborn sons can be related to the special importance of the male heir, as reflected in traditional rights of primogeniture, but we must not miss noting the fact that firstborn girls also show greater attainment than their siblings and greater achievement need than their sisters.

Attainment in school subjects has much to do with linguistic experience and ability. In this respect, firstborns probably benefit from the less diluted attention they get from parents before the arrival of a younger child and, particularly, from the more frequent conversations with adults which are possible. Furthermore, according to Bossard (1945), 'the family seems to adjust its age level to the older children and to ignore the younger ones, especially if the age differential is not large. Questions on word-meanings raised by the younger children are given less consideration'. Koch (1956) found that among six-year-olds the firstborns were the ones to speak more clearly. Eldest children may also benefit from the more frequent demands on them to interpret things to their younger siblings, a process that, it is claimed, gives them more practice in data-processing. Related to this greater verbal proficiency, firstborns are found to have a tendency to adopt a more synthesizing, conceptualizing approach to learning, in which they get more effectively to the critical characteristics of things. In comparison, later-borns have a more perceptual and imitative learning style in which they tend to match the outward form but miss that deeper understanding which can lead to more effective transfer or generalization (Sutton-Smith and Rosenberg, 1970, pp. 110-12).

Another factor in the greater scholastic success of firstborns is their greater identification with parents and parental norms. This generalizes to a closer identification with adults, so that firstborns interact more easily with those adults, such as teachers, who are important to their academic progress. They are more adult-oriented, whereas younger siblings are more peer-oriented (McArthur, 1956). Firstborns are also more capable, according to Lees and Stewart (1957), of working individually. As they put it, 'Eldests and Onlys are (equally and) most, and Intermediates least, successful in scholastic activity which, in the last resort, is individual activity'.

Differences in personality

Definitions of the term 'personality' are many and varied*. Some, for instance, would include 'intelligence' or 'intellectual ability' as part of one's personality; according to this view we have already, in the previous section, been dealing with some of the relationships between birth order and personality. In this section we go on to deal with other, but related, aspects such as the relationship of birth order to anxiety, affiliation need, conforming, relationships with authority, aggression, conscience and popularity.

We mentioned, in the previous section, that 'anxious intrusiveness' of mothers toward firstborns could be one of the factors leading to a greater need for achievement in these children. It may also lead to other personality characteristics. For instance, Solomon (1965) reported that firstborn male teachers tend to be more critical but also more nurturant towards their pupils and suggested that this might reflect the critical but nurturant treatment they received from their parents. Such inconsistency in parent-child relationships may also partly account for some of the personality differences

*See e.g. G. W. Allport (1961), ch. 2.

we now describe, such as the greater anxiety and affiliativeness of firstborns.

With regard to anxiety, interesting evidence comes from a study by Cushna (1966; see Sutton-Smith and Rosenberg, 1970, pp. 92-3) in which the behaviour was observed of some middle-class children aged between sixteen and nineteen months. It was found that first-borns were the ones to be more upset when the mother left the room and that firstborn boys were significantly more sensitive to the pain of an immunization 'jab'. Other studies (Sutton-Smith and Rosenberg, p. 85) have shown adult firstborns to reveal greater anxiety on the Galvanic Skin Response test and to perform less well than others when under stress (see pp. 55-57 on anxiety and performance). It may be that this greater anxiety arises partly from the greater stress placed by parents on independence training; it is the firstborn who is more likely to be encouraged into independence prematurely and without the reassuring company of his siblings. Cushna found that parents' expectations in this respect were two standard deviations higher for firstborns than the mean of their expectations for all children of the same age.

As we shall see in the next chapter, there is a significant relationship between amount of anxiety and amount of yielding to group pressures. We would not, therefore, be surprised to be told that firstborns have been found to be more conforming in Asch-type situations (see pp. 59-61). However, Rhine (1968), has suggested that firstborns may conform more than the average in such non-achievement situations but less than average in situations where, presumably, their anxiety is more than counterbalanced by their stronger achievement needs.

Since the publication of Schachter's book there has been an impressive accumulation of evidence that firstborns have a greater desire to affiliate with others. According to Hilton (1967), 'interference and inconsistencies both undermine the child's opportunities to develop reference points for internal evaluation'. This leads to a greater tendency to affiliate for the purpose of 'social comparison' (see p. 93), that is, the assessment of one's own abilities and emotions by comparison with others around us. It could be that greater affiliation-need also arises from the greater loneliness often associated with the authority roles taken by firstborns. A further possibility is that dethronement of the eldest leads him to develop a greater desire to join in and please in order to regain the attention of parents and, later, of others. Certainly, the evidence (Sutton-Smith and Rosenberg, pp. 82-3) is that they do affiliate more readily when in stressful or ambiguous situations. In particular, it has been found that they volunteer more readily to take part in experiments and to undergo psychotherapy. Involved in this may be their greater conformity, especially in the presence of adults whose authoritativeness may be reminiscent of that of parents.

We mentioned earlier that firstborns are more adult-oriented whereas later-borns tend to be peer-oriented. Firstborns identify more closely with authority and are more conservative and conventional. They find it easier to interact with others in a clearcut, hierarchical relationship where they are either dominant or submissive. Such situations reflect the clearcut divisions of power and dependency which they experienced in their early years in the family. They also identify more with those adult roles which involve responsibility and leadership: in fact, eldest children also get more direct training for this when acting as 'junior parents' to their siblings.

It is firstborns who, in their more intensive interaction with parents, are most likely to develop a strong conscience in which the norms of parents are internalized (Palmer, 1966). Firstborns are said to be easier to train, less impulsive, more serious and more law-abiding. They are more introverted and inhibited. They may not harbour any less hostility than later-borns but their manner of expressing hostility is more adult in its greater restraint and verbalization. The aggression of later-borns tends to be more overt, primitive and physical (Sutton-Smith and Rosenberg, pp. 66-8). The greater inhibitedness of firstborn boys and girls is also reflected in the way they tend to avoid rough-and-tumbles (Koch, 1956). Among boys, it is the later-born who have been found most likely to become fighter aces and aquanauts (Nisbett, 1968).

When we consider popularity, the evidence seems, at first sight, to be contradictory. Sells and Roff (see Sutton-Smith and Rosenberg, p. 75) used sociometric measures (see p. 112) with 1000

Texan children in grades 3 to 6 (ages 9 to 12) and established the following order for popularity, from most to least: youngest, only, second of two, second of more than two, oldest, middle. Alexander (1967), on the other hand, found, in his study of 1410 high school males that firstborns were the most popular. One possible explanation, for which there is some evidence, is that firstborns are more introverted and sensitive and that these qualities do not lead to popularity at the pre-adolescent age. This greater sensitivity in interpersonal relations may, however, pay off to a greater degree in adolescence, when it may become a more valued attribute. It is also possible that introverts are late developers who change more in their personality as they move into the 'teens.

In summarizing the ways in which firstborns are different from later-borns, we may say that they show higher attainment and achievement motivation, are more verbal and conceptual in their learning style, more anxious, conforming, affiliative, responsible, conscientious and inhibited in personality and more adult-oriented in general.

In all the research that has been carried out on birth order effects, the position which has consistently been revealed as being most different from others is that of 'firstborn', but there are also some characteristics which have been found to be consistently related to the 'middle-born' and 'youngest' positions. Middle-born children are the ones who seem to get least encouragement from parents and to do least well in school (Lees and Stewart, 1957) and in popularity. They are the ones least likely to be given affectionate nicknames by parents. They tend to be one of the crowd, to imitate rather than initiate and to indulge most often in negative attention-getting (Sutton-Smith and Rosenberg, p. 75).

Youngest children, partly because they may have a few years of greater maternal attention when their elder siblings are at school, avoid many of the drawbacks suffered by middle-born children. In fact, youngest children may, if the gap between them and the next sibling is large, share many of the attributes of the firstborn, such as in achievement and popularity, while avoiding their anxiety. Bayer (1967), in a study in which differences in family size and economic status were allowed for, found that youngest children had as much chance as firstborns to get to college (quoted in Sutton-Smith and Rosenberg, pp. 73-5). Where, however, the gap between the youngest child and the next eldest sibling is small the youngest is more like the middle-born child.

Sibling effects

So far this chapter has concentrated mainly on the interaction between parents and their different children. The child whose interaction with parents is the most intense and who, as a result, reveals the strongest link between birth order and personality, is the firstborn, whether he is an only or an eldest child. Irving Harris has made the interesting point that Freud was a first son and that this might have contributed to his central concern with parent–child relations, as instanced by his emphasis on the rivalry between father and son for the affections of the mother and on the development of the superego by internalization of the voices of the parents. Adler, on the other hand, was a fourth son and he broke away from the Freudian camp largely because he interpreted human behaviour more in terms of sibling rivalry. Adler's emphases were, therefore, on the struggle for power and status and on mechanisms such as overcompensation for feelings of inferiority.*

Adler also paid much attention to the 'dethronement' of the eldest child, which occurs when the arrival of a second child deprives him of what was once the almost undivided attention of parents. The effects of such dethronement may be greatest for the two- to four-year-old. Lasko (1954), for instance, suggests that a mother who is forced to concentrate her attention on a new infant might find a four-year-old easier to deal with than a three-year-old and might be perceived as more rejecting by the latter (Sutton-Smith and Rosenberg, p. 137).

Evidence from a number of studies points to dethronement causing the eldest child to turn away from the mother and towards the father. Houston (*ibid*, p. 101), in one such study, used forty boys aged between five and eleven, all from two-child families.

*See Sutton-Smith and Rosenberg, p. 3, for a brief discussion of literary analogues such as those numerous fairy-tales in which the youngest child wins in the end.

He gave each one forty statements to sort into three boxes; one box was for the mother, one for the father and one for the sibling. Each statement belonged to one of four categories.

10 Positive Outgoing Feelings, e.g. This person deserves a present.
10 Positive Incoming Feelings, e.g. This person always listens to what I have to say.
10 Negative Outgoing Feelings, e.g. This person is bad-tempered.
10 Negative Incoming Feelings, e.g. This person is always complaining about me.

It was observed that the firstborn boys put more statements into parent boxes than did secondborns, that firstborns showed more positive intake from the father than did secondborns as well as more negative intake from the mother, and that seconds showed more negative interaction with firsts than vice versa. It may be, of course, that we should expect boys of this age to be perceiving the father as an increasingly important model with whom to identify but this does not explain the difference between firstborn and secondborn.

Further confirmation for the reaction-to-dethronement theory comes from a study by Hamid (1970) in which 150 children were used, with roughly equal numbers of boys and girls. All were aged between five and eleven; fifty were eldest children, fifty were second-born and fifty were third or later born. Each was given a series of felt figures, representing a father (F), a mother (M), self (S) and younger sibling (Y). They were asked to place the 'self' figure on a felt board, followed by the other figures. Average distances from self to Mother were found to be: eldests 11·1 cm; secondborn 9·36 cm; thirdborn 8·2 cm. Eldests also placed themselves nearer to fathers. The relative placements of the groups also merit attention. The commonest arrangement in all groups was FMsy but it was significant that two of the possible arrangements, each involving placement of self next to father and a separation from mother by one intervening figure, were used by eldest children only. These arrangements were yMFs and FsyM. The former, which also involves the maximum displacement of the younger sibling, accounted for 26 per cent of placements by firstborns.

It seems, then, that dethronement may result in the eldest child perceiving himself as rejected by the mother in favour of the second-born. This may be why the eldest child has a rather low self-esteem whereas an only child esteems himself highly. The only child is also more overtly aggressive than the eldest child and this may be because he can escape the inhibitions upon physical violence which parents have to teach the eldest child.

Sex role training

Rosenberg and Sutton-Smith, on whom we shall lean heavily for this section, have made the point that the tendency is for firstborn to learn largely through operant conditioning or shaping of their behaviour by parents and for secondborn to learn largely through a process of modelling one's behaviour on that of the older sibling, by imitation or matching. Thus, secondborn, who also have more models available, are found to have more role-taking flexibility. For instance, they have been found to be somewhat better at acting, despite the fact that it is the firstborn who are usually the earlier and clearer speakers.

Among the most important of the roles into which the process of socialization eases the young is the sex role. This consists of sets of behaviours which are thought to be appropriate to the different sexes in our society.* Much of the ease with which the appropriate sex role is learned depends, as we shall see, on one's position in the family and the sex of the closest models.

Among firstborn children, there is probably more difficulty and anxiety in store for the boy than for the girl, since the closeness to parents and adoption of 'junior parent' responsibilities, both of them characteristics of firstborns, are more appropriate to the female sex role in society. Appropriate sex roles are most easily learned by MM2 and FF2. The former, who has been described as being, typically, the 'happy younger brother', is the least dependent, least affiliative, least conformist, least anxious and most 'masculine' of all boys. His family position is a fortunate one in that he has an appropriate model to follow; he can easily learn the

---

*In the rest of this chapter, the words 'masculine' and 'feminine' will refer to the stereotypes of behaviour, attitudes and interests that are widely held in our society.

behaviours approved of by society. FF2, similarly, suffers less anxiety because she, also, has an appropriate model although this time the appropriate behaviours which she learns make her less independent, less competitive and less domineering than most girls. MM2 is the most masculine of boys and FF2 is the most feminine of girls. In both cases, this leads to less conflict with social norms and, hence, less anxiety.

If we turn to FM2 and MF2 the picture is different. The brother who has an older sister may wish to play with her and to play as she plays. Society, however, soon makes its disapproval felt when he persists in pushing the doll's pram. FM2 is the boy who gets the most feminine ratings and who reveals himself as most anxious at the ages of eleven and nineteen. He suffers from having an inappropriate or confusing model.

MF2, the girl with an older brother, has the least feminine ratings for girls at the ages of six, eleven and nineteen. She tends to be more athletic, tomboyish, quarrelsome, popular and enthusiastic, and less affiliative and conforming than other girls. She, like FM2, has an older model who is, judging by social norms, inappropriate and confusing. Yet, she shows much less anxiety than FM2. The probable explanation for this is that our society is much less tolerant of deviation from the male sex role than it is of deviation from the female sex role. There is much more disapproval for the 'sissy' than for the 'tomboy'.

One of the factors complicating this picture is the tendency of humans to 'counteract' or compensate (Sutton-Smith and Rosenberg, pp. 34-8). When they come to realize that their self-image is out of line with social expectations, they may counteract this by adopting an exaggerated stance in the approved direction. For instance, it may be FM2's realization that his behaviour is less masculine than expected that leads him to become more domineering after the age of ten and to show marked masculine interests when he gets to college. Again, M1F is less dependent than one would expect of a firstborn; according to Koch, he is, at the age of six, more aggressive, self-confident and curious than average. These characteristics may arise from a strong counteractive identification with his own sex-role following dethronement by a girl; it is as though he seeks to regain the attention of his parents by becoming a more extreme version of himself. Yet another example of possible counteraction may be found in the cases of the father of two or more daughters or the brother of more than two sisters; in each case, the male reports a greater than average number of masculine interests for himself. There is even some slight suggestion that some male delinquency results from counteractive sex role behaviour, what Adler might have called overcompensation.

There is evidence that the differential acquisition of conventional sex roles by children in different family positions carries through to their occupational choices. Girls from all-female dyads (groups of two) are attracted more often into secretarial-type jobs; boys from all-male dyads end up more frequently in entrepreneurial occupations such as buying and selling, as also does MF2 (e.g. as a store-buyer). Children from mixed-sex dyads have a greater tendency to prefer 'creative' occupations such as artist, musician, author or architect. Creativity is also found more frequently in children with inconsistent sex role patterns and in children for whom the opposite sex parent has been the major influence. Turning now to the topic of interpersonal attraction (which will be dealt with more fully in chapter 6), we find a growing body of evidence that sibling positions, which are 'a person's earliest, most regular and inescapable peer experiences', tend to become the pattern for contacts with peers in new settings outside the family. For example, Koch (1957) found that, among six-year-olds, older siblings preferred younger playmates, while those with opposite sex siblings made more frequent opposite sex playmate choices.

Evidence that such findings represent more than merely temporary states comes from studies such as one by Toman (1971), in which he hypothesized that the chances of establishing a stable marriage would be influenced by the degree of role complementarity of the partners. A highly complementary pairing would be between M1F and MF2, where the male is used to leading and protecting a younger female and the female is used to accepting such behaviour from an elder brother. Another complementary pairing would be FM2 with F1M; in this case, he gets leadership and care from his wife and she has somebody to guide and care for. 'In both matches, the partners duplicate for one another a former sibling'. Examples of low role complementarity would be pairings of M1M and F1F, where neither is used to an opposite-sex peer and each is used to being the senior partner. Similarly, MM2 and FF2 are used to being junior partners. To test his hypotheses, Toman compared a group of sixteen couples whose marriages had lasted for over ten years with another group of sixteen couples whose marriages ended in divorce in less than ten years. In the 'stable marriage' group, twelve of the sixteen couples showed high complementarity and four medium to low complementarity. Of the sixteen divorced couples, only one showed high complementarity and fifteen showed medium to low complementarity.

Conclusion

Genetic factors have a very important place in the making of personality or temperament and it is no part of the aim of this chapter to call this into question. What is also, however, undoubtedly true is that environmental factors play an important part in influencing our behaviour, and we have tried to illustrate this by looking at one narrow sector of the social environment, namely, birth order and its associated roles and expectations within the family. No doubt, the nature-nurture controversy will go on interminably, but parents and teachers can rest assured that they have plenty of scope for influencing the way that genetic potential is developed and guided. What recent empirical findings have been doing is to elaborate the details of processes of social influence which were described in a more general and speculative way by earlier social psychologists such as Cooley and Mead. We shall be referring again to the importance of position, role and expectation in chapter 8, on leadership, and chapter 12, on pupil perception of teacher expectation.

The details described in this chapter do not give us any lisence to predict personality or behaviour from a knowledge of birth order alone. There are too many factors involved. However, we may draw some tentative conclusions of considerable theoretical interest. Some children are more adult-oriented, others more peer-oriented and this can have a bearing on such important characteristics as conscience, learning styles (synthesizing or perceptual), academic achievement, conforming, popularity and sex role behaviour. In general, the firstborn is the one likely to be most different and the middle-born is the one most likely to be disadvantaged. However, a judgment such as this latter one is a matter of values and one of the interesting points emphasized here is that some personality characteristics which may not be highly valued at a particular age, e.g. as a young pupil or as a student, may come into their own when the social environment changes or when the evaluations by others come to be made on a different basis.

Discussion and further study

1. List and discuss the differences likely to exist in the upbringing of a first child and his sibling who is three years younger. For example, can a garden gate be left open for the elder but kept closed for the younger? how may going to school for the first time be a different experience for each?
2. In what ways is the upbringing of an only child likely to differ from that of an eldest child and with what possible results? (A recent British study, in the *Journal of Biosocial Science*, Jan., 1973, provides interesting data on this, to judge by the review!)
3. Some tests are designed to measure achievement or attainment, others to measure 'ability' or 'intelligence'. What is the distinction between them?
4. How many patterns of social behaviour be learned through operant conditioning, imitation and modelling? Useful books to consult include Millar and Dollard (1941), *Social Learning and Imitation*, Bandura and Walters (1963), *Social Learning and Personality Development*, E. L. Walker (1966), *Conditioning and Instrumental Learning*, and Zajonc (1966), *Social Psychology: an experimental approach*. A more advanced book is Hoppe *et al*, eds (1970), *Early Experiences and the Processes of Socialization*.
5. What personal attributes may be evaluated differently at different ages or in different social contexts?
6. The following table is taken from Eysenck and Cookson (1970).

Family position: mean english scores

Family size	1st	2nd	3rd	4th	5th	6th+	P
1	97·52						
2	96·68	95·86					NS
3	96·09	94·94	93·83				0·05
4	95·69	94·32	93·75	90·94			0·01
5	94·72	94·89	92·26	91·64	90·75		NS
6+	89·83	90·61	91·47	91·14	87·67	88·19	0·05
P≤	0·01	0·01	NS	NS	NS		

The scores are on a mean of 100 with a standard deviation of 15. Explain, or get someone else to explain to you, what the figures and symbols reveal in the way of trends and significances. If possible, read the article.

7. Are our society's sex role expectations more stringent for boys than for girls?

8. Little has been said in this chapter about parents' patterns or regimes of child-rearing. Useful on this are Sears *et al*, (1957), *Patterns of Child-rearing*, Mussen (1963), *The Psychological Development of the Child*, and Gabriel (1968), *Children Growing Up*.

Further reading

Sutton-Smith and Rosenberg (1970), is detailed and comprehensive, but not an easy read. Useful articles are by Eysenck and Cookson (1970), Hamid (1970), Lees and Stewart (1957), Rothbart (1971), Sampson and Hancock (1967), Toman (1970, 1971) and those by Warren in Wrightsman (1968); see also the work of Adler (1945) and Schachter (1959).

4

Behaviour in the presence of others

The first part of this book is concerned with social influences upon the individual and we began, in chapter 1, with a wide-angled look at society and self. In chapter 3, we changed to a more powerful lens and narrowed our field to some aspects of interaction within the family. In this present chapter, we go even farther from the macro to the micro and focus on some of the finer threads of interaction processes. We consider, firstly, evidence relating to factors which have a fairly direct bearing upon the sort of learning which occurs in classrooms, particularly the effects of audience and coaction. In the second half of the chapter we look, under the headings of social reinforcement, conforming and crowds, at some of the processes of more general influence which can be detected wherever people congregate, whether it be the classroom, the school or any other social situation.

The main question before us is this: in what ways and to what extent is the behaviour of an individual influenced by the presence and behaviour of others? We shall be referring, of course, to the effects of those who are physically present, but it is an interesting exercise to consider how far, if at all, we can divorce our behaviour from the psychological presence of others even when we are physically 'alone'. For example, how influential are other people in our thoughts and behaviour when we are sitting alone in a room, studying or writing?

Effects of others on classroom learning
Audience and coactors
Let us begin by looking at an experiment by Pessin (1933), in which sixty subjects were asked to learn lists of nonsense syllables. They

learned one list when alone and needed an average of 9.85 repetitions before being able to successfully repeat the list. Another list was learned in the presence of an audience who observed but were otherwise passive. This time the list was learned successfully only after, on average, 11·27 repetitions. It seemed that the presence of an audience somewhat impaired the learning.

A few days later, Pessin asked the same subjects to relearn the same lists in the same 'alone' and 'audience' conditions. This time, the evidence was that the presence of an audience improved, rather than impaired, the learning. Seemingly contradictory results like these were also obtained by other experimenters. How could this puzzling situation be resolved?

Zajonc (1966) suggested that these results could be embraced in one generalization provided that we differentiated between two processes which were involved. The word 'learning', he proposed, should be restricted to those tasks which were new or difficult. Where, on the other hand, one was already fairly accomplished at the task, by reason of having acquired much of the necessary basic skill or information, the word 'performance' would be more appropriate.

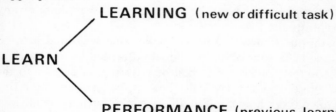

LEARNING (new or difficult task)

LEARN

PERFORMANCE (previous learned task)

The generalization could now run thus: 'Learning is impaired and performance facilitated by the presence of an audience'.

Zajonc goes on to discuss the possible reasons for this difference. The presence of others is known to be associated with increased adrenocortical activity, as measured, for instance, by the secretion of hydrocortisone. The individual's reactions are marked by greater tension, alertness and responsiveness. 'Audience enhances the emission of dominant responses'. But, we may ask, what sort of responses will be the dominant ones?

In many cases during the early stages of the learning process, a subject gives a greater number of wrong responses than right ones; the wrong responses are stronger and predominant. But once the individual has successfully learned the task, his behaviour is dominated by correct responses. If correct responses are dominant, the presence of an audience will increase the likelihood that correct responses occur; if wrong responses prevail, then the presence of an audience will enhance them.

In short, in the presence of others the bad tends to become worse and the good tends to become better.

A variation on the audience situation has been used by a number of experimenters who have compared the performance of subjects working alone with their performances in the presence of coactors. Coactors would be persons seated around the same table as the subject, working at the same task but independently. As with the audience experiment, coactors were found to impair learning but facilitate performance. One of these experiments, by F. H. Allport (1920), is worth looking at more closely since the differentiation of tasks is instructive.

Allport asked his large number of subjects to work alone on one occasion but in coaction on another occasion. In each situation they were given the following series of tasks:

1. Chain association; i.e. given a stimulus word, how many associated words could you write in a given time? e.g. BIRD–feather–quill–pen–ink–black . . .

2. Vowel cancellation; crossing out vowels in a newspaper article.

3. Reversible perspective; how often, in a given time, can you alternate your perception of the orientation of this cube:

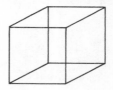

4. Multiplications; the process would be known to the subjects.

5. Problem solving; refuting false syllogisms.

6. Judgment; e.g. rating the pleasantness of odours or the magnitudes of weights.

It will be seen that tasks 1 to 4 fall into Zajonc's 'performance' category, and these were the tasks more successfully done in the 'coaction' situation. In task 5, which requires novel, less obvious, answers, most of the early attempts would be wrong and it was this wrong responding which was strengthened by the presence of coactors. In task 6, judgments were more extreme in the 'alone' condition and became more moderate in the presence of coactors, a phenomenon to which we shall return later in this chapter.

Further interesting evidence along similar lines came from Dashiell (1930). He gave his subjects a series of multiplication problems, analogies items and chain association tests. He found that in the following categories of situations speed decreased from (*a*) to (*b*) to (*c*).

(*a*) Groups of fifteen, working face-to-face and told not to compete.
(*b*) Individuals working simultaneously but in separate rooms.
(*c*) Individuals reporting separately to the experimenter and being taken to separate rooms.

Presumably, subjects (*b*) were more aware than subjects (*c*) of the 'psychological presence' of others. A further point to note is that although work in the (*c*) situation was slower it was more accurate.

From work of which the experiments by Pessin, Allport and Dashiell are examples, it seems that the presence of others has an energizing, intensifying or motivating effect but may depress accuracy. Of course, it has to be borne in mind that the time involved in these experiments was relatively short; given more time, a subject may adapt himself to the presence of others and the effect may be reduced in magnitude. However, it seems useful as a first generalization to realize that in relatively simple 'performance' tasks the presence of others is facilitating, whereas in relatively difficult 'learning' tasks the presence of others is disruptive.

For teachers, the implication would seem to be that we should be more discriminating about when to organize pupils to work 'on their own' as against organizing them to work with an audience or coactors. Most of us have had the experience of saying to ourselves, when faced with a complex task: 'If only he would go away, I could do it'. There are probably times when a teacher, having first prepared his class sufficiently, does better to reduce tension by keeping out of the way; there comes a point where a pupil may more easily master a difficulty on his own, perhaps for homework or with the aid of a teaching machine. On the other hand, there are times when there is benefit to be gained from the tension produced by an audience. Contrast, for example, the effect on a struggling pianist of learning a difficult piece while under his tutor's gaze with the effect produced in a well-rehearsed concert pianist by the presence of an audience. In what conditions should 'lines' be learned, or the polished performance be given, so as to produce the optimum degree of tension which maximizes the achievement while avoiding paralytic stage fright? One of our aims as teachers should be to sensitize ourselves to the factors involved, to discriminate more finely on behalf of our pupils and to set the stage accordingly.

Anxiety and the interaction of factors

At this point, we must digress a little to emphasize the complex nature of the relationship between learning, on the one hand, and 'arousal', 'tension' or 'anxiety' on the other. A general basic finding is that when a person's level of anxiety is very low, he learns little; he is not sufficiently aroused, motivated or discontented, as may have been the case with the slowest-learning boy in Lawrence's (1971) study (ch. 2). Where a person's level of anxiety is very high, he may again learn little; overanxiety may be too distracting and may even lead to conditions akin to the paralysis of stage fright. In general, the greatest learning occurs in the presence of moderate anxiety.

These findings are embodied in the Yerkes-Dodson Law and may be expressed by saying that there is a curvilinear relationship between learning and anxiety, giving us a graph with an inverted U-shape. (See fig. 4.1.)

We need, however, to go further in considering what factors, apart from the presence or absence of audience and coactors, can raise or lower a pupil's anxiety. What we find is that for the promotion of effective learning we need the best match between the task, the social situation and the characteristics of the individual learner.

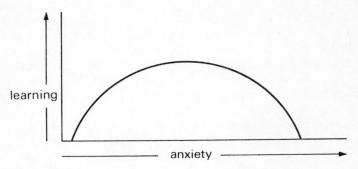

Fig. 4.1

We may summarize our considerations as follows:

1. Tasks may range in difficulty from simple to complex. High anxiety is facilitative for simple tasks but disruptive for complex tasks.

2. The presence of others, especially those others who are 'significant' to our self-concepts, can raise anxiety even to a level where 'performance' tasks are disrupted.

3. Learners themselves are, when they begin any task, variously predisposed to anxiety. The same task may be difficult to one person but easy to another, depending on the person's intelligence and his experiences with that sort of problem material. Furthermore, individuals come to a learning situation in different states of anxiety as a result of variations in constitutional make-up and in experiences of (and anticipations of) success and failure.

Thus, factors of 'objective' task difficulty, intelligence, experience and personality (such as 'neuroticism' and self-esteem) may be interacting, in any classroom, with the audience and coactor effects previously described. These interactions are complex and as yet very imperfectly mapped out (Entwistle and Cunningham, 1968), but this does not absolve the teacher from attempting to create the optimum match between the material to be learned, the characteristics of the learner and the physical and social context in which the learning is to take place.

It can also be pointed out that student-teachers (and their tutors) have many opportunities for firsthand experience of the effects of points 1, 2 and 3 on anxiety and performance in classroom teaching practice. When does the student's good become better, or his bad become worse? How difficult for the student were the subject matter and the class? What difference did variations in the audience make—pupils, teacher, head teacher, tutor? How did these points interact with the student's own personality characteristics? Such an analysis of one's own behaviour may help in the understanding of the behaviour of one's pupils.

Some processes of social influence

So far in this chapter we have looked at some social factors operating on the type of learning with which the school is traditionally and specifically concerned, with what for convenience we have called 'classroom' learning. Such learning accounts, however, for only a part of our total learning and behaviour within and outside the classroom and we therefore look now at some of the social factors which are at work in this wider context.

Social reinforcement

The rewards that are important in most teaching situations are socially derived. Social reinforcement may include verbal behaviour such as using words like 'good' or 'right', or sounds like 'mm-hm', and non-verbal behaviour such as smiling, nodding, frowning or leaning forward. The effect is, to use Professor Skinner's terminology, the 'shaping' of the other person's behaviour in a desired direction. Let us take an example.

Greenspoon (1955) used seventy-five college students in an experiment in which they were asked to say, individually and for a period of fifty minutes each, all the words they could think of, but not sentences or phrases. The students were randomly assigned to five categories of fifteen and with each category the experimenter behaved differently. This is how he spent the first twenty-five minutes with each category:

Category 1.   He said 'mmm-hmmm' after each plural response
Category 2.   He said 'huh-uh' after each plural response
Category 3.   He said 'mmm-hmmm' after each singular response
Category 4.   He said 'huh-uh' after each singular response
Category 5.   Control group; he made no sounds.

Results showed that 'huh-uh' had the effect of reducing the frequency of the plural or the singular whereas 'mm-hm' increased the frequency.

Other experiments have provided support for the following ideas:

1. One can reduce or increase, by such social reinforcement, the number of opinions expressed by a subject in speech.
2. Subjects are more likely to be affected by such social reinforcement after periods of social deprivation or isolation.
3. Anxious subjects are more responsive.
4. The status and sex of the interviewer is a factor.
5. More effective than verbal elements such as 'right' and 'mmm-hmm' are non-verbal elements such as bodily proximity, orientation and posture (e.g., leaning towards or away from the subject), gestures, head nods, eye movements, emotional tone of speech and 'looking interested'.

These verbal and non-verbal cues, which have been studied in fascinating detail by Argyle and his co-workers at Oxford, may occur at both conscious and subconscious levels. At any rate, this was the considered opinion of Argyle (1969), who said: 'The effect is rapid and can occur without the knowledge of the influencer, so that both parties are constantly influencing one another in the direction of producing the desired behaviour' (p. 179).

It is interesting to speculate that in responding to non-verbal cues in this way, 'rational' man is revealing more dependence upon a primitive, prelinguistic form of communication than his conceit will let him readily admit. The pupil who likes or dislikes a teacher may be picking up the minute signals of approval or disapproval which confirm or give the lie to the words uttered by that teacher. This non-verbal communication may also be important in conveying to the pupil the expectations the teacher has for him. That is a topic to which we shall return in chapter 12.

Conforming

We look now at that form of social influence or pressure which is concerned with the conformity of an individual to the norms of a group. This is a topic of perennial interest to the layman and it has also attracted the attentions of a number of experimental social psychologists. One of the first was Sherif, who, in 1935, published an account of his experiments into social influence on perception (see chapter 5). Other classic experiments were conducted in the early 1950s by Solomon Asch (1952) and it is to these that we now turn.

What Asch investigated were the effects on individuals of majority opinions when the latter were seen to be in a direction contrary to 'fact'. Subjects, all of whom were male college students, were asked to pick from three lines the one which matched a standard line. In a typical example, the standard line was 8 inches and the comparison lines were $6\frac{1}{4}$, 8 and $6\frac{3}{4}$ inches. A control group of thirty-seven subjects found these to be very easy tasks, getting about 95 per cent correct. Their answers were written and were done without any knowledge of other subjects' answers.

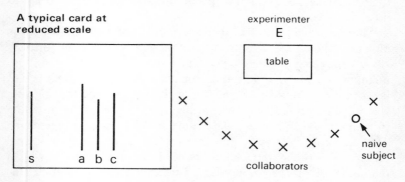

Fig. 4.2

Fifty groups of about eight subjects each were then formed. The eight consisted of seven who were collaborators of the experimenter and one who was a 'naive' subject. They were seated in an arc facing the stimulus cards. Starting at one end, each subject would in turn call out a, b or c, whichever he thought to be the correct answer. The naive subject was placed next to the last caller. On most trials all eight called out the correct answer but at certain pre-arranged times the collaborators would all call out a wrong answer. What would be the reaction of the naive subject when following six fellow-subjects who were giving a wrong answer in this way?

Altogether, there were fifty of these naive subjects and each faced twelve critical trials in which the collaborators called wrongly. An analysis of results was followed by intensive interviews with each subject. The analysis showed that one-third of the calls were distorted towards the majority call, but there were marked individual differences. A quarter of the naives remained completely unswayed whereas at the other extreme a third were swayed towards the majority on over half the critical trials. Among the non-yielders, some remained confident throughout, others manifested considerable tension and doubt. Among the yielders, a very few were quite unaware of conflict; most distorted their judgment largely because they came to believe their perceptions were inaccurate; some others kept on believing that they were right but yielded to an overmastering need 'not to appear different from or inferior to others'.

The experiment just described was concerned with 'the condition of being exposed alone to the opposition of a "compact majority"'. Asch conducted further experiments into the effects of a non-unanimous majority. He found, for instance, that the presence of just one other individual who did not collaborate with the majority was sufficient to reduce yielding calls from 32 per cent to anything from about 10 to 5 per cent, depending on the precise arrangements. This, according to Asch, 'points to a fundamental psychological difference between the condition of being alone and having a minimum of human support'. A further interesting finding was that when one collaborator in the midst of sixteen 'naives' gave predetermined wrong answers his actions were greeted first with amusement and later with contagious laughter. 'Of significance is the fact that the members lacked awareness that they drew their strength from the majority, and that their reactions would change radically if they faced the dissenter individually' Asch (1958).

A last point worth quoting relates to the systematic variation of the perceptual difficulty of the task. Asch found that the majority effect grew stronger as the differences between the lines was made less distinct. This suggests that where issues are complex or ambiguous (and social issues are usually this) we can expect a good deal of conforming behaviour.

To disagree with a majority, particularly if one is 'out on one's own', can, as Asch has shown, produce stress in most, if not all, of us and yielding in some. But who are the ones most likely to yield? This question has been tackled by many experimenters and although the evidence is complex one could risk summarizing as follows. Yielders tend to be more authoritarian, more anxious, lower in self-esteem and more in need of social approval. Many studies confirm, for example, that those most likely to conform to the norms of a group are those who are least secure in the group and particularly those who are trying to enter the group. The more intelligent subject may be more self-dependent where judgement of incoming information is concerned but is probably just as willing to conform for social gain. Females, in general, conform more than males but this may be no more than their acquiescence in the culturally prescribed sex role in which docility, submissiveness and compliance are stressed. One study suggested that women conformed more in situations which were perceived as being essentially male domains but no differently in neutral or feminine domains.

The type of result summarized above occurred not only among American students but also, as Crutchfield (1955) found, among American military officers, engineers, writers, scientists and architects, most of whom would, presumably, take pride in being independent-minded. Of course, one has to bear in mind that the American culture may be one in which the pressures to conform are more than usually strong. Interesting in this respect are the findings by Milgram (1961) of between 50 and 75 per cent yielding among Norwegian students and between 34 and 59 per cent among French students, on the same tasks.

Having described some of the work of Asch and pursued briefly the 'conforming personality' line of Crutchfield and others, it is time to discuss the matter of definitions. Is conformity the relatively simple issue we have, perhaps, so far implied? What of Asch's findings that whereas a few subjects were unconscious of what was happening others complied knowingly? The work of Kelman (1958) is a good example of the many studies and formulations of this problem.

Kelman distinguishes between (1) mere public conformity comprising superficial changes on a verbal or overt level and (2) private acceptance which he describes as being more general, durable and integrated with the person's own values. He also makes the point that to be influenced by another may mean that one considers the other's information to be valid or it may be a normative process in which the influenced person is concerned with meeting the positive expectations of the influencing group or person. It is in the latter case that, according to Willis (1965), we should use the word 'conformity', which he defines as 'behaviour intended to fulfil normative group expectations as these expectations are perceived by the individual'.

Kelman distinguishes further between compliance, identification and internalization, three processes which somewhat overlap. Compliance involves public but not private acceptance. The subject complies not because of a belief in the intrinsic value of the content or action but because compliance gains for him a satisfying social effect. Compliance occurs under surveillance, as any school-boy would tell you.

Identification implies an acceptance that is both public and private but which is restricted to the role relationship which is in being at the time. It is not integrated with the subject's broader value system but remains 'encapsulated', tied to a particular external source and dependent on social support. Identification is particularly likely in role relationships that form part of the subject's self-image. For instance, some of those who were 'brainwashed' by Chinese Communists identified with their captors partly in an attempt to regain orientation or identity. They came to talk and believe like their captors and this went deeper than mere compliance. But when freed of the situation, their new beliefs remained 'encapsulated', that is, in some way apart from their integrated value system. The process of identification also occurs in the socialization of children, 'where the taking over of parental attitudes and actions is a normal, and probably essential, part of personality development' (Kelman, 1958), and in the context of occupational role-modelling where what is at stake is the individual's 'professional identity'.

Internalization, in Kelman's view, occurs when the individual accepts influence because the induced behaviour is congruent with his existing value system. He may, for example, adopt the recommendations of an expert because on rational grounds he finds them relevant to his own problems and congruent with his own values.

Having looked briefly at some of the behaviours or processes which have at various times been labelled 'conforming', we may as well at this point look at our definitions of independent or non-conforming behaviour. One interesting formulation is that by Willis (1965) in which he isolates four basic response modes: conformity, anticonformity, independence and variability. The conformist makes a consistent attempt to behave in accordance with normative expectations. The independent is one who can resist social pressures and judge issues on their merits. The anti-conformist is one whose response is the antithesis of the norm; he is, however, reacting to the group as strongly as the conformist; he is actively opposing the group and compulsively dissenting from it; he is 'cussed for the sake of being cussed'. Variability, unlike the independence where one 'sticks to one's guns', is represented by the individual who changes his mind incessantly without reference to a group norm.

In all this, it must be borne in mind that a person is usually being influenced by more than one group and that conformance to one may involve non-conformance to another. Cooley (1909) pointed out that the non-conformist is the one who seems to be out of step with his present company; but he may, nevertheless, be in step with 'another more distant drummer'. The group of which he is a member, perhaps non-voluntarily, may not be his reference group, i.e. the group which means most to him in terms of aspirations, values, etc. As an example, we may think of an adolescent whose non-conformance with the norms of his family or school may represent conformance with the norms of his peer group.

This brings us to the point where we must look critically at the idea that people may be divided, on the basis of personality traits, into conformists or independents. A number of writers have emphasized that a person may conform in some situations but not others. What are these situational factors?

First, we should note how the situation may vary according to the importance the group has for the individual. If a person conforms with a majority view it may be because he accedes to pressures to conform in order to gain social benefit from a group which matters to him, or it may simply mean that he 'goes along' because it matters little to him. In relation to Asch's experiments we may believe that conforming behaviour would have been less likely if the groups had been groups of friends. On the other hand, we could argue that conforming would have been even more marked if the subjects had formed real psychological groups rather than aggregations of unrelated persons. To disagree with one's friends is, in general, more productive of stress than disagreeing with those upon whose regard and favours we are less dependent.

Another point, one made by Jahoda (1959), is that the 'customary operational criterion by which independence is distinguished from conformity,—agreement or disagreement with a presented opinion not previously held by the individual', is perhaps not wholly adequate. She says that one and the same position taken by different individuals can have completely different meanings. To take a position on an issue in which one has much 'intellectual and emotional investment' is very different from taking up the same position on an issue which is of little importance. Housewives, she maintains, have a much stronger interest in coffee and cosmetics than in international relations, so that although they may fall in with the majority on both types of issue, it may be that two rather different processes are involved. What is wanted is a repetition of earlier experiments with the addition of some assessment of the degree to which the individual's intellect and emotion are invested in the issue. How much did it matter to Asch's subjects that they disagreed or agreed with their particular cosubjects over the particular question of the length of lines? We come back to this question in chapter 10, when dealing with attitudes which are ego-involving.

What of the distinction between conformity and convention? Barker and Wright (1954), in their very thorough survey of the behaviour of children in a Midwest town, concluded that 95 per cent of this behaviour on a typical day was determined by the settings in which the children found themselves; they responded in a way appropriate to the situation and this meant largely similar responses from different children. This is conventional rather than conforming behaviour.

Conventional ways of acting represent established solutions to problems; conventions are well-oiled grooves of social conduct which are provided ready-made and often followed with minimal conflict. . . . The essence of conformity, in distinction to uniformity and conventionality, is the yielding to group pressures. For there to be conformity there must be conflict— conflict between those forces in the individual which tend to lead him to act, value and believe in one way and those pressures emanating from the society or group which tend to lead him in another way.

Summarizing this section on conformity, we can say that although some people tend to be more generally conformist than others, situational factors are probably just as important. People tend to conform in one situation and not in another, depending upon the salience of the issue and the group. This becomes clearer when we analyse the concept of conformity and discriminate between a number of processes which are often subsumed under that one heading.

Crowds

Our treatment of the influences of others on the individual would not be complete without some reference to crowds, or 'collective behaviour'. This is one of the longest-studied topics in social psychology; for instance, in Ross's (1908) book it accounted for about one-third of the contents. Since then, interest and progress have fluctuated and it must be admitted that there is not yet a fully articulated theory to embrace the various regularities observed. Whether or not the recent intensification of work on scientific and quantitative observation, recording and analysis (for example, measures of the densities of crowds or studies of the psychological effects of crowding on animals) will lead to better insights and theory construction remains to be seen. The aim of this brief section is rather to indicate the field than to outline any firm conclusions; nevertheless, the importance of trying to understand the behaviour of an individual in a football crowd, pop concert or lynch mob is apparent.

A crowd is not merely an aggregate of persons; its members show some measure of focus on a common stimulus, and are also in various ways stimulating each other. One variable in such inter-stimulation may be the size of the crowd, as suggested by Argyle's finding that in revivalist meetings the *proportion* of those who indicate conversion rises as the crowd becomes larger. Crowds are not, of course, all alike, and various attempts have been made to categorize them; Brown, for example, produced a detailed taxonomy in which the main distinction is between mobs, which are active, and audiences, which are more passive (Brown, 1954).

Early writers, like Le Bon (1898), stressed the unattractive features of crowd behaviour and more recently a Harvard survey, using a semantic differential technique, showed that students looked more unfavourably on the word 'crowd' than upon the word 'person'. The early writers stressed irrationality, the release of antisocial feelings under the cloak of anonymity, the easily swayed uniformity of the 'collective mind' and the intellectual inferiority of crowd activities. Later writers have questioned whether the crowd produces these effects or whether the crowd acts as a convenient convergence point for those who are already antisocial. Hofstätter (1957) suggests that an individual can be just as irrational and emotional as a crowd. Perhaps the most persuasive view is that of F. H. Allport (1920), who maintained that an individual in a crowd behaves as himself, only more so.

Freud was impressed by the writings of Le Bon and developed his ideas, giving additional importance to the part played by the leader, the one who takes over the superego or conscience of the followers. This is a point to which we shall return briefly in chapter 8 on leadership.

What are the processes by which a crowd produces effects in an individual member? The interstimulation aspect has been studied by such writers as F. H. Allport (1920), and Miller and Dollard (1941). The latter pair take the view that repetitive stimulation and circular reaction lead to an amplification of emotion. One person makes some response such as booing or clapping or screaming; this acts as a stimulus to those around and their reaction stimulates the first person to an even more intense reaction. 'The mob, then, becomes a catalytic medium that reverberates interpersonal stimulation to higher and higher levels of intensity'. Attention has also been drawn to the fact that the larger the crowd the greater is the possibility of there being in it an extremist or group of extremists, perhaps from the 'lunatic fringe', who may take the lead in this circular reaction.

Conclusion

The effects of society on the individual are mediated largely by face-to-face groups, such as the family, and by processes such as those we have just described. At the simplest level, the mere presence of others can arouse us and affect our learning. Verbal cues from others can shape our behaviour, as also can their conscious or unconscious non-verbal behaviour.

It may be in these subtle ways, as well as in numerous more obvious ways, that members of a group convey to an individual pressures to conform to their norms (see chapter 7), or that teachers convey their expectations to their pupils (see chapter 12). Conforming implies succumbing to social pressures, but the depth to which conforming behaviour pervades the personality can vary from compliance to identification and internalization. Some persons, especially those who are less sure of their acceptance by others, may be more generally conformist or persuasible, but any individual is likely to vary in conformity according to the situation and the salience to him of the group and issue involved. These are matters which are central to the discussion, in Part 3 of this book, of the ways in which attitudes are formed and changed.

However, before embarking on that discussion, we need to look in more detail at the nature of an individual's attraction and attachment to groups, in Part 2. This is because attitudes are so intertwined with group allegiance. For example, the teacher who is struggling to induce in an adolescent pupil an internalization of (or, at least, compliance with) the values of the school must appreciate how much that individual's attitude is a reflection of the peer group's power of attraction. The teacher is faced not with one simple question but with a complex series. In this situation and on this type of issue, he must ask himself, which is the group to which the individual pupil is conforming? The answers to at least some of our problems, as teachers, may lie in the locating of such 'reference groups', but how many of us are sufficiently tuned-in to these 'distant drummers'?

Discussion and further study

1. Discuss the following, using personal illustrations where appropriate.

   (*a*) Examples of effects upon behaviour and learning of differing levels of anxiety which may be related to the presence of (i) any others and (ii) 'significant others'.

   (*b*) Non-verbal cues from various others which encourage or discourage you in conversations.

   (*c*) Asch's claim that there is a 'fundamental psychological difference between the condition of being alone and having a minimum of human support'.

   (*d*) Being disloyal to one's family, friends, school or country may be a result of a stronger loyalty to 'more distant drummers'.

   (*e*) Disagreeing with friends is more difficult than disagreeing with strangers.

   (*f*) The part played by social factors in the taking of drugs, tobacco and drink.

2. On a political dimension, the communist and the fascist may seem poles apart, but may they have more in common with each other at a more basic psychological level than either has with a centre-

party man? (see, e.g. Eysenck, 1957, ch. 7). If so, may a similar point be made about conformist/counterconformist or about religious/atheistic persons?

3. Are the terms 'compliance, identification and internalization' useful in describing (i) the varying acceptances by pupils of the norms and values of a school and (ii) the expectations or aims of various teachers? Which is most desirable in a pupil and in what conditions is it most/least likely to occur?

Further reading

Zajonc (1966) on audience, co-action and social reinforcement. Open University, E.281, unit 5, on neuroticism and school attainment, including the article by Entwistle and Cunningham (1968). Argyle (1969), especially chs. 2 and 3 on non-verbal communication. Hollander and Hunt (1967, 1971) for Kelman (1958) and Hollander and Willis on nonconformity; Asch (in Maccoby *et al*, 1959); Bettelheim on life in Nazi concentration camps and Schein on Chinese 'brainwashing' (also in Maccoby *et al*); Miller and Dollard (1941) on crowd behaviour and lynch-mobs; and Bandura and Walters (1963) on behaviourist approaches to modelling, imitation etc.

Part 2

Interpersonal processes and structures

In Part 1 our emphasis was on the way in which the individual's personality and behaviour are influenced by other individuals, groups and culture. Thus, the teacher who seems to be dealing with an individual pupil is in fact dealing with what is merely the visible tip of a social iceberg.

In Part 2, our frame of reference widens to encompass two or more people in interaction. We begin by considering how individuals perceive one another and how these perceptions guide them into attraction or rejection. Where they are attracted into groups, these groups soon develop structures which give pattern to individual inter-actions and guide, constrain and crystallize the liking, communication and power processes between individuals. Of the positions and roles which develop within the group structure, the most important is that of leader and the leadership of a group is one of a number of factors we shall have to look at when considering what makes some groups more effective than others.

The teacher is, of course, vitally concerned in this study of group dynamics. He spends most of his time dealing with groups; not only is he involved in the interaction between himself and the pupils he leads, he is also involved with interaction between pupil and pupil and between himself and his fellow-teachers. His most distinctive skills, one could argue, are his interpersonal ones.

5

Interperson perception

It would be as well to begin by attempting to clarify the use of three terms often encountered in social psychology; namely, social perception, person perception and interperson perception.

A famous experiment by Sherif (1935) illustrates 'social perception'. A number of subjects were asked to sit in a room which was perfectly dark apart from one pinpoint of light. This light was in fact stationary, but after such a light has been looked at for a short time it seems to the subject that it moves, the so-called 'autokinetic effect'. Sherif asked the subjects to estimate the amount of this imagined movement and found that estimates given individually were much more wideranging than those reported in the presence of other reporting subjects. This has been labelled a 'social perception' process but it is perhaps better understood as a process of conforming, as also is the case with the Asch experiments described in chapter 4.

'Person perception' occurs when one person is perceiving another. Studies in person perception have made use of such techniques or stimuli as a one-way screen, a photograph or film, or voice recordings. These are useful in laboratory-type studies but lack the important element of reciprocal interaction which characterizes so much real-life perceiving. If, for instance, A was interviewing or teaching B, then A is not perceiving a B who exists apart but a B whose behaviour is at least in part being produced by A's behaviour or presence. The process would be evident even if A and B were two strangers sharing a railway compartment; A might be perceiving a B who is in some way responding to his own perception that A is looking at him. So, we get a 'recycling dyadic process' similar to what happens when 'I think he thinks I think . . .'. It is partly to emphasize such reciprocal influence that some social

You may prefer to complete activity 1 (p. 89) before reading this chapter.

psychologists prefer the term 'interperson perception' to 'person perception', but the two terms are often used interchangeably.

In either case, perceiving another person is in a number of ways different from perceiving an inanimate object such as a tree. For one thing, the other person reacts to us. For another, we are more like another person than we are like a tree and we draw many inferences from our own feelings and thoughts to those of the other person.

Person 'perception' is a complex cognitive process in which we hope to get to 'know' the characteristics of another person. What we are doing is processing the vast amount of information about the other person, forming it into manageable generalizations which can become a basis for appropriate prediction and interaction. The paranoid who, because of his selective hypersensitivity, magnifies cues of hostility from others is likely to interact inappropriately with them. Perception precedes prediction which, in turn, precedes action.

One way in which we generalize about other people, or 'pigeon-hole' our information about them, is by inferring intentions, traits or attitudes. Thus, we might forge links between a large number of separate behaviours by saying that a person has a mean streak or an antischool attitude. We do not, normally, attribute such traits or attitudes on the basis of all the events with which the person is associated but only on the basis of those which he has the ability to cause and which, we think, he had the intention to cause. Such, at any rate, is one of the chief propositions of 'attribution theory'.

One of the chief aims of this chapter will be to try to indicate some of the more systematic ways in which our generalizations about others may be inaccurate or irrational. Heider, one of the chief figures in attribution theory, held that we are generally overeager to think of events as being intentionally caused by particular people rather than as being outcomes of complex situational factors. Even adults are too prone to attribute intentionality and to find someone to praise or blame. The sort of irrationality which can affect our perceptions is suggested in an experiment by Walster (1966), who showed that where subjects considered one of four versions of a story of a runaway car, each version having different consequences but the same cause, the group which heard of the most serious outcome attributed the most intentionality to the driver.

In reviewing the main research findings on person perception, it may be useful to follow, approximately, the historical line of development. In the late nineteenth and early twentieth centuries, the greatest concern was with the judgment of emotions, some of the impetus coming from the view of Darwin that expressive movements of the face, such as smiling or snarling, represent remnants of movement which may have been functional in earlier stages of man's development. Alongside this was a concern with the question of who were the good or accurate judges. The difficulties of establishing a satisfactory criterion for accuracy led to this question being shelved and replaced by a greater interest in the processes of impression formation.

Judgment of emotional states

One of the earlier experiments was conducted by Gates (1923), who found that the ability to recognize emotional states varied according to the emotion and to the age of the judge. Thus, three-year-olds showed 50 per cent accuracy in judging laughter, but it was only later, at approximately two-year intervals, that such a degree of accuracy was obtained for pain, anger, fear/horror, surprise and contempt, in that order.

Woodworth (1938) realized that 'accuracy' of differentiation of emotions depended partly on how fine or how broad were the categories to be used. He produced a scale of six categories in which the categories most often confused with each other were adjacent; they were: (1) love—happiness—mirth, (2) surprise, (3) fear—suffering, (4) anger—determination, (5) disgust, and (6) contempt. Using these six broad categories, Woodworth showed that subjects could discriminate pretty accurately, particularly between those which were farther apart on the scale. Later, Schlosberg (1952) realized that since categories (1) and (6) were quite often confused with each other the list could justifiably be presented as a circle.

That the perception of emotional states can be influenced by social context was demonstrated by Cline (1956), who used simple drawings of three faces, one glum, one smiling and one frowning. These he presented in pairs to his subjects. When paired with Glum, Smiler became a dominant, vicious, gloating, taunting bully, but when Smiler was presented along with Frowner he was perceived as peaceful, peace-making, helpful and friendly.

The question of accuracy

Much of the earlier work, on the lines discussed in the previous section, was concerned with getting subjects to judge 'accurately" what emotion was being expressed. Gradually, however, it came to be realized that the various criteria for being correct, such as the opinions of the experimenter or of the actor or of a group of other judges, were all unsatisfactory. Who is to know what the other person really feels or is really like? It might be thought that we could put subjects into certain situations where the emotion and its expression could be easily identified. Landis (1929) did this when he had a number of subjects photographed while they watched a rat being decapitated; the difficulty was that a number of subjects 'smiled'. Again, there are individual and national differences in the degree to which people allow their feelings to show.

Another difficulty lay in the fact that many of the earlier experiments used judges and subjects who were from rather homogeneous groups, for example American female students judging American female students. 'Accuracy' in such cases is likely to be higher than otherwise because of what Fiedler (1954) has called the 'assumed similarity' phenomenon. It is thought that we often assume others to be like ourselves and to infer their emotions from our own. In the case of judge and judged being from a homogeneous group, the chances are that such assumptions and inferences will happen to be pretty accurate.

It has been suggested by some psychologists that such processes as 'motor mimicry', 'empathy' and 'recipathy' are involved. In the first, we would unwittingly mimic some part of the other's behaviour, such as slumping the shoulders, puffing out the chest or limping. Then our mimicry would become the unconscious basis for empathy, that is, for feeling the other person's feelings. In recipathy, we would judge that the other feels depressed because he makes us feel depressed.

The difficulty of establishing a valid criterion for accuracy, together with a realization that in 'real life' we perceive others not on the basis of arrested animation as in photographs but on extended sequences of events, led to a shift of interest to the processes involved in forming and maintaining impressions. It is to these processes that we now turn.

First impressions

Probably many people overrate their ability to 'read a face', being insufficiently aware of how their first impressions are very dependent upon other cues from the social context. This context is usually highly structured and we are receiving cues from the person's role, the place, the occasion and the people with whom he is seen. 'You can judge a person by the company he keeps'. Presumably, the good 'con' man appreciates many of these points, as does the social climber. Some sources of cues, such as dress and appearance, which once helped us greatly in impression formation, are becoming more ambiguous, so that we are being forced to realize more clearly how useful the length of hair was in perceiving the sex of a person, or how the beard helped us decide who was the student.

Where role is concerned, it can be argued that where it is perceived we can ascribe certain personality traits with some accuracy; for example, the civil servant may be seen as methodical, prudent and disciplined (Merton, 1959). This would be either because a role is chosen to suit one's personality or because the personality is shaped by continued enactment of the role; or both. We are usually aware, however, that the role does not encompass all of the person's personality; in fact, we often consider his 'real' personality to be revealed more by those acts which lie outside that range of behaviours we normally associate with the role. Thus, we might consider that we had learned more about the 'real' personality if we saw the vicar in a night-club than if we saw the businessman there.

Another important contribution to a first impression is made by the perceiver's own commonsense or 'naive' personality theory, which he brings readymade to the particular act of perception. We all try to delve below the surface to discover relationships between various items of a person's behaviour. We conceive of these relationships in terms of causes, motives or traits. In this pattern-finding we are helped by the sense we have of which traits go together. Some of the commonly held associations are indicated by the frequent occurrence in our language of such phrases as 'fat and jolly' or 'mean and grasping'. These traits may or may not be correlated in 'reality'; the point is that all of us have implicit theories of personality in which they *are* related. When Wishner studied the correlations existing between a number of trait adjectives he found high correlations between such pairs as unjust/unintelligent and conscientious/practical. In Wishner's (1960) terms, the implicit personality theory would be a complex correlational matrix which we carry in our heads and by means of which we are unconsciously making inferences about the object-person's personality.

Implicit theories of personality may also be described as stereotypes, where certain characteristics are ascribed to a category of persons such as Negro, old person or policeman. When we recognize in a person a cue which is central to a category, we assign the person to that category and impute to him those traits which form our stereotype of the category. An illustration of this comes from experiments by Secord (Secord and Backman, 1964). He used a series of photographs of faces varying in Negroidness along a dimension from extreme Negroid to Caucasoid. He found that a wide range of Negroidness would be lumped together under the label of 'Negro' and that a common stereotype of 'Negro' would be applied to the whole of this range.

Prejudice consists of a negative stereotype and attitude towards a certain category or group (see chapter 11), but stereotyping in itself is a common process of generalizing which is probably necessary if we are to get to grips with our complex world. We may have stereotypes about old people, owners of sports cars, headmasters or any other conceptual grouping of people. In so far as they are accurate, stereotypes allow us to move into action promptly and appropriately, as would be the case at a party where we had correctly distinguished between the vicar's wife and the publican's wife. But, like all generalizations, the categorization and the stereotype may be inaccurate or may do injustice to individual cases.

Central traits in impression formation

So far we have said nothing about the way in which some traits seem to be more central or influential in the process of impression formation. The classic study in this field was by Asch (1946). He took a Gestaltist view and held that even a first impression is an impression of the whole person. Even when the factual basis is meagre, the impression is striving towards completeness, reaching out to other compatible qualities. Again, traits, when ascribed to a person, do not exist in isolation but are mutually defining and interacting in such a way as to produce meanings not found in the individual traits. The 'intelligent' component of 'warm and intelligent' suggests a creative, spontaneous brightness whereas when 'intelligent' is linked with 'cold' it suggests craft and calculation. A change in one trait affects the others, particularly if that trait is a central one.

In an experiment, Asch asked subjects to give their impressions of a person whom he described as intelligent, skilful, industrious, cold, determined, practical, cautious. He asked other subjects to do the same except that in their case he substituted the word *warm* for *cold*. What he found was that the two sets of impressions were significantly different and he argued that in this list the trait-names 'warm' and 'cold' were central in that they had a greater share in organizing the other traits and in polarizing the two sets of impressions. As an example, 65 per cent of the subjects given the 'warm' list saw the person as 'wise' whereas of those given the 'cold' list only 25 per cent saw him as 'wise'.

If, however, the words 'warm' and 'cold' were used in the list— obedient, weak, shallow, unambitious, vain—they had less centrality or influence than they had had in the previous list. Again, if the words 'polite' and 'blunt' were used in place of warm and cold in the original list, the percentages seeing the subject as wise differed less; 30 and 50 per cent respectively. Thus, a central trait is one which is important in organizing a given stimulus list in relation to a given trait ('wise') in a checklist. Wishner later defined a central trait as one which organized the other traits because of its intercorrelation with the trait to be judged, e.g. warm and wise.

An experiment by Kelley (1950) explored the effects of Asch's warm–cold variable in a more 'live' situation. He prepared three groups of students for their meeting with a new instructor by giving them brief biographical notes about him. The notes were identical except for one item; half the students in each group read that the new instructor was a 'rather cold' person, whereas the other half read that he was a 'very warm' person. The instructor then appeared and led a twenty-minute discussion with each group. Following this, the 'warm subjects' rated him more highly than did the 'cold subjects' on the following traits: considerate, informal, sociable, popular, good-natured, humorous, humane, sincere, industrious. Furthermore, it was noted that 56 per cent of the 'warm subjects' entered the discussions as against only 32 per cent of the 'cold subjects'. It seemed that differing perceptions had led to differing behaviours.

To illustrate further the way in which a classical experiment, such as Asch's, can generate a whole line of further research, we can refer to an experiment reported by Huguenard *et al* (1970). In this experiment, 377 pairs of students were formed, with each student being a stranger to his partner. One selected student in each pair was told either that his partner was (*a*) intelligent, skilful, industrious, cold, determined, practical and cautious *or* (*b*) the word 'warm' was substituted for 'cold', as in Asch's original work. Then the selected student interviewed his partner for ten or twenty or thirty minutes and, finally, rated him on an eighty-item pairs comparison form where warm-related words were paired with neutral adjectives. It was found that there were significant differences in the ratings, corresponding to the use of the words *warm* and *cold*, and that these differences according to initial 'set' persisted even through the thirty-minute interviews. Thus, a central trait can affect a first impression and this first impression can maintain its influence right through a period of intensive interaction.

This brings us to a more detailed consideration of the ways in which first impressions may or may not be revised in the light of further experience.

Maintaining and changing impressions

We have, perhaps, been implying that the various bits of information which are unified into an impression are experienced at one and the same time. What is much more likely is that the various bits are received in some sequence over a period of time. Various models, such as the additive, averaging and weighted-averaging ones, have been proposed to account for the way in which a sequence of bits of information are absorbed into a unitary impression, but to consider these in any detail is beyond our scope. We should, however, before concentrating on the phenomenon of 'primacy', make the point that probably a number of different processes are involved at different times.

In experiments where subjects have been asked to form an impression from a short list of trait-names, just two or three words, they tend to combine the words in a simple, additive fashion. Thus, as shown by Bruner *et al* (1958), it is possible to predict with reasonable accuracy the impression of responsibility a subject will form from the words 'intelligent' and 'inconsiderate' if one knows the strength with which each one separately is correlated with 'responsibility' in the subject's mind. As we have seen, however, where lists are seven words in length there occurs a differential weighting in which some words assume a centralizing influence. Differential weighting of items is also found in the 'primacy effect', in which the first items tend to dominate the final impression, probably by giving the subject a 'set' which influences the reception, or non-reception, and interpretation of later information. The process resembles that by which a self-concept is sustained (see ch. 2).

On of the earliest demonstrations of the primacy effect was given, again, by Asch. He presented some subjects with the following stimulus-list, in which the 'good' terms come first: intelligent, industrious, impulsive, critical, stubborn, envious. He found that the person so described was likely to be viewed as happy, humorous, sociable and restrained. Another group, who were given the list in the reverse order, tended to form a different impression, one in which 'bad' traits were dominant.

Luchins (1957) extended this idea by giving subjects two paragraphs describing a stimulus-person called Jim. One paragraph described him as friendly, outgoing and extraverted, (E), whereas the other paragraph described him as shy and introverted, (I). Jim was perceived as more friendly by the groups given the paragraphs in the E-I order than by the groups in which the order was I-E. In each case, the first paragraph was the one which had the greater influence on the final impression.

Other experiments explored the effects of early crystallization of impressions. Asch asked one group of subjects to make ratings of a stimulus-person who was described as intelligent—industrious—impulsive. After these ratings, he asked them to rate a person who was critical—stubborn—envious. After the two separate ratings, they were told that the two sets of traits belonged to the same person. This group had greater difficulty in reconciling the two sets of traits into a unified impression than did a second group who were given the six traits 'at one go'. Dailey (1952), in another experiment, showed that where subjects were pressed to make a more 'premature' judgment of another on the basis of early and rather trivial information, they made less use of later information and were therefore less accurate in their predictions. On a somewhat similar line, Cohen (1961) found that subjects who believed that they were expected to transmit their impressions to others tended to suppress contradictory elements and polarize their evaluations. One must wonder if a teacher, expected to produce an early report on a pupil, would react in the same way!

The ways in which early impressions survive are probably similar to those by which the self-concept is maintained (ch. 2) and by which attitudes harden after public commitment (ch. 10). Incoming information tends to be received, rejected or distorted according to how well it fits the existing impression. It is true that in a number of conditions the primacy effect can be overcome as where, for example, subjects are warned that they are expected to recall *all* the stimuli presented. Nevertheless, there is now a weight of evidence to underline the commonsense view that first impressions are difficult to erase. The commonsense we refer to is, of course, ours; the impressions are those held by others.

The perceiver's part

This brings us to the point where we must consider more closely the part played by the perceiver in person perception. It has often been said that all people tell us something about *themselves* as they describe others. We have already discussed the way in which such descriptions are given in terms of categorizations. We shall now describe a study by Dornbusch (1965) in which he investigated the importance in person perception of the way in which the perceiver categorizes his world.

Dornbusch's subjects were white, Negro and Puerto Rican boys and girls, aged between nine and eleven, at three summer camps. Previous to the camps, the subjects had been strangers to one another. He recorded non-directive interviews in which, one week after camp started and again a week later, each child described a number of other children. The recorded interviews were analysed and all the ideas contained therein were coded, making sixty-nine categories. Further analysis revealed that where one subject described two others he tended to use the same categories so that there was an overlap, from the description of one to the description of the other, of 57 per cent in the categories used. Where, on the other hand, an analysis was made of the amount of overlap in categories used by two different children in describing a common subject person, the average overlap was only 45 per cent. There was, in other words, a greater overlap with a common perceiver than with a common stimulus person. This was interpreted by Dornbusch as meaning that 'the most powerful influence on interpersonal description is the manner in which the perceiver structures his interpersonal world'.

This structuring of the interpersonal world has received increasing attention since the publication in 1955 of George Kelly's *The Theory of Personal Constructs*. His approach, which is being increasingly used as a basis for psychological assessment, is perhaps best illustrated by a brief and simplified consideration of his 'grid technique'. The subject may be asked to supply perhaps twenty names of significant people or objects or events. If it were people, he might write one name on each card; e.g. his mother, his wife, the girl-friend he nearly married, his boss, his closest friend, his favourite teacher, and so on. These cards would then be presented to him three at a time, these triads either being completely different or overlapping, and he would be asked to state some important way in which any two people in a triad might seem alike and in contrast to the third. He might, for instance, say 'I can sit and chat to A and C but not to B'. A succession of triads would elicit from him his 'repertory of constructs', the bipolar dimensions according to which he categorizes, interprets, evaluates and anticipates his experiences. Only with schizoids and very complex people, says Kelly, are more than twenty or thirty triads needed to elicit these repertoires of constructs which as 'used in everyday life are generally quite limited'.

By exploring a person's 'phenomenological' world (see chapter 12) in this way, we see not only what his chief constructs are but we can also arrange them hierarchically: see e.g. Hinkle's 'laddering technique' (Hinkle, 1965, p. 73). Whereas some are core or super-ordinate constructs, others are peripheral or subordinate. Those people whose constructs are more numerous and more hierarchically integrated are sometimes referred to as 'cognitively complex' (see Crockett, 1965), but the validity of this term as a generalization should not conceal from us the fact that a person's subsystems may vary considerably in degree of complexity. For example, a lepidopterist may be cognitively complex with regard to moths and butterflies but cognitively simple with regard to people; according to Kelly, a man may differentiate finely among other men but see only unidimensional differences among women. Miller and Bieri (1965), in their 'vigilance hypothesis', have suggested that more distant or less familiar objects are more closely attended to, possibly because they are perceived as a greater potential threat, and therefore more finely categorized. Some support for this comes from a study by Soucar (1970), in which he found that disliked teachers are more differentiated by their pupils than are liked teachers.

Personality studies of cognitively—simple perceivers have shown them as more likely to be authoritarian (see Steiner and Johnson, 1963), to be more intolerant of ambiguities and to be more extreme in the judgments they make. To them, people are right or wrong, good or bad, black or white. Their highly stereotyped impressions tend to form rigid but brittle structures which eventually give way or 'about turn' in the face of inconsistent information. There is some evidence that their impressions often show a recency effect rather than a primacy effect. They probably make more use of irrational procedures such as the discounting of contradictory evidence; that is, until they 'about turn'. Cognitively—complex perceivers, on the other hand, are more capable of assimilating seemingly contradictory facts into their impressions and probably make more use of additive processes to achieve a balanced picture. On the whole, the cognitively complex person seems better able to perceive finer differences between people, but his very complexity may lead him to be still reflecting when action is called for.

What we are arguing in this section is that the perceiver, with his own peculiar categorizing and interpreting style, is a vital factor in our consideration of what is perceived. We perceive and evaluate the 'same' phenomena in different ways according to our varying cognitive complexity and our varying personal constructs. An interesting illustration of the way in which this can be a cultural or group variant was given recently when the troubles in Ulster were reported and analysed in two documentary films, one Polish and one Belgian. Whereas the former based its analysis on social class differences between the workers and their exploiters, an expected Communist viewpoint, the latter 'saw' the events in terms of Protestant versus Catholic, a reflection of the dissensions in their own country. Perhaps there is more than a little truth in Sullivan's (1955) assertion that 'one can find in others only that which is in the self'.

Who is the good judge

The question whether there is a general ability to judge others accurately is one which is still hotly debated among social psychologists. What does seem likely is that there are factors at work which could make us believe that we are better judges than we really are. For example, it is likely that in our society, at least, politeness dictates that other people are likely to confirm our impressions rather than question them. It is probable, also, that people are more variable in their personality and behaviour than we normally accept; we tend to overgeneralize or overstabilize our perceptions. The well-known 'halo' effect is an illustration of this.

Even if it is difficult to prove the existence of a general ability at judging, there is a variety of evidence suggesting that we may have more success in judging some types than other types. An early study by Vernon (1933) showed that the personality traits of those who were good raters of themselves, traits such as a good sense of humour, were not the same as those traits which characterized good raters of friends or good raters of strangers. Those who were good raters of strangers tended, for example, to be less sociable. Twenty years later, the socially detached were again picked out, by Taft (1955), as being more accurate judges of others.

Taft also concluded that there was no general difference in judgment ability between men and women. Bronfenbrenner *et al* (1965), however, later distinguished between sensitivity to one's own sex and sensitivity to the opposite sex and decided that women who were accurate in judging their own sex were less successful in judging men, whereas men who could accurately judge other men tended to be accurate in judging women also.

There is also evidence that any given person may be better at judging some traits than other traits. Argyle (1967), has suggested that people are more accurate in assessing whatever qualities concern them most so that, for example, anti-Semites are better at identifying Jews. Taft decided that intelligent people were better judges of the intelligence of others but were not necessarily better at judging other traits.

It may well be that there are two major types of judgment ability which contribute to accuracy and these may not be possessed in equal degree by the same person. They are sensitivity to individual others and sensitivity to generalized others. The latter is similar to that 'stereotype accuracy' possessed by the person who is good at perceiving general social norms and trends. To take an example given by Bronfenbrenner, a store manager might be a good predictor of which items will sell but be a poor predictor of just which customers will buy. It has been shown more than once that in certain conditions 'stereotype accuracy' can lead to better predictions than can interpersonal sensitivity. It could be that, within certain limitations of time, a live situation might present the interpersonally sensitive perceiver with so much information that he is more confused, at least temporarily, than if he based his predictions on a perception of the norm.

Interpersonal elements in person perception

We have been seeing that any question of accuracy in person perception must take account of who and what is the judge and who and what is the judged. Person X may be able to make accurate perceptions and predictions for person Y but not for person Z.

Furthermore, most human encounters are examples of interaction, characterized by a 'recycling dyadic process' in which reciprocal feedback modifies further perception. An example of what we have in mind comes from a study in which subjects were paired with partners with whom they had equal scores on a dominance measure (Davis, in Jones and Gerard, 1967). The subjects were led to believe that their partners were either more dominant or more submissive than they themselves. In a cooperative context, the subject who believed her partner to be dominant was herself quite submissive, and vice versa. In a competitive context, the subject who believed her partner to be dominant tended to be dominant herself whilst her partner tended to be submissive.

Summary

First impressions tend to stick. They may, of course, be valid but they can arise from 'chance' situational or contextual cues which may have no real relevance. They may also owe a great deal to our individual systems of personal constructs and our varying degrees of cognitive complexity. Even when contradictory evidence appears, it may be ignored. If the evidence on which we made up our mind is removed we may still, in a complex issue like judging another's personality, quite easily find alternative evidence or excuse for not admitting that we were mistaken. In particular, it is the cognitivaly simple who are less willing to revise their first impressions or to let the evidence before their eyes modify the stereotype with which we all usually begin our interactions.

Often, what we are seeing is the behaviour of the other in a particular type of situation of which we ourselves are an important part. We assume that this is their usual behaviour but, given a different situation or different behaviour from us, this behaviour could alter considerably. Once our first impression is signalled to the other, usually subconsciously, there is set in motion a 're-cycling dyadic process' through which these first impressions come to function rather like self-fulfilling prophecies. The fact that the rude noise may in truth have come from over the wall and not from the only boy in view may not prevent him from reacting to your freezing look by slinking 'guiltily' by the next time you see him.

In schools, it is a common experience to find two pupils disagreeing about the friendliness and efficiency of a particular teacher. Similarly, two teachers may perceive different traits or abilities in a particular pupil or class. Of course, each teacher may be describing correctly the situation in which he is a participant. The importance of this is seen when we link it to the teacher's great power to influence events. He is, for instance, often required to pass on his evaluations of pupils in the form of reports to parents, prospective employers and others. Perhaps even more important is the fact that his perception of a pupil, even where kept private, is guiding his behaviour towards the pupil and the pupil's reactions to him. For these reasons, it is essential that a teacher should be continually questioning the origins and validity of any impressions he has formed of his pupils or classes. Yet, although we are advocating that impressions should always be open to revision, it is realized that a teacher must of necessity be making decisions every hour on the basis of these impressions as they exist, and must often implement his decisions in anything but a tentative manner. What he must beware of, however, is the danger that the necessity of deciding and acting may polarize and harden impressions in such a way that teacher and pupil are led to interact along a narrowing and deepening channel. It is in such ways that vicious circles remain unbroken.

Discussion and further study

1. (*a*) Get together with about four others. Choose three persons (X, Y, Z) known to each of you and with whom you interact. If, for example, you are at a college you might choose a male student, a female student, a tutor or a porter. Do *not* divulge names to anyone outside the group. Then, working independently, write down three important ways in which two of the three are similar and in contrast to a third—they need not be the same pair each time. Now compare the constructs you have used.

(*b*) Pool the constructs and add to them until you have about ten different bipolar dimensions related to personal qualities. Set out the dimensions like this:

PERSON X

intelligent |⎿___|____|____|____|___⏌| dull

humorous |⎿___|____|____|____|___⏌| humourless

Then, working absolutely individually, grade person W on each dimension, placing a tick where you think appropriate. Now pool your ticks on to a master-sheet using colours to distinguish ticks from different graders. Find any marked discrepancies between graders and attempt to explain them. Then do the same for persons Y and Z. (If marked discrepancies do not arise from these three, choose as a perceived person someone about whom you think the group will be divided in liking/disliking). Summarize your conclusions.

2. List the sorts of statements that various teachers could make which might indicate what their core constructs are for perceiving pupils.

3. How far are we justified in judging an individual by the company or place in which we see him?

4. 'What you look hard at seems to look hard at you' (Hopkins, *Journals*). Discuss.

5. Is it a good thing that a student-teacher or probationer should be warned that a class he is about to teach, or a group within it, are 'trouble-makers', etc.?

6. How important may the first impression be that is given by a teacher to a class?

7. What are the pros and cons of stereotyping?

8. In a small group, list individually and then compare and discuss any words or phrases which trigger off fairly strong stereotypes for you, e.g. middle-aged.

Further reading

General: Hastorf, Schneider and Polefka (1970), *Person Perception*; M. Cook (1971), *Interpersonal Perception*.

Specific: On 'personal constructs', Bannister and Fransella (1971) is excellent. Also useful but more advanced is Bannister and Mair (1968) *The Evaluation of Personal Constructs*. Maher, ed (1965), *Progress in Experimental Personality Research,* Vol. 2, contains two moderately long and useful articles, Bonarius, on personal constructs, and Crockett on 'Cognitive complexity and impression formation'. On styles of perception, categorization and cognition, there are excellent though advanced articles in Warr (1970); see also the articles in Part IV of *Wrightsman* (1968). Articles Asch (1946), Wishner (1960), Dornbusch (1965), Huguenard *et al.* (1970) and Kelley (1950) are also worth reading.

6

Interpersonal affiliation and attraction

Traditional commonsense has many and varied things to tell us about how people attract or reject one another. We would all agree, presumably, that 'birds of a feather flock together'. Would we also agree that 'opposites attract' or that 'politics make strange bedfellows?' Does familiarity really breed contempt? Does absence make the heart grow fonder or does being out of sight imply being out of mind? If we bear in mind the contradictions that occur in that wide pool of commonsense from which we draw as suits us, we are less likely to think that the answers being provided by, or stressed by, psychologists are as obvious as some people might, in retrospect, claim.

Affiliative needs

Before discussing why it is that people affiliate, we should observe that there are times when we are impelled towards company and other times when we seek to escape from company. The effects of isolation, solitary confinement, 'cabin fever' and the like, and the often-associated effects of sensory deprivation, have been well documented. These conditions can rapidly undermine the morale of most normal human beings who, it is said, thrive on the mild stress and excitement of being with others. If, however, the stress grows too great then we are soon retreating into some den or making for the nearest trout stream. Small closed communities from which people cannot easily retire, such as a kibbutz or an Arctic base, can generate more tension than is bearable. We can suffer from over-exposure to people as well as from underexposure.

Primary wants

Among the more obvious reasons for people banding together is the satisfaction of their basic physical and material wants, such as mating, food production and defence against common dangers. The young human spends a number of impressionable years in dependence on the family group, particularly in the mother–child relationship. His membership of a family group is reinforced, at first continually and later intermittently, by the rewards of food and security. In this way he becomes conditioned to being a member of groups in general. Thus, it seems appropriate for Maslow (see ch. 2, p. 4) to have put 'belongingness' as the third most imperative of human wants, following those of physiology and safety.

Reduction of fear

With regard to safety needs, the common observation that in conditions of loneliness people often suffered fear inspired Schachter (1959) to explore the relation between fear and the urge to affiliate. In his model experiment all subjects were told by the experimenter, a 'Dr Gregor Zilstein', that they would be given an electric shock. Half the subjects were told this would be painful whereas the other half were told it would be a mere tingle. The former group became more afraid, as revealed by later questioning. It was then announced that there would be a ten-minute delay for the setting up of apparatus, and subjects were given the choice of waiting either alone in a comfortable room or together with other subjects in a less comfortable room. Whereas about two-thirds of the 'high-fear' subjects chose to wait in company, only one-third of the low-fear subjects did so.

An interesting supplementary finding from Schachter's experiments was that fear generated a stronger urge to affiliate in firstborn than among later-born children. This has been explained in terms of the greater attention given by parents to the firstborn's aches, pains and fears. The firstborn thus learns, more than the others, to turn to other people for the reduction of fear.

A later experiment, by Sarnoff and Zimbardo (1961), was concerned with the differentiation between fear and anxiety.

They used the word 'fear' to describe what one felt when faced with a 'realistic' danger, such as an impending attack by a bull, and the word 'anxiety' to describe the sense of nervousness or dread that may arise without any obvious or understandable external cause. The experimenters hypothesized that fear, as defined, would be more readily understood by others who might in any case be experiencing the same external fear-provoking event. Fear could thus be more easily shared than anxiety which, being more personal, vague and 'unrealistic', would be difficult to discuss without the risk of embarrassment and the further anxiety arising from this. This being so, they argued, 'anxious' subjects would prefer to be alone, in contrast to 'fearful' subjects who would seek company. The subjects in the experiment were male students. Fear was aroused in some of them by the threat of electric shock, while anxiety was aroused in other subjects by asking them to suck a variety of emotionally-laden objects such as a breast-shield. As hypothesized, high-fear subjects tended to choose to wait together whereas high-anxiety subjects chose to wait alone.

Social comparison

Apart from the reduction of fear, affiliation is thought also to satisfy a need for 'social comparison'. This idea owes most to Festinger (1954), who argued that in many situations there are no clear, objective means of establishing what is right or good or acceptable, and that in such situations the actions of other people become our guide. The social norm becomes the criterion of 'right', as many of us may realize when asked to donate to a charity or towards a gift for a departing colleague. Festinger maintained that we all desire to evaluate ourselves, our actions, abilities and opinions, and that we do this mainly through the social comparisons we are able to make. Frequently, we do not know just how we should react except by taking our cue from others similarly placed.

We can illustrate these general points by reference to a couple of experiments. In one (Zimbardo and Formica, 1963), examinees-to-be were found to prefer to wait with those in the same condition than with others who had already tried the examination. In another (Schachter and Singer, 1962), subjects were given an injection of a drug which aroused them physiologically; it was found that they became either angry or euphoric according to the 'staged' behaviour of a person who was waiting with them. It seems that where they were aroused but felt unsure of *what* they were feeling they would take the cue, or label the emotion, from the example of others who were thought to be in a comparable situation.

Affiliation to a group, apart from giving opportunity to compare one's emotional responses with those of others, is also very important for the attainment of 'social reality' (Kelvin, 1969, pp. 33-6), the 'consensual validation' of opinions, attitudes and beliefs. To perceive others in agreement with oneself is very satisfying and reassuring and we tend to avoid those who too often disagree with us. The group is also a source of esteem and a vehicle for self-development, the fourth and fifth factors in Maslow's list (p.   ). In many ways, a group is necessary for the development of identity and the definition of one's self. A number of experiments have shown how a threat to the status and esteem of one's group is seen as being also a threat to one's self-concept.

The need for social comparison usually helps to draw us into the company of others similar to ourselves, for it is with these that we usually compare ourselves. To mix with people dissimilar to ourselves is to run greater risk of disconfirmation of our opinions, attitudes and beliefs as well as a greater risk of loss of appreciation from others. It has been shown that the psychologically secure can more often take this risk; it is those, such as adolescents (see ch. 2), whose self-concepts are most precarious who are most dependent on approval from others of their kind. There are, of course, considerable individual variations in self-esteem, as we have seen in chapter 2, and there is evidence (Reese, 1961) that those whose self-esteem is low are the ones who are most sensitive to group reaction in that they find acceptance most rewarding and rejection most frustrating.

Interpersonal attraction

From a consideration of a person's attraction towards others in general, we now turn to the question of who, in particular, a person will be attracted to or repelled by. We shall look at the following factors: popularity, similarity, complementarity, proximity, reward-ingness of others, and frequency of interaction.

Popularity

A useful distinction can be made between popularity, which is an evaluative factor describing a more general or collective attractive-ness to others, and friendship, which is an interactive factor describ-ing, usually, interpersonal attraction in a dyad (couple) or small group. Thus a person may be popular, in that he is held in high esteem by many, but may at the same time have few or no friends with whom he interacts closely. A further point about popularity is that it may be specific to the group or groups with whose norms the individual con-forms; he may not be popular in other groups. Nevertheless, there are people who are more generally popular than others and they tend to be the ones who are more extraverted, adjusted, socially sensitive and intelligent (Argyle, 1969, pp. 332-3).

There is also a relationship between self-acceptance and popularity, as indicated by Reese (1961) in a study he made of four hundred elementary and high-school pupils in the United States. He found that the most popular were those with a moderate degree of self-acceptance; less popular were those whose self-esteem was high; least popular were those with the lowest self-esteem. The relation-ship between the two factors is, at least partly, a circular one in that either can be cause or effect.

Similarity

If we now look more closely at the question of who befriends whom, we find that one of the most frequently stressed factors is similarity of values, attitudes and interests. One of the chief proponents of this line of reasoning is Newcomb (1961), whose data came mainly from a study of male students who shared a hostel for sixteen weeks. He found that analysis of an attitude questionnaire, completed by the students before they met one another, gave a pretty good prediction of who would like whom in the latter part of the sixteen-week period. What was most predictive was similarity in attitudes that were central (see ch. 10) and the attractions that developed during the period did so particularly where there was a similarity of attitude towards the self and towards other members of the hostel.

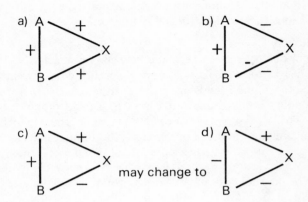

Fig. 6.1

At its simplest, Newcomb's model may be represented by a triangle where A and B are the two persons and X represents the issue, event or other persons towards which or whom they each have an attitude. If their attitudes towards X are both positive, (*a*), or if they are both negative, (*b*), there will be less difficulty in A and B becoming friendly than in the case (*c*), where A has a positive attitude towards X but B's attitude towards X is negative. Greater strain would be generated where X represented an issue which was central to the self-concept or attitude system. If, in our diagram, A and B were pupils and X represented school or a school subject or another pupil, the imbalance in (*c*) might be resolved in a change to (*d*). In what other ways might (*c*) change?

As part of his study, Newcomb asked each subject to describe himself and the others and also to describe how he thought the others would describe him. From this, Newcomb derived a measure of perceived similarity regarding the self and found that this related even more closely to interpersonal attraction than did 'actual' or 'real' similarity. That A's picture of himself should be similar to B's picture of A was important, but even more important was the similarity between A's picture of himself and A's perception of how B pictured A. We like others who, we think, view us as we view ourselves. This has been found to apply even where the descriptions of the self have contained unfavourable elements. (cf. ch. 2, p. 25). Perceived confirmation of one's attitude leads to attraction which is likely to lead to reciprocation and a rewarding relationship.

The evidence on similarity of attitudes between friends, and on the part played by perceived similarity, is plentiful and convincing. Evidence as to similarity between friends on personality traits, such as extraversion, or authoritarianism or ascendancy (G. W. Allport, 1961, pp. 347-8), is much more equivocal. That friends are often perceived by others as being more alike in personality traits than they really are is suggested by Miller *et al.* (1966), in an article which concludes as follows: 'Friends' common navigation through time and space and their true similarity on attitude, interest, value, skill and socio-economic dimensions is mistakenly generalized by the raters to personality trait dimensions'.

Complementarity

An alternative to the 'similarity' argument is that which stresses complementarity of needs and skills. Needs and skills can differ in kind or intensity. It has been proposed that, for instance, a dominant person and a submissive person, or a nurturant person and a succorant person, would make good pairs of friends since their needs are complementary in kind. It can further be argued that a person who admires a quality with which he himself is weakly endowed may be attracted towards a person who manifests that quality or ability to a higher degree. Such a difference in intensity or quality might attract a physically weak person to a physically strong person, a power-seeking but relatively powerless person to a leader, or a socially inept individual to a socially skilled one.

The complementarity theory has been advanced mainly by Winch and his co-workers (1955), who drew their data largely from studies of married couples. Arguments raised against their standpoint include the following. Firstly, what is described as complementarity may be but a special case of similarity. A married couple one of whom is dominant and the other submissive in the relationship may in fact be in agreement about how the marriage roles should be played; they may, for instance, agree that the husband should take the lead in many matters. In this way, they are sharing a similar attitude. The same may be said about a number of professional roles, e.g. doctor and patient, teacher and student. Secondly, it has been shown that married couples show more complementarity than do friends or engaged couples. Complementarity may, then, characterize long-lasting or clearly established dyadic relationships in which there are mutually accepted complementary roles but, in general, it is thought that 'similarity' is much the more important factor in initial attraction between people.

Proximity

Before people can perceive similarities or complementarities between themselves and others they must come into some form of contact. This brings us to what some authorities consider to be the most basic condition for attraction, namely, physical proximity or 'propinquity'. This factor may seem very obvious and yet its applications are often neglected in classrooms and elsewhere. In Newcomb's study, referred to earlier, it was found that in the early part of the sixteen-week period propinquity was a very important factor in determining preferences, and that only after the first fortnight or so did perceptions of similarity in attitude outweigh it.

Evidence of the strength of the proximity factor comes from a number of studies conducted by Festinger, Schachter and Back (1950) in the late 1940s, in which they investigated friendship choices among families of war veteran students. Families were allocated in random order to houses or apartments. Where ten families in each apartment block were housed five to a floor it was found that friendship choices between next-door neighbours on the same floor amounted to 41 per cent but fell to 22 per cent among next-but-one neighbours and to 10 per cent among those separated by two or three other doors. In other cases, families lived in five units, each arranged in a horseshoe shape with all houses except the end ones facing inward to a grassy court. It was discovered that those who lived in the ten end-houses, facing away from the rest of their unit, had fewer than half as many friends as did the others. Another finding in these studies was that those who lived adjacent to focal points such as mailboxes or stairway exits were more often named as friends.

It has been suggested that when people become neighbours, or realize that in some other way they are going to be interacting frequently, they try to convince themselves that such interaction is going to be pleasant. This can lead to a more positive evaluation of the other person, as demonstrated in an experiment (Darley and Berscheid, 1967) where subjects were given information about two others and told that they would be interacting, later, with one of them. As hypothesized, a subject's evaluation was higher for the one with whom he anticipated interaction.

Rewardingness of others

Having looked at similarity, complementarity and proximity as factors in determining who is attracted to whom, we now turn to the rewards that are provided by some people more than by others. An interesting standpoint is that taken by Homans (1958) and by Thibaut and Kelley (1959), who look on social behaviour as an exchange of goods, material and non-material. Put at its simplest, they hold that A will maintain interaction with B so long as the transaction is profitable enough to satisfy the expectations he has developed from past experiences (his 'comparison level') and more profitable than any available alternative promises to be (his 'comparison level for alternatives'). Profitability is not just a matter of rewards or income; it is the excess of rewards over the costs incurred. Thus, we may avoid a relationship which promises high rewards if we think the costs are likely to be too great; we may prefer a less rewarding but less costly and, therefore, more profitable relationship.

Rewards may include the satisfaction of our primary needs for food and drink and of our need for secondary, generalized or social reinforcers such as approval. Costs can include fatigue, boredom, anxiety and fear of embarrassment and loss of reputation. Homans quotes an example of a person asking a colleague for advice; the consultant measures costs such as disruption of work against rewards such as enhanced prestige; the consultee weighs rewards such as accrue from the advice against the cost of some acknowledgment of his relative inferiority. One of the interesting points about exchange theory is the application it makes of ideas from operant conditioning to the maintenance, strengthening or extinction of bonds between people.

It might be thought that a complimentary remark would always be rewarding. In most cases it is, but we can reach satiation point beyond which another compliment means nothing, as would be the case in giving another pellet to a satiated pigeon. Furthermore, humans are, as we stressed in the previous chapter, prone to interpret an act in terms of the motive or attitude which they think lies behind it. We are less pleased by a compliment we perceive as ingratiating and may be suspicious of one we think is undeserved.

The place of a compliment in a sequence of behaviour has also to be considered, as illustrated in an experiment by Aronson and Linder (1965). Each subject (S) interacted over a series of seven meetings with a confederate (C) of the experimenter. It was arranged that S should 'accidentally', after each meeting, overhear an evaluation of S given by C to the experimenter. The evaluation followed one of four sequences.

P–P Positive in all sessions
N–N Negative in all sessions
P–N Positive in early sessions; negative in later ones
N–P Negative in early sessions; positive in later ones

After the end of the seventh session, each subject was asked to rate his liking for the confederate.

On the basis of a naive application of reinforcement theory, we might have predicted that the greatest liking would follow the sequence which contained the greatest number and greatest consistency of rewarding statements, i.e. the P–P sequence. The greatest liking, in fact, occurred after the N–P sequence followed by P–P, N–N and P–N, in that order. What is important, according to the experimenters, is the feeling of gain or loss in esteem. A gain in esteem may be more potent as a reward partly because a formerly critical person who becomes complimentary may be seen as a more discriminating and reliable judge. A person who has come to be relied upon to produce consistent and frequent praise may lose some reward-value.

Frequency of interaction

This discussion of the rewards provided by others leads us to a consideration of the effects of 'familiarity', or interaction frequency, on liking. Some social psychologists maintain that interaction is in general more rewarding than punishing and that in consequence increased interaction leads to increased liking (Newcomb, 1967). This is the argument behind the proposition that where two people, two pupils or two cultural groups dislike each other, dislike will be lessened if only the two are engineered into closer proximity and more frequent interaction (see ch. 11 on prejudice). Newcomb accepts that this generalization holds over a wide range of situations. We should, however, take note of an important limitation to this generalization.

In an experiment by Freedman and Suomi (Freedman *et al.*, 1970) it was arranged, successfully, that a confederate would stage an incident by which he would cause subjects to either like him or dislike him. After this, the confederate and the subjects met for three, six or twelve sessions after which the subjects again voted their liking for the confederate. The evidence from this and other experiments was that where there was initial liking, or neutrality, or even mild dislike, an increased number of meetings led to an increase in liking; where, however, there was an initially strong dislike, this remained unchanged even after twelve meetings. In chapter 11 we shall discuss in more detail the possibility that where there is an initial strong dislike or a marked conflict of interests, needs or personality, more frequent contact may increase conflict rather than decrease it, at least in the short term (Zajonc, 1968).

Summary

Man finds in the company of his fellow humans satisfaction of his instrumental and expressive wants, reduction of fear and an opportunity for social comparison and the establishing of 'social reality'. His attraction to others is, however, selective. Important factors in this selection process are:

(a) similarity in central attitudes, particularly in the eye of the beholder;

(b) complementarity, of lesser importance;

(c) spatial proximity, worth bearing in mind when, in the next chapter, we discuss applications of sociometry, which is the measurement of social attraction;

(d) differential reward value of others;

(e) frequency of interaction, which seems to ameliorate all but the more extreme incompatibilities.

For the teacher, an awareness of the factors influencing inter-personal attraction should help him to make wiser use of his considerable powers to encourage or discourage this or that grouping of pupils. This awareness should, for example, make him better able to ameliorate the attitudes (see ch. 10) of pupils to one another and to form groups which are effective (see ch. 9). Before dealing with the latter point, however, we need to look more closely at some of the structures and processes which characterize the groups into which people are drawn or directed.

Discussion and further study

1. Do the commonsense adages quoted in the first paragraph help or hinder us in our understanding of human behaviour?

2. Do you agree that we may suffer from overexposure as well as underexposure to the company of others? If so, may this be linked with the effects of others as described in the early part of chapter 4?

3. How far does the material of this chapter follow lines indicated by Maslow's 'ladder of wants'? (ch. 1).

4. How may the Behaviourist concepts of reinforcement and conditioning help explain the adult human's almost universal affiliation with groups?

5. Does the distinction between being 'fearful' and 'anxious' (p. 92) seem valid?

6. 'I didn't know whether to laugh or cry'. Does a statement like this make sense in relation to the Schachter and Singer experiment?

7. Do you agree that we tend to avoid those who often disagree

with us? If so, what are the implications for the maintenance of impressions and stereotypes as discussed in ch. 5 (and again in ch. 11)?

8. With reference to Newcomb's ideas on balance or congruity or consonance in attitudes, in what various ways might the dissonance in Fig. 7. (*c*), p. 96 be resolved? Consider real-life or hypothetical examples.

9. What is the importance of distinguishing, as on p. 96, between (*a*) similarity of attitude and (*b*) perceived similarity of attitude? Relate this to ideas discussed in ch. 5, e.g. the 'recycling dyadic process'.

10. Do you agree that complementarity of behaviour (p. 97) in a dyad (pair) may be underpinned by similarity in a more basic attitude? (cf. ch. 4, question 2).

11. Why, in the Festinger, Schachter and Back study (p. 98), was it important that allocation to residences was random? What limitations might there be in applying conclusions from this sample of people to other groups of people?

12. Do Homan's ideas on 'exchange theory' apply to your friendships?

13. Suggest explanations for the varying degrees of liking which followed the four sequences in the Aronson and Linder experiment (p. 100). What may the implications be for teacher-pupil interaction?

14. Discuss examples, either small-scale or large-scale (e.g. Ulster or Cyprus), which might indicate that the findings of Freedman and Suomi (p. 101) may have wider application.

Further reading

Berscheid and Walster (1969); Newcomb on attraction and balance —(1961, 1967); Festinger (1951, 1954) and Festinger *et al.* (1950) on social comparison and propinquity; Schachter on 'Affiliation and isolation'—e.g. in Wrightsman (1968). Homans on 'exchange theory' (1958); also Thibaut and Kelley (1959). Articles by Miller (1966) and Aronson and Linder (1965); Button (1971) on friendship and sociometry, especially ch. 4 and Appendix 2. A useful general account which has served as an unavoidable model for some of this chapter is in Freedman *et al.* (1970).

7

Groups: general characteristics and internal structures

This chapter will be mainly descriptive of the general characteristics of psychological groups and of their internal structures. It will also introduce a number of concepts and terms which are useful in the classification of groups. We shall in this way hope to prepare the ground for the next two chapters, in which we discuss important group processes.

General characteristics of groups

Affiliative needs and the forces of interpersonal attraction, the subjects of the previous chapter, serve to draw people into clusters or groups, although it is well to remember that there are groups which are involuntary and which *may* be neither satisfying nor attractive. For a child, one such involuntary group would be his family, and another could be the school he attends. The study of small groups, whether voluntary or involuntary, has become a distinctive concern of social psychologists and in this chapter we shall be describing some of the chief characteristics of such groups.

The group, in a psychological sense, differs from a mere aggregation of individuals in that from the interaction of its members comes a relatively stable pattern of relationships, with some agreement about common goals, a degree of cohesion, and the evolution of norms and structures. Thus, a crowd would not qualify as a psychological group because it is relatively unstructured; in the words of Kelvin (1969, p. 252), it 'does not interact, it acts in unison'.

Goals and wants

Some groups may be described as formal and may, ostensibly, have an explicitly stated and agreed goal, as in the case of a football

105

club or an amateur orchestra. However, this probably does not blind us to the realization that such a group is in fact satisfying a number of different wants, with the admixture being somewhat different for each member. In the case of a political club, for example, one member may have joined merely out of interest in politics, another to further his personal career and another 'just for the beer'. Yet, given some time for interaction, the beer-drinker may be led by stages into involvement and identification with the club's political activities, whereas the politician may find increasing satisfaction in the bar. Other groups may be better described as informal and may, for instance, pursue a succession of temporary goals while satisfying a basic want of belonging and friendship. All groups, if they are to function smoothly, must satisfy some of the varied wants of each member; in the case of a voluntary group, if the satisfaction given does not reach the member's 'comparison level' (p. 99) he may leave or transfer to a more profitable alternative.

Cohesiveness

The degree of attraction a group holds for its members and the amount of commitment the members have to each other and to the group's goals and norms are referred to as the group's cohesiveness. In a cohesive group there would be low absenteeism, a low turnover of members, a high reciprocation of sociometric choice among members (see p. 115), and greater conformity to a group's norms. One way in which the cohesiveness of an in-group (the 'us' group) can be increased is by increasing the threat, or perceived threat, from an out-group (a 'them' group); There are numerous examples from history of this being done deliberately by politicians and it may be suspected that some of the presentday international border incidents, whether the 'border' is physical or psychological, are fomented and maintained in the interest of diverting attention from internal dissensions and of increasing national cohesiveness.

Group norms and conformity

Where a number of people cluster together long enough for inter-action to develop, patterns of behaviour and expectations will evolve; these are known as group norms. These norms represent shared ways of seeing the world. In order to be compatible with one another, in order that the group functions shall be performed smoothly, members must to some extent share perceptions of and attitudes towards others and themselves. They need to be able to predict with some accuracy the behaviour of the other members, in order that all behaviour may synchronize smoothly. 'In essence, a group consists of people who know, or believe they know, what to expect from one another' (Kelvin, 1969, p. 233). The way in which this applies to the agreed division of tasks within the group is a topic we return to shortly, when discussing positions and roles.

The smooth running of a group, based on accurate predictions of each others' behaviour, is only possible where members conform to the norms. Since the common goals of the group are to some extent compromises between the wants of individuals, it is unlikely that group goals and activities are at all times satisfying to an individual member. Conformity to all the norms is therefore difficult, at times, for each individual and most groups have worked out explicit or implicit sanctions to be applied to individuals who deviate and thus threaten the basis of the group's functioning. Studies (Schachter, 1951) have revealed that other members direct more communication towards a deviate or potential deviate in an attempt to bring him back into line. This increased attention ceases at a point where it seems hopeless, whereupon the individual is ignored and rejected. The processes involved include those of 'social reinforcement' which we discussed in chapter 4.

Deviance is most threatening, of course, when it involves norms that are central to the group concerned. To flout a norm concerning dress and appearance would be tantamount to suicide in one group but cause hardly a stir in another. Deviance from peripheral norms is less unacceptable and is, in fact, found with some frequency among the leaders of groups, presumably because their allegiance to central norms is unquestionable. In this way a leader may be given 'idiosyncrasy credit', whereas a fringe member has to consolidate his acceptance by the group through stricter conformity to its norms. The outsider trying to get in is probably the one to show the greatest conformity to the norms, or, at least, to those which are most easily identified and paraded; he has the job of establishing his credentials to the club gatekeeper.

Reference groups

This brings us to the concept of 'reference groups'. This name is given to the group or groups with the goals and norms of which a person identifies. From such a group he would absorb values, attitudes and norms of behaviour. The point to note is that a reference group need not be also a membership group. Adolescents, for example, seem often to be identifying with their stereotype, accurate or inaccurate, of groups or classes of people they would like to join. Equally, there may be membership groups which do not serve as reference groups; this may be the case with an adolescent in a non-voluntary group such as the family or the school. Some non-voluntary groups may even become negative reference groups where the enforced member is, so far as he can be, a counter-conformist (ch. 4, p. 63). Another interesting case is that of the 'marginal-man' (ch. 11) such as a second generation immigrant, a foreman, a prefect and, perhaps, a deputy headmaster. The 'marginal man's' dilemma consists of his having conflicting reference groups, neither of which is he able or willing fully to reject or join. It is usually attractive but sometimes difficult to be 'one of the boys'.

How large is a small group?

So far we have described small groups in terms of their being voluntary or non-voluntary, formal or informal, 'in' or 'out', membership or reference. But how do we define 'small'? One rough definition which reflects much usage is: 'greater than the Graces and fewer than the Muses'; i.e. between three and nine. However, dyads (groups of two) show many of the characteristics of small groups, such as patterned interaction, norms and roles, and are included in the same category by many social psychologists. Some writers, however, seem to prefer to treat the dyad separately, emphasizing the much greater complexity that exists where a group has three or more members. A third member can provide audience, mediation and the threat of a cleavage into two and one.

At the upper end of the size scale, it is very difficult to say where a group ceases to be small. This question is linked with the distinction between a 'primary' and a 'secondary' group, a distinction which owes much to Cooley (1902). The 'primary group' is one which is small enough for face-to-face interaction of all the members and which involves a member as a whole person, cognitively and emotionally. The family, the peer group of friends and some work groups have these characteristics, though not to an identical degree. A 'secondary group', in contrast, is mainly one of contractual association for the attainment of specific goals; relations between members would be relatively more formal, impersonal and cool; only a segment of the member's personality would be involved. It is to primary groups such as the family, the army platoon or the church-going-wives' group that most of us give our deepest loyalties rather than to the secondary groups or social organizations such as state, army and church. It is the primary group, the 'great incubator of human character' (Cooley, 1902) which mediates the values of society most effectively and which anchors our attitudes most firmly.

The distinction between primary and secondary groups, though useful, is not always easy to make. Few groups fall clearly into one category. One supposes that a political party would be a secondary group whereas a political club, which involves its members in a great variety of interaction, is nearer to being a primary group. Presumably, a school class would be better described as a primary group where its size and the amount of time it is in being allow the development of cohesion and structure. It is difficult, however, to fit a secondary-school second-year mathematics set C into the same category.

Coming back to the definition of the psychologist's 'small group', we can, perhaps, say that the critical thing is not the size in itself but the quantity and quality of interaction or mutual influence between members. This may be why the term 'face-to-face group' seems to be gaining some preference over 'small group' or 'primary group'.

How groups are studied

Many of the characteristics we have been describing were stated in general terms by 'armchair' social psychologists around the turn of the century. Since then, and in keeping with its chosen image as a young science, social psychology has seen a great expansion in the use of controlled laboratory situations for the study of groups. These have added a good deal to our knowledge and we shall make considerable reference to some of them in later chapters. But there are limitations to what artificial laboratory experiments can teach us about the complexities of everyday behaviour in groups. For instance, a 'natural' group is usually one in which interaction has developed over a longish period of time and to which the individual has a strong commitment. This may be very different in important ways from a laboratory 'group', which may be an aggregation of relative strangers who may care little about the effects their actions have on the others and which may be in existence for only half-an-hour. Because of such limitations, field studies of 'natural' groups have also played an important part in extending our knowledge of group structures and processes.

Whether studies have been carried out in the laboratory or in the field, it is worth looking briefly at some of the chief techniques employed, such as rating systems, category systems for interaction analysis, participant observation and sociometry.

Rating methods

These have been fairly widely used by, for example, army and civil service selection boards. Typically, a trained observer watches a group and then gives a rating to some aspect of group behaviour which interests him. He might, for example, be observing a group solving a number of problems such as building a bridge out of barrels, planks and selotape while he rates individuals on some such aspect as 'leadership'.

Category systems and interaction analysis

These systems are designed to enable a trained observer to categorize and record all the significant acts likely to occur in small face-to-face groups. If we take as an example one of the earliest and best-known systems, Bales's 'Interaction Process Analysis', the significant behaviour is that related to problem-solving processes in the group

Bales's System of Observational Categories*

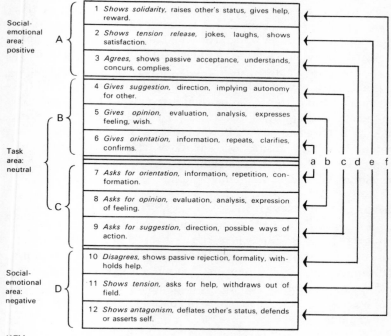

KEY

a   Problems of communication   d   Problems of decision
b   Problems of evaluation   e   Problems of tension reduction
c   Problems of control   f   Problems of reintegration

A   Positive reactions   B   Attempted answers   C   Questions
D   Negative reactions

*Robert F. Bales, (1950), p. 9.

Fig. 7.1

(Bales, 1950; Bales *et al.*, 1951). Bales identified six interlocking functional problems applicable to any interaction system; these are labelled *a* to *f* (see Fig. 7.1 and Key). Problems *a*, *b* and *c* relate to the task of the group; *d*, *e* and *f* relate to socio-emotional problems.

The trained observer would first number the members of the group, e.g. 1 for the chairman or leader, 2 for the person to his left, 0 for the group as a whole. He would then categorize each unit of verbal behaviour, such as a single sentence or a phrase, or a significant non-verbal act, such as a deliberate yawn, a laugh or a nod, and record these units at a rate of perhaps twenty or thirty per minute. For instance, a chairman's remark to the group: 'At the end of our last meeting we decided . . .' would be entered as 1-0 in category 6. Observations recorded in this way can be used to draw profiles by which groups or individuals can be compared. In chapter 12 we shall look at category systems specially designed for the analysis of teacher–pupil interaction.

Participant observation

A classic example of participant-observation is that carried out by Whyte (1941) in Boston, where he spent three and a half years in close contact with various street-corner groups. He joined in many of their activities, such as bowling, but did not hide his purpose of studying their activities. Among the techniques he used for recording his observations was the mapping of spatial groupings. Figure 7.2 is an example.

The participant-observation method, with its tricky 'semi-detached' role, is costly in time and effort. It is also open to criticisms such as that the known presence of an observer changes the behaviour of the observed and that subjective elements can creep in where there is a sizeable lapse of time between observation and recording. Nevertheless it is a most useful complement to laboratory studies. (See J. Patrick (1973)—A Glasgow Gang Observed.)

Sociometry

This, the last method we describe, is the one which has been used most widely in education. Developed by Moreno (1934), it involves

The Cornerville S&A Club

February 29, 1940 8–8:15 p.m.

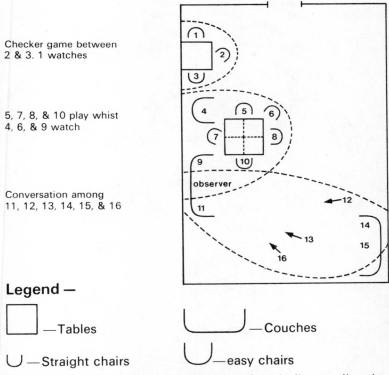

Checker game between
2 & 3. 1 watches

5, 7, 8, & 10 play whist
4, 6, & 9 watch

Conversation among
11, 12, 13, 14, 15, & 16

Legend —

☐ —Tables

⊔ —Straight chairs

⌣⌣ —Couches

⊔ —easy chairs

Direction in which chairs and couches face indicates direction in which men face.

Arrows indicate direction in which standing men face.

Dotted lines enclose those interacting.

Fig. 7.2

asking subjects to name up to three, four or five others with whom the subject would like to work at some specified type of task. such as constructing a boat, or sit next to or go on holiday with, etc.

(Gronlund, 1959; Button, 1971). These choices can be plotted on a matrix or depicted on a target sociogram such as illustrated in Fig. 7.3.

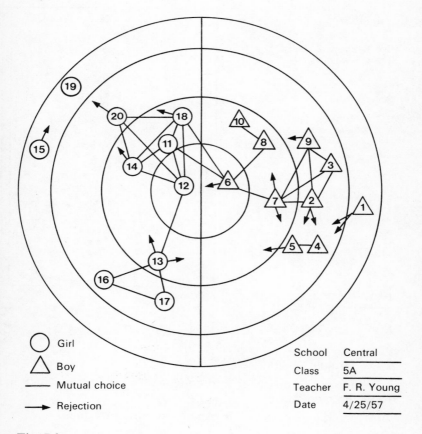

○ Girl	
△ Boy	
—— Mutual choice	
⟶ Rejection	

School	Central
Class	5A
Teacher	F. R. Young
Date	4/25/57

Fig. 7.3

With the use of such a method, it can more clearly be seen who is the 'star', who is the 'isolate' and who form the cliques. It is thought advisable to avoid asking children to name those they would *not* like to work or play with, as there is a danger of crystallizing dislikes. In the hands of a cautious and sensitive teacher, the information gained can be a basis for some social engineering. In the case of an isolate, for example, an arrangement to involve him in a joint task (proximity and frequency, p. 98) with another pupil with whom there is some promising similarity or complementarity (p. 97) stands more chance of success if the teacher knows there is at least some oneway attraction. Sociometric data can also be analysed to reveal the amount of cohesiveness in a group, as indicated by the proportion of total choices which are in-group or mutual.

Sociometry, like all methods, has its dangers and limitations. One relates to a point we made earlier regarding the distinction between a dyad and a larger group. Argyle (1969, p. 238) puts it thus: 'Sociometry treats a group as the sum of a number of dyadic relationships; however, this is only part of the story—A's relation to B may be quite changed if C is going to be there too'. A somewhat similar point was made by Whyte (1941), who found that observing who originated more interaction in a pair told him little about their relative hierarchical ranking, whereas this *could* be determined from observation of the amount of interaction originated by each member in a group of three or more.

Internal structures of groups

All of the methods considered briefly in the previous section have contributed to our knowledge of the structure of groups and of the processes which generate the structures and work through them. As we discussed earlier, the word group, as used by psychologists, implies systematized interaction. Among many members of informal groups, realization or, perhaps, acknowledgement that there is a structure and hierarchy in their relationship is absent or resisted. Whyte found that his 'corner-boys', asked if they had a leader or boss, invariably replied 'No, we're all equal'. More recently, a student making a study of an 'alternative society' group in a Midlands town was told much the same thing; yet when, for example, he asked one member for his views on a topic which was fairly central to the group ideology he was referred to member X—'he's the expert on that'.

In any group, formal and informal alike, a number of structures develop. One is the sociometric structure, the pattern of interpersonal liking. This affects the cohesiveness of the group and has an influence on the other structures. For example, it affects the communication structure in that information and rumour tend to spread along chains of friends.

The power structure

Another structure which develops is that of power and status; the 'pecking-order'. One illustration of this is in the differential distribution of acts, especially verbal acts. Interaction process analysis has shown that in a number of types of decision-making, problem-solving and discussion groups, ranging in size from three to eight, one person does about 40 per cent of the talking, irrespective of the varying size of the group. In an eight-man group, for example, one member is likely to contribute 40 per cent, a second member 20 per cent, a third member 14 per cent and the other five members 26 per cent between them. The most active contributors also receive the most communications and tend to address their remarks to the group as a whole, whereas less active members direct their contributions 'up the line', i.e. to higher-status individuals rather than to the group. High-communicators also differ in that they give out more information and opinions than they receive, whereas the remarks of low-communicators are characterized by agreement or disagreement or requests for information.

The communication structure

In more formally organized groups, especially when they are larger, this pattern of communication is more explicit and rigid, with more emphasis on the 'proper channels'. A number of possible communication networks in experimental groups have been explored, particularly by Bavelas (in Smith, 1970) and Leavitt (1951). In a typical set-up, group members would be placed in cubicles interconnected by slots in the walls; through these slots, written messages could be passed. Some of the networks in five-man groups are shown in Fig. 7.4.

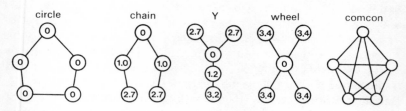

Fig. 7.4

The lines represent channels of communication, from which it can be seen that some positions in the first four structures are more central while others are more peripheral. The figures inside each circle are the 'peripherality' indices for those positions. In chapter 9 we shall consider some of the implications of studies such as these but for the moment it is worth noting one of Leavitt's conclusions, namely, that 'the positions which individuals occupied in a communication pattern affected their behaviour while occupying those positions,—one's satisfaction with one's job and with the group, the quantity of one's activity, and the extent to which one contributed to the group's functional organization'.

In all groups, then, a communication structure is found, whether it is imposed, as in laboratory and formal groups, or whether it emerges, as in informal groups. Each individual has a position in this structure and positions carry varying degrees of centrality, influence, power and status.

The role structure

Overlapping or coinciding to some extent with the power and communication structures of a group is its role structure. This represents a division of labour or function to allow specializations which either further a group's task or increase the socio-emotional satisfaction of its individual members. Both aspects are important and have to be kept in balance; greater specialization may seem to promise greater task effectiveness but this may be at the cost of decreased satisfaction which can adversely affect productivity.

A role represents the expected behaviours associated, in many cases, with one's position in the power structure. For example, different behaviours may be expected of a leader, a lieutenant and a follower. In other cases, roles capitalize on the varying expertise or personality strengths of individuals for specific subtasks. Some may be task experts on this or that, like the 'natural' secretary or treasurer; others may be cast in socio-emotional roles such as clown or comforter. Role differentiation is seen clearly, even today, in most British families; there are, in general, different patterns of expectation for father, mother, son, daughter and eldest child (see ch. 3).

In essence, those roles or norms which are attached to positions in the group and reflected in the structures within groups make possible the prediction and coordination of behaviour. Where such patterning is relatively absent we may have a crowd or mere aggregate; at the other end of the scale is the social organization, characterized at its extreme by 'bureaucracy' (Albrow, 1970).

The social organisation

The term 'social organization', which seems to have superseded the term 'secondary group' (p. 109), is used to describe an integration of a number of small groups into a system designed to accomplish a stated and limited objective. Examples would be an army division, a political party, a local council administration or a large factory. Although one could argue that a school's objectives may be much more comprehensive than those of organizations such as we have mentioned, there can be no doubt that large schools and colleges share many of the characteristics we shall describe.

To gain the maximum advantage from greater size and resources, the organization has to pay much attention to problems of inter-action and coordination. It tends to develop formal and rigid structures into which the individual is slotted. His position becomes a rank or office; norms become formalized into explicit rules; 'proper channels' dictate to a considerable extent who talks with whom and what about.

One interesting model for an effective organization, based on a study of management in America, is the one proposed by Likert. In this 'linking-pin model' (Fig. 7.5), the link men are those who hold overlapping group membership; they are superior in one

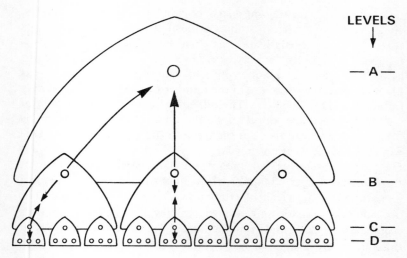

Fig. 7.5

group but subordinate in the other. In a large secondary school, for instance, the Head of Humanities and the Head of Science could be at one level, say level B, and would attend decision-making meetings with their superior, who could be the Head or the Deputy Head. They would also organize meetings with their subordinates in the power hierarchy, such as the heads of the English, History and Geography departments in the former case, the heads of the Chemistry, Physics and Rural Science departments in the latter case. These would be at level C and would, presumably, hold formal or informal meetings with their assistants who would be at level D. In reality, a simple model such as this would not cover all the hierarchies in a large school; other positions, with their associated roles, would be found in separate or overlapping hierarchies; e.g. Senior Mistress, Careers Master, Senior House Master, Head of Lower School.

A model such as Likert's can help us visualize and analyse the sorts of problems met with in social organizations, particularly if used along with concepts such as 'span of control', 'minimal number of levels' and 'chain of command'. In the model, each

119

link-man is shown as having a span of control of three subordinates. Evidence from American studies of business and industry suggests that if a span exceeds five or six then the link-man may be overloaded. To avoid this, it may be thought expedient to subdivide so as to have a greater number of smaller groups. This, however, is likely to lead to an increase in the number of levels in the hierarchy (levels A to D in Fig. 7.5). The difficulty then is that the 'chain of command' becomes longer, with the danger of too many levels intervening between those at the top and those at the bottom. One can conceive a situation in a large school where a young assistant Geography master has an unconventional idea; he has to route it through the proper channels, which might mean via the Head of Geography to the Head of Humanities to the Deputy Head. The decision may be made only after a lengthy wait while the idea moves from desk to desk and is sieved through a series of meetings at different levels. If and when the young assistant gets the go-ahead, his opportunity may have gone or his enthusiasm may have been dissipated.

This sad tale brings us to a crucial dilemma which faces social organizations, the danger of impersonalization and personal frustration. Two big problems to be faced are how to keep all members identifying with the common goal and how to cope adequately with their socio-emotional needs. Sometimes, these needs are satisfied only outside the organization, on 'Saturday night and Sunday morning'; in other cases, sociometric groupings within the organization can bring some satisfaction. Internal sociometric groupings often cut across the hierarchical lines, partly because it may be more difficult to be friendly with one's immediate boss than with equal-ranking close colleagues or members of higher or lower rank in a different chain.

The best managements, of course, try to cater for some self-fulfilment of members within the organization and realize that this has to come through more than mere financial reward. Good management understands the fundamental part played by face-to-face groups in processes of identification and self-fulfilment. According to Likert, management will be successful 'only when each person in an organization is a member of one of more effectively functioning work groups that have a high degree of group loyalty, effective skills of interaction, and high performance goals'.

A developmental sequence

In any group which is sensitive to changing circumstances and is capable of adaptation, internal structures will only be relatively stable, representing states of relative equilibrium in the interaction processes which are going on continuously. Even this relative equilibrium is not achieved all at once; groups go through a development sequence. This consists, according to Tuckman (1965), of early stages of *forming*, *storming* and *norming*, during which there is great concern with internal problems, when the dependence hierarchy, the norms and the roles have to be worked out. Only when this internal jockeying is over can the group concentrate its attention on the external goal and reach the *performing* stage. If one considers a school staff, it is true that one can picture a situation where a firmly settled hierarchy can give rise to complacency in some and frustration in others (not necessarily at top and bottom, respectively). But, it may be equally true that on a staff where pecking orders and roles are not clearly settled one may witness a considerable diversion of energy away from the task to competitive infighting in which task furtherance becomes incidental or is distorted in the service of individual gain.

In a group's developmental sequence, one of the first internal problems which needs to be settled is that of determining the dependency or power relationship and the first position and role to be established is usually that of leader. His influence can be so crucial in the subsequent development of structures that will harmonize the group and harness the energies and skills of its members to the common task that it seems appropriate to deal with the concept of leadership in some detail in chapter 8, before discussing group effectiveness in chapter 9.

Discussion and further study

1. In any formal or informal groups to which you belong, can you

list and then compare some norms, central or peripheral, stated or unstated, which affect behaviour? e.g. approved or disapproved attitudes or topics of conversation.

2. 'Two's company, three's none'. In what important ways does the addition of a third member change a group?

3. What are the pros and cons of studying real life as opposed to laboratory groups?

4. Analyse the target-sociogram in Fig. 7.3. What might the analysis suggest to the teacher?

5. Unobtrusively observe a small group and see if you can determine and, perhaps, represent diagrammatically (*a*) a pecking order in verbal communication as described on p. 116 and (*b*) a role structure as described on p. 117. If two of you could observe independently, you could compare notes afterwards.

6. If you work in, or know well, a large school or college, try representing in diagram form the staff power and communication hierarchy(ies), on the lines of Likert's linking-pin model (Fig. 7.5). Does analysis in terms of 'minimal levels' and 'span of control' suggest any points of possible strain or frustration?

7. Why might power and friendship roles be sometimes difficult to combine? (p. 120).

8. Discuss the relevance of the section on 'The social organization' to any large school(s) you know. Consider especially the needs of staff and pupils in terms of Maslow's 'ladder of wants' (p. 4).

Further reading

Articles by Shaw and by Tuckman, both in Smith, ed., (1970). Also worth reading are articles by Schachter (1951), Bales (1950) and Bales *et al.* (1951), Leavitt (1951) and Likert (1961). On socio- metry, Gronlund's (1959) book is comprehensive, and Button's (1971) has some interesting pages.

8

Leadership: changing concepts; varying styles

Changing concepts of leadership

Teaching has been described as 'institutionalized leadership' (Waller, 1932). Leadership in schools is not, however, confined to teachers but is part of the expectation attached to a whole range of positions at different levels, from the headmaster to the football captain and from the house master to the pupil who edits the magazine or leads the project group in class. Recent developments, such as the growing use of small group work and team teaching, or the application of management principles to the running of our enlarged schools, are causing many people to re-examine the concept of leadership, as we shall do in the first part of this chapter.

Definitions and functions

The leader is that member of a group who has the most influence over the behaviour of the other members and whose position is usually the first to emerge as a group becomes structured. However, it is difficult to divide people into those who are leaders and those who are not: leadership is not an all-or-nothing matter. For one thing, any one individual is usually a member of more than one group and each of these groups may have a structure which represents a state of dynamic equilibrium in which the group is continually adapting to changes in membership, task and situation. Nor does leadership consist of just one skill; it consists of many and these may be based on a variety of intellectual, physical, moral and artistic abilities or qualities. Our main purpose in breaking down the wide and complex concept of leadership into a number of subconcepts will be to suggest that a place can be found in our schools for just about anyone to exercise some type or level of leadership and, in so doing, to develop some of those interpersonal skills of which it is composed. For instance, one of the common ingredients of leadership is social poise and confidence and this can, presumably, be fostered in any pupil through leadership tasks carefully graded and selected for him by the teacher.

We need to begin by introducing some terms which are useful in an analysis of the leadership concept. Some leaders are 'appointed', others are 'emergent'. The appointed leader holds office formally; he is the titular or institutional leader such as a king, a chairman or a teacher; at least part of his authority is derived from his position or office. The 'emergent' leader is one who rises in an informal way from within the group as a result of interactions between the members. Many groups may be observed which have both an appointed or titular 'head' and an emergent or informal leader who is the real centre of influence.

If we were to argue that in such a group the 'real' leader was the one who *functioned* as a leader, we should have to consider the great variety of functions possible in a leader. He may be one or many of these: 'executive, planner, policy maker, expert, external group representative, controller of internal relations, purveyor of rewards and punishments, arbitrator and mediator, exemplar, symbol of the group, substitute for individual responsibility, ideologist, father figure, scapegoat (Krech *et al.*, 1962, ch. 12). Some of the later items in this list have been highlighted by the psychoanalytic school. For example, Fromm (see J. A. C. Brown, 1961, ch. 8), in talking of an 'escape from freedom' by the individual who, 'freed from the bondage of tradition and fixed status and role, . . . was also freed from the ties which had given him security and a sense of belonging', was emphasizing the way in which a leader may be satisfying dependency wants in his followers.

The functions we have listed are so many and so diverse that it is only rarely that one person can perform them all. What happens, therefore, is that they are distributed more widely among members of the group, although the more crucial functions tend to become centred around two positions and roles, those of the 'task specialist' and the 'socio-emotional specialist' (Bales and Slater, 1955). The task leader may also be called the instrumental leader, initiation specialist or ideas specialist. The socio-emotional leader may be referred to as the expressive, maintenance or consideration specialist, or as the 'best-liked man'.

Some of the evidence for such a dichotomy (task/socio-emotional) comes from the work of Zelditch (1955), who studied the nuclear family in fifty-six societies and concluded that the father is usually a task specialist and the mother a socio-emotional specialist. He says that even in the U.S.A., where this differentiation is least obvious, 'the cult of the warm, giving "Mom" stands in contrast to the "capable", "competent", "go-getting" male'. The same dichotomy of functions has been identified in a large variety of small, informal groups, including in the army, schools and colleges and it has been suggested that this role structuring is modelled after the father–mother role differentiation in the family, that small group which has been the centre of so much of our early experience and conditioning.

If we consider the small group as a social system responsive to its environment, like one of those cells which float below the biologist's microscope, we can see that it has an outside and an inside. The task leader is the one who specializes in the 'outside' aspect; he is the most influential member in such functions as perceiving and diagnosing problems, initiating and planning, directing the group towards achievement of the external goal and preventing irrelevant activities. In pressing the group towards its goal, or towards a better adaptation to its environment, he is often forcing members to change their behaviour and to re-examine their ideas and values. The tension he generates may result in some transferring of liking from him to the expressive leader. Tensions created by external demands may also add to tensions already existing between members and it is the particular function of the expressive leader to maintain cohesion and morale, improve communication between members and reduce friction within the group. He it is who keeps the group 'sweet' and this he may do by mediating, lending a considerate ear or shoulder or releasing tension by a timely injection of humour.

It may be that these two major roles we have described are almost incompatible and that few individuals can encompass both. It is difficult to drive and be sympathetic at the same time. Much depends, however, on the group and the situation. If, for instance, the salient motivation of the members is towards the achievement of an external goal, then the one who gives the lead in this, who helps promote satisfaction through success, may be well-liked, at least until the goal is attained.

Who becomes leader?

Personality and leadership

'Prior to the 1930s it was widely believed that leadership was a property of the individual, that a limited number of people were uniquely endowed with abilities and traits which made it possible for them to become leaders. Moreover, these abilities and traits were believed to be inherited rather than acquired' (McGregor, 1960). This 'Great Man' theory led to a great volume of leadership studies which attempted to find the degree of correlation between various personality factors and emergence as a leader. Much of this literature was reviewed by R. D. Mann in 1959 and it is worth while to look in some detail at his findings.

Mann grouped the results of a large number of studies to arrive at correlations with leadership for each of seven personality factors. If we take, as an example, studies concerned with intelligence and leadership, Mann studied twenty-eight of them and found the positive association between intelligence and leadership to be highly significant, statistically. 'However', he says, 'the magnitude of the relationship is less impressive; no correlation reported exceeds ·50 and the median "r" is roughly ·25'. A further conclusion that verbal intelligence was a better predictor of leadership than 'such non-verbal factors as memory and numerical ability' should not surprise us when we remember the importance of the verbal communication network to a group's functioning.

Another five of the seven personality factors—adjustment, extraversion, dominance, masculinity and interpersonal sensitivity —were found by Mann to be positively related to leadership, but all correlations were of even lower magnitude than those for intelligence. The seventh factor, conservatism, was found to be negatively correlated.

Another approach to the question of what type of person becomes leader is to consider the perceptions of the followers, subjective as these may be. According to Krech *et al.* (1962, pp. 438-9), the leader is perceived as being 'one of us', 'the most of us' and 'the best of us'. He needs to be 'one of us' because members need to identify with him: he should, therefore, share the same pattern of interests, attitudes and reaction tendencies with the group. But if he is too much 'one of us' he may lose some of the power to lead. So he should be 'the most and best of us' in incorporating the norms and values of the group to a special degree and in being something of an expert at what matters to the group. But here again we are warned that the gap between leader and led can be too large. Hollingworth (see Krech et al., 1962) found that among children 'the leader is likely to be more intelligent, but not too much more intelligent, than the average of the group led'. If the gap in intelligence is too large, the leader is likely to have different interests or goals; problems of communication arise and the leader would cease to be 'one of us'.

One difficulty in the attempt to identify one 'leader personality' type is suggested by our earlier discussion of the separation of functions among members. The functions of the task and socio-emotional leaders are different and probably, in most cases, require different types of personality for their execution. According to Fiedler (1958), 'the person who readily forms deep emotional ties with his subordinates, who needs to be liked and supported by his men, will find it difficult to discipline or to discharge them'. The socio-emotional leader may have a strong need to be liked and so may like everyone in order to be liked back, whereas task leaders may be able to tolerate more negative feeling and may not feel the need to like all equally.

In general, the leader personality approach has met only limited success. For one thing, the validity of predictions based on those traits which have been studied can at best be only as good as the preliminary grouping of people into leaders and non-leaders or into good and bad leaders. Furthermore, we should bear in mind that these studies have concentrated upon those who *are* leaders; it is possible that any traits which they possess may help a person to *become* a leader but need not be the traits which make for good leadership. An individual may possess qualities which make him a good leader when appointed yet may not possess those qualities most necessary for his 'emergence'. Again, if we consider Likert's 'linking-pin' model we can see that in many of our complex and hierarchical social organizations the effective leader of those below him must also be an effective follower of those above him. At least one study (Hollander and Webb, 1955), concerned with naval aviation cadets, did indeed find that the good leader also tended to be the good follower.

The influence of followers

When, earlier, we were discussing intelligence and leadership, we stressed the interrelationship between leader and followers. We were not simply saying that a leader tends to be intelligent; we were saying that he tends to be more intelligent than his followers but not too much more. This point illustrates the interactionist approach to leadership where the emphasis is upon the realization that leadership depends on the characteristics of the particular group as well as of the individual leader.

It seems to be a fairly commonplace belief that a person who is a good leader of a small group may be a poor leader of large groups. For instance, a lecturer may be excellent with small discussion groups but may be unnerved by large lecture groups. That the reverse can sometimes be true seems less obvious but can be observed. In a large lecture group, it may be the common expectation or norm that no one should interrupt or voice disapproval; in such a situation, a lecturer might be able to keep many interpersonal difficulties at arm's length while he wades non-stop through his prepared material. In a seminar, on the other hand, the followers may expect the right to question and criticise and may more easily undermine the confidence of a tutor who is either inexpert or extrasensitive to criticism. Thus, followers may in some situations display different expectations which put pressure on an appointed leader to display skills which we normally associate with an emergent leader. Bavelas (1960) has suggested that an officer may be no leader in a less structured situation, that a person who can lead well where planning and deliberation are called for may fail where immediate action is called for, and that an individual who may lead well in a friendly group may not succeed where he perceives the atmosphere as hostile.

One illustration of the interaction of leader and follower personalities comes from a study by Haythorn (1956) in which sixty-four male undergraduates were used. Half were high scorers on measures of authoritarianism (e.g. the F-scale); the other half were low scorers. Eight groups of high-scorers and eight groups of low-scorers were then formed; half these groups were given low-F leaders and the other half were given high-F leaders.

	F plus leaders	*F minus leaders*
F plus followers	4 groups	4 groups
F minus followers	4 groups	4 groups

Comparisons of the observed behaviour of leaders and followers indicated, firstly, that the behaviour of individuals 'can be predicted, to some extent, from measures of those individuals' attitudes or personality characteristics'. Secondly, Haythorn found that when the high-F leaders had low-F followers the behaviour of these leaders was less authoritarian than it was when they had high-F followers.

This finding indicates that the behaviour of leaders is, to a significant degree, a function of the attitudes or personality characteristics of the followers. Conversely, the behaviour of followers is found to be significantly a function of the attitudes or personality characteristics of the leaders. The latter, of course, is almost a 'sine qua non' for the concept of leadership, but the former has received less attention theoretically and almost none empirically.

The type of task

A number of researchers have asked whether 'Who becomes leader?' depends at least partly on the situation facing the group. These researchers have often employed the leaderless group technique in which groups are faced with different problems modelled as closely as possible on real life situations, e.g. discussing problems or assembling some physical structure from given materials. The groups are observed and the behaviour of individuals is categorized.

In this way, it is possible to make a fairly objective judgment of who emerges as the leader in each situation.

Some of the most interesting work in this field has been done by Carter and his associates (1950). In one experiment, subjects were grouped and each group was observed working at six different tasks. These tasks were described as: reasoning, intellectual construction, clerical, discussion, motor cooperation, mechanical assembly.

The correlations between the leadership ratings given the subjects on six different kinds of tasks were computed. Almost all of the coefficients were positive, indicating a certain generality of leadership performance from task to task. At the same time, there were noticeable groupings of relationships between certain tasks. By the use of factor analysis it was indicated that there were two different kinds of tasks apparently calling for different leadership abilities. These two factors were called an 'intellectual leadership' factor and a 'doing things well with one's hands leadership' factor.

The fact, suggested by this and other studies, seems to be that leadership is neither wholly general, a function of the leader's personality only, nor wholly specific, determined solely by the nature of the task.

Can leadership be learned?

In chapter 1, we discussed briefly the part played by role in the development of personality and suggested that within limits people can eventually become what they do. Does one become more of a leader the more one goes through the motions of leadership? To what extent does the office make the man? This is a difficult and complex question, but an experiment by Berkowitz (1956) throws a little light on it.

From a pool of over 200 volunteer students, Berkowitz selected forty on the basis of the Guildford-Zimmerman Temperament Survey and of observations of their behaviour in a mechanical assembly task. Ten of these subjects he described as characteristically 'high ascendant', ten as 'low ascendant' and twenty as 'moderate ascendant'. These forty were formed into ten groups, each having one high, two moderates and one low. Each group was then given three problems to solve, the solutions depending on the cooperation of all four members, each of whom had some of the necessary information. The group was set in a 'wheel' pattern and all inter-communication had to be through the central position. In half the groups a 'high ascendant' subject was in the central position; in the other five groups the central position was occupied by a 'low ascendant' subject.

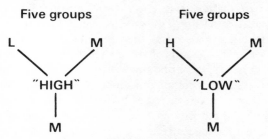

Communications from the central position to other members were analysed and grouped into: (i) passive; e.g. simply relaying information, and (ii) active; e.g. asking for information or proposing solutions. It was found that in problem one the low ascendant leaders were more passive but that by problem three this difference had been eliminated. 'Under the high press of common situational requirements, both the high and low ascendant subjects behaved in a somewhat similar fashion by the third trial'. Further, by the third trial the lows in the centre were more 'active' than highs in the peripheral positions of the group and expressed just as much satisfaction with being in the central position as did the highs. Berkowitz interprets the data as follows.

The high and low subjects differ primarily in that ascendant responses are higher in the response hierarchies of the former. . . . The former are initially more likely to behave in an ascendant manner. However, ascendant responses *are* in the response hierarchies of even the low-ascendant subjects and ascendant behaviour tends to occur by trial three.

Leadership opportunities in schools

In schools, three leader relationships may be found: teacher–pupil, pupil–pupil and teacher–teacher. The problem of who shall do the leading applies to the last two of these.

Whereas relatively few children may reveal a general aptitude for leadership on the lines of the 'great man' theory, many will have the abilities to exercise leadership in at least some situations. Different leader roles, such as those mentioned earlier in the chapter, may require different combinations of physical, intellectual, artistic and social skills. The discerning teacher will encourage one pupil into leadership where the task is intellectual but another where the task is more 'physical' in nature. Two groups which differ in the intellectual level, attitudes or needs of their respective members may be successfully led by two pupils of somewhat dissimilar personalities. Different leaders may be appointed according to any differential weighting of task and socio-emotional goals. Emergent leaders may on occasion be given their head whereas on other occasions a teacher may lend authority to a less ascendant type of pupil by appointing him to a leader role and giving him clearly mandated functions. In this way, a pupil may be perceived as being an agent of the group rather than as someone who is asserting himself for personal glory; this may reduce his fear of losing the friendship of other members of the group. As one simple illustration, we may think of the teacher appointing a different pair of pupils each half-term to the position of form captain and vice-captain, the order being dictated by the register.

An important consideration is the avoidance of the 'self-fulfiling prophecy' whereby those who are first chosen, or who first emerge, get all the subsequent practice and special knowledge available to them as leaders and are thus able to maintain and strengthen their positions. Leadership is something to which many can contribute and from which many may gain in social confidence and skills, and it is in schools, more perhaps than anywhere else, that possibilities exist to manipulate positions and roles to these ends. Nowhere is the old idea of a dichotomy between leaders and followers more harmful than where it appears in our schools.

What sort of person is best fitted to become a headmaster? It depends, at least partly, on whether the school is large or small and on whether it is changing or static in size and ideas. In industry, according to McGregor (1960), 'the leadership requirements of a young, struggling company . . . are quite different from those of a large, well-established firm', and the same may be true of schools. As a school or college changes in size, constitution or curriculum, so its head or principal may find himself less or more suited to be its leader.

What are the main functions of a head teacher as a leader and are these, functions changing as schools become larger? One headmaster (Mather, 1968) writes that 'one of the head's main roles is an enabling one; to enable his staff to exercise effective leadership'. He would accept McGregor's 'Theory Y', particularly where this states that 'the average human being learns, under proper conditions, not only to accept but to seek responsibility'. The leadership function is 'distributable over the whole field of the staff and is not a monopoly of the head'. Acceptance of these views is spreading as the rapid enlargement of schools forces more headmasters to delegate more of their functions and powers.

The idea of rotating leadership has some adherents both abroad, e.g. in Russia, and in this country. For instance, in the Rudolf Steiner schools

it is typical . . . that there is no headmaster, and there are no offices that need be permanent. The control of the schools is in the hands of the collective body of teachers. . . . In most schools . . . there is an executive for assembling and scrutinising the agenda for the week; also a chairman, a secretary and a treasurer; the personnel for these may change from time to time, allowing entry for new points of view and new initiative. . . . No one is bound irrevocably to an office (Edmunds, 1963).

No one imagines that ideas such as these are applicable in all. schools, but what is likely is that there is much room for experimenting on these lines, particularly at levels of leadership below that of headmaster, e.g. in team teaching.

This section has dealt with the position, role, emergence and selection of leaders. The question of leadership styles and how these may contribute to the effectiveness of a group is what we turn to in the next section.

II Leadership styles and group performance

In our consideration of varying styles of leadership and how these affect group performance, we shall begin by discussing the authoritarian-democratic studies which dominated the scene during the forties and fifties and then consider a more refined development of these in the form of Fiedler's 'Contingency Model'.

The authoritarian-democratic studies

The classic early study of this authoritarian-democratic dimension was carried out in the late 1930s by Lippitt and White (1939). It has been so frequently and fully described in the literature that we shall limit ourselves here to a brief summary.

Four groups of ten-year-old boys, each group containing five members, met after school for hobbies such as mask-making. Four adult leaders were 'trained to proficiency' in three leadership styles, viz. 'authoritarian', 'democratic' and 'laissez-faire'. These leaders were rotated from group to group every six weeks, each leader 'changing his leadership style at the time of this transition. Thus, each club experienced each of the leadership styles under different leaders'. In authoritarian leadership, the leader determined the policy, techniques, activities, organization and work partners and was aloof except when demonstrating. The democratic leader encouraged group discussion of policy, outlined the whole plan, made alternative suggestions, gave freedom to choose work partners and subdivide tasks and participated in the spirit of the work without doing too much of it himself. The laissez-faire leader gave almost complete freedom for groups to make decisions and was generally passive and non-participant.

The researchers' conclusions about behaviour under the three 'climates' or regimes may be summarized thus. Groups under laissez-faire did less work and poorer work, and expressed preference for their democratic leader. Groups under autocracy, when compared with those under democratic leadership, were a little superior in quantity of work but showed a sharp decline in work when the leader absented himself: they were more submissive or dependent towards the leader but more unfriendly to each other: they were less contented than when under 'democracy'.

Much research on similar lines came during the forties and fifties and there was a fairly widespread belief that 'democratic' procedures, although a little less productive, were associated always with higher morale and were altogether to be preferred. A major criticism of these views came from Anderson (1959), who reviewed forty-nine studies of this dimension and came to the general conclusion that 'the authoritarian-democratic construct is an inadequate basis for research because, for one thing, it presumes to summarize the complexity of group life into a single dimension'. We can include some of his views within the following points.

1. There is no certainty that teacher-centred approaches are superior or inferior, for learning, to pupil-centred ones. Anderson found eleven studies favoured pupil-centred approaches while eight favoured teacher-centred approaches and thirteen showed no difference.

2. Too many researchers have set out to prove the superiority of the 'democratic' approach. This would be the expected reaction of many Americans in the face of physical and ideological threats from totalitarian powers during the 1940s and 50s. These researchers may, however, have trained their authoritarian leaders to be untypically harsh and hostile, and this may have brought about the lower morale of those groups. In fact, it may be possible to be an autocratic and yet friendly leader with a high group morale.

3. There is evidence that democratically led groups may have higher morale when the group goal is social but that autocratically led groups may have higher morale when the group's primary commitment is to some external task goal. Classes highly motivated towards an impending examination often reveal this.

Fiedler's contingency model

An approach which has sought to recognize the complexity of the relationship between leadership and group performance is that developed by Fiedler (1962, 1965a, b) during the 1950s and 60s. He formulated a means of measuring a person's perception of, or attitude towards, his co-workers. The individual would be asked to think of all others with whom he had ever worked and then to describe first the person with whom he had worked best and then the person with whom he worked least well (his least-preferred co-worker, or LPC). Typically, the descriptions would be made on twenty eight-point bipolar adjective scales of which the following are examples:

Pleasant	8	7	6	5	4	3	2	1	Unpleasant
Friendly	8	7	6	5	4	3	2	1	Unfriendly

From these ratings, Fiedler obtained two scores. The first was the ASO score—Assumed Similarity between Opposites—which indicated the degree to which the individual perceived his most and least preferred co-workers as similar or different. Where the two profiles are very different, the ASO score would be high. Fiedler later found that this score correlated highly (0·80 to 0·95) with the simpler measure of how favourably or unfavourably the individual perceived his least preferred co-worker; the LPC score. The two scores can be treated as interchangeable and we will refer only to LPC scores. A low-LPC scorer is one who differentiates more between his group members, being very favourable to some but rejecting to others.

A leader who is a high-LPC scorer tends to be accepting, permissive, considerate, anxiety-reducing and person-oriented. A low-LPC leader is directive, controlling, managing, anxiety-inducing and task-oriented in his interactions. One notes, of course, a high correspondence between this LPC concept and the democratic/autocratic dimension and, perhaps even more so, the socio-emotional leader/task leader dichotomy discussed in the previous section. Fiedler's researches led him to realize, however, that the relationship between a leader's LPC score and group productivity was complicated by three major factors, in this order of importance:
1. the relations between the leader and the members
2. the degree of structuring of the task, and
3. the strength of the leader's position.

Leader-member relations (*a*) could be measured by sociometric indices or by group-atmosphere scales which indicate the degree to which the leader experiences the group as pleasant and friendly towards him. Tasks (*b*) could be highly-structured where, for instance, they had clear goals, were programmeable, had verifiable results and obvious procedures; or, they could be weakly-structured as where there were infinite solutions and procedures, e.g. as in writing a good play. The leader's position (*c*) could be weak or strong according to the support or lack of support he got from the rules, or the control or lack of control over rewards and punishments rested in his position, e.g., power over promotion.

Fiedler represented these factors in a three-dimensional model with each dimension subdivided. Thus, his model represented eight possible combinations of the three factors (Fig. 8.1). Note that on the lefthand side, octant I, all three factors are favourable (good, structured, strong), whereas in octant VIII, all three are unfavourable (poor, unstructured and weak).

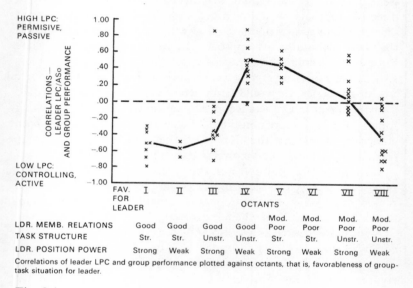

	I	II	III	IV	V	VI	VII	VIII
	FAV. FOR LEADER					OCTANTS		
LDR. MEMB. RELATIONS	Good	Good	Good	Good	Mod. Poor	Mod. Poor	Mod. Poor	Mod. Poor
TASK STRUCTURE	Str.	Str.	Unstr.	Unstr.	Str.	Str.	Unstr.	Unstr.
LDR. POSITION POWER	Strong	Weak	Strong	Weak	Strong	Weak	Strong	Weak

Correlations of leader LPC and group performance plotted against octants, that is, favorableness of group-task situation for leader.

Fig. 8.1

Fiedler analysed the performance of a large number of varied task-groups in terms of these eight types of situation and calculated the mean correlations between the group performance and leader's LPC for each one. The results, as shown in Fig. 8.1, indicate that the low LPC (autocratic) leader has the more productive groups in the most favourable and least favourable situations (octants I,

II, III and VIII), but that the high LPC leader (democratic) does better where the mixture of the three factors adds up to a moderately-favourable situation (octants IV, V and VI).

Let us consider the case of a college lecturer who is lecturing to a group of headmasters on the use of a new piece of equipment such as a video-tape recorder. An assumption that prior relations are good would take us to octants I to IV. The task is one which could be highly structured; i.e. organization into logical procedural steps is possible and acceptable; this narrows us down to octants I and II. His 'position power' vis-a-vis the headmasters is ambiguous and weak but this need not matter; in either case (I or II) his adoption of a directive approach would be accepted by the headmasters without displeasure or non-cooperation and with greater chance of success than with a non-directive approach. If, on the other hand, the same lecturer was leading the same headmasters in a discussion on a less structured, more 'divergent' topic, such as how best to organize teaching-practice, he would be in octant IV. In this case, he would probably incur less resistance, in a situation which is ego-involving for all, by being a more non-directive chairman. Had the group been composed of students and his position power been relatively strong, (octant III), he might find a directive style more efficient.

We may or may not agree on the precise analysis of this or any other case, but we can see, from this example, how Fiedler's model is more articulated and discriminating than the cruder authoritarian-democratic model from which it evolved.

A study by Sample and Wilson (1965) is interesting in the way it combines the use of Fiedler's model with Bales's Interaction Process Analysis (p. 111). Groups of subjects were given a number of fairly routine rat-training problems and the overall results from ten sessions showed no significant difference between the groups led by low-LPCs and those led by high LPCs. During the eighth session, however, the situation was deliberately made more difficult and stressful; on this occasion, the low LPC groups did significantly better. For this eighth problem, observers using the Bales system noted little *overall* difference in the behaviour of the two types of leader. For instance, the mean percentage of leader-to-member acts classified as positive socio-emotional (p. 111, categories 1 to 3) was 24 for high LPCs and 21 for low LPCs. When, however, they separated out the initial planning stage and the rat-running phase which followed, two quite different patterns emerged.

Type of leadership

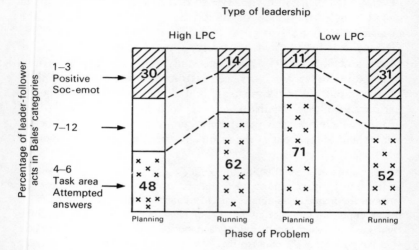

Fig. 8.2

In the planning phase, the low-LPC leaders were more task-oriented and directive than the high-LPC leaders, but in the second phase of 'running the rats' they were the ones better able to relax and see to the socio-emotional aspects of group life. The roles were played by the two types of leader in reverse order and on the 'stress' problem the task–socio-emotional sequence was the one to bring better results.

Conclusion

In its greater concern with the follower and the task, Fiedler's model reflects more closely the interactionist view of leadership discussed in the previous section. It brings home the point that there is a place for more than one style of leader and leadership. Either the leader can select, or be selected for, those situations which suit his style or he can try to change his style to suit different situations and tasks.

What would seem useful for the intending classroom teacher is the development of flexibility in style so that he can switch styles from task to socio-emotional, or directive to permissive, to suit the occasion. An important point to realize is that whichever style is adopted can be adopted positively, a point made in a study by Maier and Solem (1952). In their study, some discussion groups were led by leaders who had been instructed not to contribute their own opinions but to try to ensure that all members had a chance to participate. Other groups were 'led' in a laissez-faire style. The groups which had the positive leaders showed results of better quality and an analysis of the results led the researchers to conclude as follows:

A discussion leader can function to upgrade a group's thinking by permitting an individual with a minority view time for discussion. In a leaderless discussion, the majority dominates and this condition releases pressure which has an important influence on opinion [cf. ch. 4 on conformity]. Without the right kind of leadership, therefore, a minority cannot effectively compete with the pressure of the majority. . . . The quality of thinking in a democracy is thus dependent on the opportunities it affords minority opinion to be heard.

The point to make is that the teacher, no less than the government or the mass media, should not confuse 'democracy' with 'laissez-faire'. Even when he is non-directive, the teacher should have a clear and positive function in promoting group and individual development by, for instance, nurturing minority viewpoints within his classroom and protecting them from the tyranny of the majority.

Discussion and further study

1. How commonly, in your experience, may an individual (*a*) lead in one group but follow in another or (*b*) lead a group in some situations but not in others?
2. Do you agree that social poise and confidence can be fostered in *any* pupil through leadership-type tasks *carefully graded and selected* for him by the teacher? Discuss, itemise and grade according

to difficulty the range of such opportunities available in a classroom and a school.

3. Discuss the phrase 'escape from freedom' (see p. 124 and Brown 1961).

4. To what extent, in our present society, do fathers and mothers take up dichotomous task/socio-emotional roles, as these are described in the three paragraphs on pp. 124 and 125?

5. How is it possible that an officer who was a successful leader in the army *may* fail as a leader of groups in some types of civilian work, e.g. teaching? (And vice versa, of course!).

6. What difficulties *might* arise where a highly intelligent pupil is appointed as leader of a group of pupils in which the others are all about average in I.Q.?

7. For what reasons could one argue that *some* teachers *may* be good leaders of one group but not the other in each of these pairs? (*a*) junior, secondary; (*b*) boys, girls; (*c*) bright pupils, slow-learners. What qualities would be most crucial in those teachers who could teach *all* such groups well?

8. Discuss the implications of the Berkowitz experiment for schools (p. 130).

9. Do you agree that in considering teacher–pupil or tutor–student relationships there is no question about who should be the leader?

10. The author's experience is that appointing form captains, etc., according to strict register order can work even where there are pupils involved who are notorious for irresponsible attitudes. Why *might* this work and be preferable to alternative systems? Does it depend on the tasks involved?

11. Consider any cases—historical or political, real or hypothetical (preferably the former)—of changes in leadership to accompany changes in a group's 'outside' or 'inside' conditions, e.g. peace to war; establishment or expansion to consolidation. Why should such changes in leadership occur?

12. Through discussion, try to pinpoint a good example, real or hypothetical, of two learning tasks one of which is highly structured and the other weakly structured.

13. What sorts of factors might contribute to a leader's position power being (*a*) strong, or (*b*) weak?

14. Discuss the Sample and Wilson experiment (p. 138) in relation to teaching.

15. Do you agree that a teacher has a special responsibility for the nurturing of minority opinions?

16. If, as a teacher, you wished, during a lesson, to switch from a directive to a non-directive style or role, or vice-versa, (*a*) how would your expectations for the pupils have changed and (*b*) how would you signal these changes to the class so that they know clearly what you expect from them? Consider verbal, non-verbal and paralinguistic cues (see ch. 12, p. 207).

Further reading

There are many useful articles in Gibb (1969); of other articles listed in the bibliography those by Anderson, Bales and Slater, Berkowitz, Carter *et al.*, Fiedler, Mann, and Sample and Wilson, are relevant and well worth reading; see also McGregor (1960) and Button (1971), ch. 7.

9

Group effectiveness

It is difficult to think of any group of people outside the armed services who have more power than have teachers to form, sustain, disband or change the groups in their charge. We can allocate work to be done by individuals or by groups; we can vary the size of groups, dictate who goes with whom, impose structure and leadership or allow these to emerge; we can encourage or discourage competition or cooperation both within and between groups. If, as can be argued, education is primarily concerned with the development of the potential of the individual, it should also be remembered, as discussed in the first section of this book, that such individual development takes place in the context of groups. Our power to influence these contexts being so great, it surely behoves us to consider carefully those principles on which we may base our objectives and our methods.

Our obvious objective is to establish groups that are effective; but, we may ask, effective at what and for whom? Social psychologists apply two criteria when judging effectiveness. They are productivity or task achievement; and member-satisfaction or morale. Satisfaction and productivity often go hand-in-hand, but not necessarily so; a satisfied group may be unproductive in terms of an external task and a productive group may suffer internal dissatisfactions. Nor is cohesiveness or solidarity necessarily correlated with productivity. A cohesive group is likely to achieve its aims more effectively but these aims may as easily be for a 'go slow' as for a 'go ahead'. In a group with a low-productivity norm, be it an industrial group or a classroom group, the 'norm buster' will become the target for subtle or unsubtle, verbal or non-verbal pressures designed to induce conformity. This increased attention directed at the deviant ceases only when he accepts the norms of the group or is rejected

143

by the group. In general, however, an increase in cohesion, which makes it possible for members to cooperate and communicate more easily, can be a preliminary to greater productivity.

Individual work or group work?

We all know that many hands make light work and that two heads are better than one, but we also know that too many cooks spoil the broth. How, then, can the teacher make the more appropriate choice between organizing pupils to work individually and organizing them to work in groups? It would be idle to pretend that social psychologists have mapped a clear path through this veritable minefield, but a start has been made and we are moving towards a better appreciation of the factors involved.

One common belief is that groups are capable of better solutions than are individuals and an example of the sort of evidence adduced might be Thorndike's (1938) finding that groups were better at solving crossword puzzles. One reason for this is that groups have a larger pool of information and ideas available, so that there is more chance of someone in the group being able to provide any one particular answer. This answer may then provide a cue for the next answer from someone else in the group. In this way, it is possible for a group to solve a problem which is beyond the capability of any one of its members.

Where a task involves a number of separable skills, work may be subdivided so that each member contributes from strength and cancels out another's deficiency. This is making use of what have been called 'uncorrelated deficiencies', as where a blind man could push the wheelchair in which sits the cripple who is guiding him. It is in such cases, however, that we have to consider our hierarchy of educational aims. If we merely encouraged mutual dependence it might be at the expense of developing independent capability. Fortunately, we should be able to cope with both aims.

One field in which groups can sometimes produce better results than individuals is in the estimation of physical phenomena such as size, weight or temperature. For example, Gordon (1923) asked students to rank-order a set of weights. The average correlation of individual rankings with the true ranking was 0·41. When Gordon 'grouped' the individual rankings into random fives and fifties, he found the correlations rose to 0·68 and 0·94, respectively. These were, of course, not live groups but nominal or 'staticized' groups, and what was being demonstrated was how a larger number of random errors can tend to cancel out. This need not happen where there is a constant bias among the members. For example, the average estimate by members of a political group of the number of votes they will win is not necessarily any better than the estimate made by one particular member. Nor need a group estimate be any better in a live interacting group where the group decision may reflect the bias of the more socially powerful members, who are not necessarily the more accurate judges.

The same argument can apply in the matter of weeding out the poorer ideas suggested by members. Groups certainly have larger pooled resources of critical capacity and can function to eliminate individual errors more quickly, but it is not always true that they select the better ideas and reject the worse ones. Sometimes, a group may not recognize or be willing to accept the best ideas, especially if these ideas are proposed by low-status members. An example of this comes from a study by Torrance (1955) in which he found, among the aircrews he studied, that when a pilot (the leader) had the right idea it was always accepted whereas when the gunner had the right idea it stood only a 40 per cent chance of acceptance. Similarly, Riecken (1958) found that a clue given to a leader or talker was more often utilized than a clue given to a relatively silent member.

Other differences between individual and group working are related to points we discussed in chapter 4 when dealing with the effects of audience and coactors. As we saw, the emotional temperature may rise in a group in such a way as to facilitate what we called performance but inhibit the learning of new or more complex material. However, it may also be suggested that in a group situation an individual might begin by imitating another's behaviour but later he may be able to go on independently. That such advantages gained in a group working may not persist into later individual work is suggested in an experiment by Gurnee (1937). On a series of six trials with bolt-head mazes, groups were quicker and made fewer errors than individuals, but on the seventh trial, when all worked as individuals, no superiority was shown by those who had previously worked in groups.

Quite often, when discussing work in schools, one hears group work being extolled because the product is better. What is sometimes overlooked here is the simple fact that although a group of four will normally produce more than an individual, it is using four times as many pupil-hours. This point is illustrated in an experiment by Taylor, Berry and Block (1958), in which they sought to compare the productivity of face-to-face groups with that of individuals.

The experimenters compared 'real' groups of four with nominal groups of four. The interacting groups were instructed to adopt 'brainstorming' techniques, where criticism was ruled out, 'free-wheeling' of ideas was welcomed, quantity was encouraged and combination and improvement of each other's ideas advocated. The problems consisted of producing as many suggestions as possible for (1) increasing the number of European tourists to the United States, (2) the benefits or difficulties arising from having two thumbs on each hand, and (3) maintaining teacher effectiveness where teacher–pupil ratios were worsening. There were twelve four-man groups in addition to forty-eight men who worked individually. Taking the mean total of responses on the three problems, individuals scored 19·6, real four-man groups scored 37·5, nominal or non-interacting random 'groups' of four scored 68·1. An analysis of the number of unique responses gave a mean total of 10·8 to real groups and 19·8 to the nominal groups. Nominal groups also produced more ideas that were judged to be of good quality.

The experimenters concluded that group participation when using brainstorming inhibited creative thinking. They suggested that this may be due to fear of criticism, even when this is expressly discouraged, and to the way in which a given number of individuals working in a group may pursue the same line of thought or develop the same set towards the problem.

We began this section by looking at the theoretical advantages possessed by groups. What advantages are possessed by *individuals* which in certain circumstances give them greater productivity per man-hour? Firstly, there may be less distraction, a greater chance to concentrate. This can be particularly important in new or difficult learning where there is the advantage of less tension caused by the presence of others. There is also less effort wasted in behaviour of an ego-defensive nature, and less status conflict. Interpersonal problems are fewer and there is less loss of potential through poor coordination. There is no chance of the slowest member delaying consensus and decision. At a simpler, but nonetheless important, level is the fact that in some tasks people cannot help get in each other's way physically; five cannot write any faster on one piece of paper than can one. Especially in complex tasks that require much coordination, individuals may do better than groups, or, at any rate, better than newly formed groups.

Thus, to qualify the evidence with which we started this section, we need to say that Thorndike (1938) found that although groups were better at *solving* crosswords, where the structure of the task was helpful and where solutions were of the 'convergent' type, groups were worse at *composing* crosswords, perhaps because the multiplicity and divergence of ideas led to confusion.

Large or small groups?

If and when a teacher does decide on organizing group work, should the groups be large or small? Some of the answers have already been suggested in the previous section. A larger group has greater resources in information and skills but as the group enlarges so it becomes more and more difficult to tap its potential effectively because of the increasing complexity of physical and psychological coordination. Davis (1969) has estimated that where a three-man group can generate sixty-four structures or relationships a five-man group can give rise to over a million.

One of the earlier demonstrations of the difficulty of realizing the potential of larger groups was given by Köhler (1927), who found that in a tug-of-war team the addition of each member, up to a maximum of twelve, was accompanied by a loss of about 10 per cent of the effort of all the other members. Again, Gibb (1969) found a law of diminishing returns operating where he formed groups of 1, 2, 3, 6, 12, 24, 48 and 96 and gave each group thirty minutes to produce as many solutions as possible to a series of problems permitting multiple solutions. Increments decreased as group size increased.

In a previous chapter, we referred to the work of Bales (1951), who showed that as a group grows in size so there is growing inequality in the amount of participation in verbal communication by members (see also Stephan and Mishler, 1952). A few become relatively more dominant and more tend to 'take a back seat'. Slater's study (1958) of twenty-four groups varying in size from two to seven looked at this from a different angle. He gave the groups 'creative' problems which invited discussion and each group met four times. Afterwards, those in groups of five expressed satisfaction at their experience. Those in groups smaller than five were satisfied except that they felt their groups were too small; observers of these smaller groups thought that members were inhibited from expressing ideas freely for fear of alienating the others; these groups may also have been less stimulating. Those in groups larger than five felt that their groups were often disorderly and time-wasting and that some members were too 'pushy' and competitive; some even asked for more central control. It seems then, that to be effective the group should be 'the smallest possible that contains all the skills required for the accomplishment of the tasks of the group' (Thelen, 1949).

Who goes with whom?

One way of trying to ensure that a group is the smallest possible that contains all the necessary skills is to encourage heterogeneity of personalities within in, but this can also bring problems if it goes too far.

Evidence we discussed in chapter 6 indicated that similarity of persons is more important than complementarity in producing dyads that are smooth-working. A number of studies suggest that the same is true of larger groups. For instance, groups of six where three were high scorers and three were low scorers on an E (ethnocentric) scale showed a tendency to division into two cliques with little intercommunication (Altman and McGinnies, 1960). Groups formed from an admixture of Calvinists and Catholics have also been found to exhibit impeded communication and more social strain (Fiedler, 1962).

In general, heterogeneous groups have the advantage of the large groups we discussed earlier, in that they can produce more ideas, have greater potential for problem-solving, can more quickly eliminate random errors, are less likely to suffer from constant biases, and have a wider critical base. Yet, like the larger groups, they also suffer from more problems of an interpersonal nature. Thus, it could be that where the task of the group is relatively highly structured and there is less possibility of conflict, the advantages of heterogeneity are greater, whereas in unstructured tasks where, for instance, more choices are necessary and more ambiguity present, it may be wiser to form homogeneous groups. Schutz (1958) found that heterogeneous groups were as good as homogeneous groups on simple problems needing little real cooperation but that on more complex tasks, where coordination was more critical, the homogeneous groups did much better.

So far we have used the term 'heterogeneity' in a very general sense. When we look more closely at the variety of skills involved we find some evidence that heterogeneity is more disruptive in a group if it concerns personality characteristics that are highly 'interpersonal', such as those related to power or dependency. An illustration of this comes from a study by Cattell, Saunders and Stice (1953) in which eighty ten-man groups were given a wide variety of tasks. They found greater accuracy of judgment in groups in which the members' personalities were heterogeneous in surgency (i.e. cheerfulness, sociability), radicalism, character integration and adventuresomeness, but found slower decision making and greater frustration in goal achievement in groups which were heterogeneous in sensitivity, suspiciousness and aggressiveness.

Before leaving this section, it is worth mentioning a study by Torrance and Arsan (1963) in which they made a link between heterogeneity of group membership and the factors of social tension and anxiety we discussed in chapter 4. On the basis of IQ and creativity tests, they sorted out classes of 4th, 5th and 6th graders into heterogeneous groups (e.g. 1st, 6th, 11th etc.) and homogeneous groups (e.g. top five scorers, next five, etc.). They found that the homogeneous groups showed less social stress and unhappiness, whether made up of the brightest or the dullest pupils. However, they argued that the homogeneous groups could also be a bit unstimulating and unproductive of new ideas. Bearing in mind what we said in chapter 4 about the possibility of low and high degrees of tension being less productive, we can see that it might pay a teacher sometimes to create moderate social tension by controlling the mixture of personalities in a group.

Group structure and efficiency

We have seen that increasing the size or the heterogeneity of group membership may provide more potential for task solution but at the same time it may increase interpersonal difficulties in such a way as to make that potential more difficult to realize. Also important to consider are the effects of the communication and status structures we discussed in chapter 7.

Networks

In chapter 7, we described structures such as wheels, chains, circles, comcons, which have been widely studied by Bavelas, Leavitt and others and which have parallels in real-life groups. The research results are complex and sometimes embarrassingly inconsistent, one difficulty being that results depend very much on the type of task with which the group is faced. As yet there is no adequate detailed task specification but we may get some general insights into the matter if we accept a rough and ready division of tasks into:

1. Simple tasks such as the pooling of information at a central point.
2. Complex tasks requiring manipulation or discussion of data after it has been collected.

We can set these against a categorization of networks into:

(a) centralized,
   such as the wheel, Y and chain;

(b) decentralized,
   such as the circle and comcon.

| | Tasks | |
	Simple	Complex
cent		
dec.		

(Networks)

Many researches have shown that simple tasks are better done by centralized networks whereas complex tasks are better done by decentralized networks, e.g. Shaw (1964) found that centralized groups did better on simple tasks in fourteen out of eighteen studies he reviewed, and explains this in terms of 'saturation' and 'independence'. In a centralized group, he argues, much depends on the central member and this person may become overloaded or saturated by the demands made upon him in a complex situation. Such difficulty on complex tasks may be aggravated by the greater resistance shown by peripheral members to this central member or leader, who is the one getting most of the 'kicks' which may satisfy such culturally supported needs as independence, autonomy, recognition and achievement. In simpler or more routine jobs there is much less prestige attached to a central role and therefore less resentment from the others. On all types of task, decentralized groups show a more even spread of activity and satisfaction and less resistance from the periphery.

On all tasks, the efficiency of a group depends to a great extent on how quickly and how well they get organized to cooperate. Wheel networks seem to settle most quickly, followed by comcons and then circles. Centralized networks have often been shown to be superior in short-run experiments but it has also been demonstrated that all the networks we have mentioned have roughly equal efficiency *once* they have settled.

Status conflict

One factor which promotes speedy organization in a group is the resolution of conflicts over status. A study by Heinecke and Bales (1953) illustrates this. They formed ten discussion groups, each of five or six members, which met for four sessions. Conflict between members was most marked during the second meeting when, presumably, the status battle was foremost. It was the four groups which reached the highest degree of consensus over the pecking order by the end of this second session which by the end of the fourth session were working with greatest efficiency and satisfaction.

A second example of status consensus promoting efficiency comes from a study by Ghiselli and Lodahl (1958). They began by giving their subjects personality tests on scales designed to measure 'decision-making' or 'supervisory' ability. They then formed groups which had the problem of running two model trains in opposite directions on a track, a job requiring much coordination for success. It was found that productivity was not related to the mean test score of an entire group, nor to the score of the highest-scoring member. What was found, however, was that the most productive groups were those with the largest *differences* between the highest and next-highest test scorers. These were also the groups making the fewest organizational changes during the experiment. It seems that those groups which contained one uncontested leader got organized more quickly. It should be noted again, however, that the time allowed for group interaction was very short, so that it is quite possible that other groups could have become just as efficient if given longer to settle the status hierarchy.

Having in a group a person who is likely to establish himself quickly as an emergent leader seems to produce results similar to those where, as in a laboratory wheel-network, a person is appointed to a focal position. In the terminology of Tuckman (1965), with the 'forming' and 'storming' over, attention can be concentrated on 'norming' and 'performing'. (See p. 121.)

Cooperation and competition

Our purpose here is not to discuss the pros and cons of cooperation and competition but to look at some of their causes and effects. Both competition and cooperation exist; both are encouraged at different times and in different contexts in all schools known to the author.

An experiment by Deutsch (1949) explored the effects of co-operation and competition in ten groups, each with five student members. These groups met for five sessions in each of which they had to reach a solution to a 'human relations' problem. Trained observers categorized the verbal behaviour and rated various aspects of group activity. Five groups, the 'cooperative' groups, were told that each was in competition with the other four groups for a prize and that every member would receive the same rank as the rest of his group. Another five groups, the 'competitive' groups, were told that the individual who contributed most in quality and quantity to the discussions and recommendations would get the prize.

Results indicated that in the cooperative groups there was more coordination of effort, diversity in amount of contribution per member, subdivision of activity, achievement pressure, attentiveness to fellow members, mutual comprehension of communication, orientation and orderliness, productivity per unit time, quality of product and discussions, friendliness, and incorporation of the attitude of the generalized other. Competitive groups showed more behaviour designed to satisfy individual goals, e.g. aggression, sympathy-seeking, domination, recognition-seeking and self-defence. There was no significant difference between the types of group in the amount of interest or involvement.

We should note that what we have here called 'cooperative' groups were actually encouraged in intragroup (i.e. within group) cooperation but intergroup (i.e. between groups) competition. Many situations involve a mixture of the two processes. For example, a football team is cooperating to defeat an opponent but at the same time the forwards in one team may be competing with one another to score the most goals. Such mixed motives, where cooperation and competition are variously balanced, have become the subject of study in 'game theory' (see, e.g., Gergen, 1969).

Sherif's summer camp studies

One of the most fascinating and instructive series of studies of inter-group conflict and cooperation was that begun by M. Sherif and his co-workers in 1948 (M. Sherif, 1966). They ran three separate camps, each for three weeks, for boys of eleven and twelve who were previously unknown to one another. The behaviour of the boys was observed and recorded unobtrusively by the 'camp personnel'. It is worth looking in some detail at these studies, although only a full reading of the original will be justice to the many excellent illustrations of interperson perception and attraction, group dynamics and structure, and attitude formation and changing, all topics we have mentioned or will mention in this book.

At the first camp, early friendships were allowed to develop on the basis of interpersonal attraction and common interest, but when the large group was then rehoused in two separate cabins the friendship choices shifted 'from strictly interpersonal attractions toward in-group exclusiveness'. The two later camps omitted this preliminary but all three camps went through the following stages, which we have summarized.

Stage One lasted for the first week, when the two groups were kept apart and many activities were arranged requiring interdependence within each group. In each group, individuals soon came to assume different roles such as 'cook' or 'athletics leader'. A leader and lieutenants quickly emerged. Each group developed its own jargon, jokes, special ways, symbols and name, e.g. Eagles and Rattlers. Wayward members became the focus for reprimands or 'silent treatment'. By the end of the week, each group had clearly established structure, norms and cohesion.

Stage Two was devoted to the promotion of intergroup conflict. The two groups were brought together to compete for prizes in games, treasure hunts and so on. Each prize could be won by one group only. Between the two groups, bad blood soon developed, as evidenced by flag-burning and the hurling of epithets such as 'stinkers'. Within each group this stage was marked by greater solidarity and cooperation, unfavourable stereotypes of the out-group and some changes in the role structure. For instance, those leaders who were found wanting in the new situation were replaced;

in one case, a former bully became a hero.

Stage Three was designed to reduce the intergroup conflict. The experimenters decided that provision of 'accurate information' about the other boys would be met with distortion. So they tried sermons on 'brotherly love', the results of which survived the chapel door by only a few minutes. More promising was the notion of creating contact between the groups on an equal footing and in pleasant activities; but, contact merely aggravated the hostility and gave more chances for its expression. For instance, meals are generally pleasant and rewarding and the effects are said to generalize, as with business lunches. In this case, however, meals turned into affrays, with food as missiles.

The answer was found in the creation of 'superordinate goals', that is, goals desired by both groups and attainable only by co-operation between them. A series of 'accidents' arranged by the camp staff led to the two groups deciding to pool their resources to rescue the food truck, mend the water supply, pay for a popular film and so on. The effects were not immediate but gradually in-group exclusiveness was breached by many cross-group friendships.

Conclusion

Assessment of success in teaching is a very tricky business. Try to put your finger on a teacher's weakness and he can move his ground like quicksilver and claim that you are pointing to a position he was not occupying. If our pupils do not achieve X, it is because we are really concentrating on Y. This can be as true of methods of organizing one's groupings of pupils as of methods of organizing one's subject matter. Where choices between individual and group work are concerned, there are at least three sorts of aims and criteria between which we can vacillate and it may pay us to identify them a little more clearly.

1. *Achievement of the external task of the group*. This is usually much less important in itself than it would be in the industrial or commercial world, but there *are* occasions when a teacher is concerned with such a criterion. For example, he may be organizing

children to do community work, put on a public production or clear some ground quickly in time for spring planting. There are ways in which the achievement of such an external goal brings educational advantages in its train in the form of greater cohesion or motivation and enhanced self-esteem. Should the teacher be concerned with maximizing the external end product, then he needs to decide between small groups, large groups, individual work, heterogeneous or homogeneous groups, appointed or emergent leaders, more cooperation or more competition.

2. *Intellectual learning.* In the last resort this is, presumably, individual and the teacher must consider how, if at all, the individual's learning is enhanced by its being done in a group. Possible advantages may include the teaching or stimulating of one pupil by another and the raising of motivation as discussed in chapter 4. On the other hand, one child may frustrate another's learning in a group, time may be wasted or emotional tension may rise too high. What is important is to consider productivity in terms of man-hours involved, in which case the answer might frequently be individual work.

3. *Social learning.* Obviously this occurs only in groups and may include learning to share, learning to control one's emotions in face of interpersonal frustrations, and learning to take a variety of roles such as leader and led.

Often the teacher will compromize in his aims, or vary them according to what he considers to be the particular needs of classes or individuals at particular times. A class whose members are socially well developed may benefit most from more individual work, whereas in other cases a teacher may deliberately sacrifice some of the cognitive learning or some of the achievement of an external group goal for the sake of letting his pupils rub some social corners off one another.

What is important is to realize that the teacher's work will be all the better for the teasing out of such aims and their reassembling in an order of priority which fits that particular lesson, project, class or individual. Our 'aims' may then really guide us rather than provide woolly rationalizations for what has already happened in a more haphazard way.

Discussion and further study

1. How satisfied should a teacher be if the pupil groups in his charge are happy and cohesive?

2. Do you agree that education is primarily concerned with the development of the potential of the individual?

3. A recent article on team-teaching (Warwick, 1973) mentions a variety of school activities and suggests: Model-making requires a group of not more than (a); drama and mime seem best done in groups of (b); the interview (of local experts by children) requires a group of (c) and the optimum size for project work is probably (d). The numbers given by the writer were 2, 4, 6 or 7 and 8. How would you allocate the numbers to gaps a, b, c and d?

4. Why is it that the best ideas do not always win through in a group? How might the studies by Torrance (1955) and Riecken (1958) (p. 145) link with the ideas of Maier and Solem (1952) in the previous chapter (p. 140)?

5. Discuss the possible relationship between audience and coaction effects (ch. 4) and the learning or problem-solving in a group.

6. Has the Torrance and Arsan (1963) study any implications for grouping and streaming in schools? (See p. 149.)

7. What factors may impede decentralized networks in settling down quickly to the task? Does this mean that the teacher should always set up centralized networks among pupil groups, e.g. by prescribing positions and roles rather than letting these emerge?

8. Do relationships between members have to become more formalized as groups grow in size? Consider, e.g. large schools.

9. Analyse any group work you have experienced, or are experiencing, in terms of mixed motives of competition and cooperation.

10. How might the section on 'Frequency of interaction' in chapter 6 be related to Stage Three in the Sherif studies, or to wider sociopolitical issues?

11. 'Politics make strange bedfellows'. Discuss examples of how superordinate goals might be used by teachers to reduce animosity between individuals and groups.

Further reading

Smith (1970), contains many useful articles, especially the ones by

Collins and Guetzkow, Shaw (1964), Tuckman (1965) and M. Sherif (1966). Other articles worth reading are those by Bales (1951), Slater (1958) and Deutsch (1949). A book that is useful but not always easy to read is Davis (1969), *Group Performance*.

Part 3

Attitudes and interaction

We looked, in Part 1, at the individual in relation to society and, in Part 2, at the way in which processes of social influence become embodied in group structures. Now, in Part 3, we look at attitudes which result from the intertwining of individual and group factors and which come to guide our interactions with others. In particular, we consider fixated attitudes and prejudices which reduce an individual's, or a society's, power to keep in touch with and to adapt to a reality which is complex and changing. The psychological comfort which comes from order, consistency and predictability needs to be leavened by a willingness to consider alternatives. In the case of the teacher, a willingness to see and to examine alternative viewpoints, without necessarily agreeing with them, would seem essential.

10

Theories of attitude change

Psychologists are committed to the belief that there are consistencies in the behaviour of individuals and that if the structures or processes underlying these consistencies can be discerned then it should be possible to predict and to guide or change much of that behaviour. It could be said that the changing of the behaviour patterns of his pupils is the central concern of the teacher.

What is an attitude?

Social psychologists tend to see patterns of behaviour in terms of a hierarchical arrangement of values, attitudes and opinions. Much of a person's behaviour will be in line with the basic values which, in the main, he would have developed during the years of early socialization but which he may still be modifying in later life. These values will embrace, and be expressed through, a number of attitudes, and these attitudes in turn will express themselves through many opinions and items of overt behaviour. Thus, if I express the opinion that more children should have supported the school team, I am probably expressing an opinion that is part of my general attitude that pupils should be loyal to a school, which itself is part of an even more general value of mine that loyalty is desirable towards those groups of which a person is a member.

What an attitude represents is an organization of the residual or significant elements of our past experiences and also an organization of our likely future responses to social objects. When we meet a person for the first time we tend to place him, on the basis of cues of speech, dress, colour and so on, into a category. Having done so, we then tend to act towards this person in terms of the generalized attitude we have developed in the past in respect of that category.

In this way, an attitude helps us 'to economize on thought' (Karlins and Abelson, 1970). An attitude is a 'set', an orientation, 'a mental and neural state of readiness' (G. W. Allport, 1961) and, as such, brings much consistency and predictability to our behaviour.

Predictability is possible only where an attitude is persistent. Attitudes tend to be persistent partly because they 'work' and thus represent a valid adaptation to 'reality', and partly because, once formed, they govern the perception and interpretation of new experiences, especially in ambiguous situations. If, for example, we have an unfavourable attitude towards a person, we tend to see only the unfavourable aspects of his behaviour. As with the self-concept, once a framework is established, the tendency is to assimilate only those facts which fit or those which can be made to fit. The attitude can then persist as a self-contained system the parts of which are in equilibrium. However, external conditions may change. For example, in the case of a person we dislike, we may be unable to go on indefinitely explaining away or blinding ourselves to a succession of good acts, especially if these are obvious to our friends. Such upsets to the equilibrium of the system are sometimes referred to as 'dissonance', and attitude systems under such strains usually have to be restructured in order to accommodate themselves to changes they can no longer assimilate. This we return to in the next section.

An attitude may be described not only in terms of being for or against, i.e. in terms of direction, but also in terms of its intensity, centrality and interconnectedness. We may wish to change an attitude from being for to being against, what we might call an incongruent change, or from being mildly for to being strongly for, which we might call a congruent change. Congruent change is much easier to achieve and in many ways the principles of change are different for the two types, a point to which we return later. An attitude is central when it is highly significant to the individual, as is the case with self-attitudes. These central attitudes are the ones most likely to be part of a system or web of interconnected attitudes and they will be difficult to change because change in one would cause reverberations throughout the system. For example, an attempt to change an adolescent's attitude towards staying on at school may be resisted or eased according to how much change this would necessitate in his attitudes toward his family, his friends and his self-image.

It is now time to consider how attitudes and changes in attitude may be measured. An attitude is an 'inferred construct', which is to say that it is not directly observable but has to be inferred from measures of one or more of its three chief components, viz., affects or feelings, cognitions or beliefs, and behaviour. The common assumption is that there is considerable consistency between these three components, but it is well to realize that inconsistencies also exist. Beliefs and feelings are usually consistent with one another in that both are favourable or both are unfavourable towards the object, but overt behaviour, being much more subject to environmental constraints, is often out of line with feelings and beliefs. Does our observation of the behaviour of a schoolboy in going to school each day entitle us to infer that he likes school and thinks his attendance is of value? Taking note of a person's opinions or beliefs may also be an inaccurate measure of his attitude, since the opinion may indicate compliance, in which case it may be inconsistent with what he feels or does; if, on the other hand, we could be more sure that the opinion was part of his identification or internalization, it would be a much better measure of attitude. Again, to measure an attitude merely through its verbal expressions may give little prediction of the person's non-verbal behaviour since it may represent a merely intellectual stance with little associated action-tendency. With some, the attitude is 'all talk'.

This difficulty of using a measure of any one of the three components as a measure of the general attitude was illustrated some decades ago by La Piere (1934). He journeyed across the U.S.A. in the company of a Chinese couple and they were refused service at only one out of 128 restaurants. When, some time later, he wrote to these restaurateurs asking 'Will you accept members of the Chinese race as guests in your establishment?' over 90 per cent of the half who replied said 'No', as did a similar proportion of a control group of other restaurateurs. It is possible that the questionnaire was tapping the feelings and beliefs of the restaurateurs but that their behaviour towards the particular couple was subject to greater restraints in a *fait accompli* situation in which the value they attached to being a host, involving, for example, the avoidance of an embarrassing scene, was greater than the value they attached to the question of colour. Other explanations may be plausible, but our point is to stress the difficulty in assuming that from a measure of one attitude component we can confidently infer the general attitude and predict future behaviour.

Despite many shortcomings, questionnaire methods are the most widely used form of attitude survey, partly because they are much more economical of time and money. Any description of attitude measures (McDavid and Harari, 1967; Zimbardo and Ebbesen, 1969, pp. 123-8) such as devised by Thurstone, Likert, Guttman, Osgood and others is beyond the scope of this book but we should stress that the theoretical and methodological difficulties involved should make us very cautious in drawing conclusions from questionnaires.

Some theories of attitude change

There is no one theory of attitude change which is both comprehensive and unchallenged. There are, however, three approaches which help us to understand at least some of the issues involved. They are:

1. Dissonance theory, as presented by Festinger.
2. The functional approach, associated particularly with Daniel Katz.
3. The assimilation—contrast theory of Hovland and Sherif.

1. Dissonance theory

A number of theories in the field of attitude change are based on the idea that a person is concerned to maintain consonance or consistency both between the various components of an attitude and also between those attitudes which form an interconnected cluster. In chapter 1, we saw how consistency and self-image or identity tend to go together. Festinger (1957), in *A Theory of Cognitive Dissonance,* assumes that dissonance or disequilibrium between attitude components, resulting from inconsistency, leads to psychological discomfort and a drive to reduce this tension by changing one or more of these components so as restore equilibrium. Few of us are happy if we are constantly caught saying one thing but doing another; the dissonance which results will have to be reduced by changing either what we say or what we do.

One of the claims for consideration made by Festinger's theory is that a number of non-obvious predictions based upon it have been substantiated. In a well-known experiment, Festinger and Carlsmith (1959) asked subjects who had taken part in a dull, repetitive task to lie to other waiting subjects by saying that the job was interesting. Some of the subjects were paid one dollar to tell this lie, others were paid twenty dollars. Afterwards, their opinions were measured on how interesting or dull they found the job. Whereas reinforcement theorists might have predicted more opinion change where more money was given, Festinger and Carlsmith predicted the opposite.

Their hypothesis was that the twenty-dollar subject would feel justified in telling the lie; the lie was balanced by the twenty dollars and no more adjustment was necessary. On the other hand, the one-dollar subject would experience greater dissonance; anyone might have lied for twenty dollars, but what sort of person would lie for a mere one dollar? Since the lie would not be counterbalanced by the one dollar, other justification would be necessary to redress the balance. This restoration of equilibrium would come if the subject convinced himself that what he said was not a lie anyway, that he really had thought the task was interesting. In this way, the one dollar subject could feel he was not being inconsistent with himself. Results of the experiment confirmed the prediction. More 'one-dollar liars' than 'twenty-dollar liars' stated afterwards that the job had been an interesting one.

Many criticisms have since been levelled at the lie experiment. For instance, it has been argued that the result could have been influenced by the suspicion which might have been aroused in those who were given twenty dollars for a small amount of work. However, a number of other experiments have produced results which, in general, confirm the ideas of Festinger. Applying his theory to the changing of attitudes, we can see that if it were possible to induce and maintain a change in one of the components of an attitude, the resulting dissonance might lead to the other components being brought into line. With this idea in mind, we shall now look at each of these components in turn.

Changing the affective component

Probably the most deepseated component, and the one most difficult to change, is the affective one, but then this also means that it is probably the most important one to change. The teacher who is liked by his pupils has probably won the major battle of his campaign. The initial affect is possibly best explained in terms of association or reinforcement theory, but our main point is that pupils will later tend to argue for and behave favourably towards the teacher they begin by liking.

An experiment by Rosenberg (1960) bears this out. His eleven subjects were students who had revealed a negative attitude towards integrated housing. After hypnotizing them, he instructed them as follows. 'When you awake you will be very much in favour of the idea of Negroes moving into White neighbourhoods—the mere idea of Negroes moving into White neighbourhoods will give you a happy, exhilarated feeling'. After awaking, the students, who had no memory of being hypnotized, showed a change of attitude from negative to positive, not only in feelings but also in beliefs. For example, they no longer believed, as previously, that integration in housing would lead to a lowering of property values. Thus, beliefs and opinions had come into line with the changed affect. Similar changes in 'rational' argument have been demonstrated where hypnotized subjects have been told they will like a work of art that they previously disliked.

Obviously, there are limits to such plasticity of belief, yet many of the most important and controversial issues that face humans are in areas of such breadth and complexity that one can find an almost limitless and unsinkable fund of arguments to support one's position, on whichever side of the fence one 'happens' to be.

Changes in the belief component

Changing an attitude by changing the cognitive or belief component is widely believed to be very effective, if we are to judge by the vast amount of energy and money expended in disseminating information and arguments by lecturing, preaching and propaganda. Research does indicate that such informational approaches *can* have the result of strengthening existing attitudes and enabling those who already support the attitude to verbalize their sentiments more easily. Preaching is often criticized because it is 'to the converted' but at least they come away with a stronger armoury of arguments and slogans and with the knowledge of social support. However, research also indicates that informational approaches seldom result in an attitude change in an incongruent direction, that is, from unfavourable to favourable, or vice versa, unless the audience has little existing information and only weakly formed preferences. If information is already possessed it is likely that it has been organized into a cognitive system or attitude which will tend to repel incongruent information and incorporate only that which is congruent.

Some of the best-documented evidence on this comes from studies of the televized debates by Kennedy and Nixon during the 1960 presidential election campaign. Viewers observed in pubs would attend to their preferred candidate but would then 'tune out' the the other by turning back to the beer and conversation. According to Sebald (1962), there occurred selective perceptions, selective remembering and selective distortion of the information presented.

Changing the behaviour component

In dealing with the inducing of dissonance through this third component of an attitude, we shall proceed farther along that continuum which runs from the so-called passive listener at one end to the active learner at the other. Most teachers can attest to the wisdom of the old Chinese proverb which states: 'I hear and I forget; I see and I remember; I do and I understand'. But, do 'activity' methods work simply through better cognition or do they work by providing also a more effective penetration of the ego defences? Let us consider (*a*) discussion-methods and (*b*) role play methods.

Discussion methods

Mitnick and McGinnies (1958) conducted an experiment where,

first of all, they tested students on the California Ethnocentrism Scale (E-scale) which measures prejudice. They then formed nine-person groups, some groups being formed entirely of high-scorers and some entirely of low-scorers. Some of these groups then saw a film about group prejudice while other groups saw the film and then discussed it among themselves for thirty minutes. If we ignore other groups of medium-scorers, controls, etc., the set-up was like this:

	High-E	*Low-E*
Film alone	2 groups	2 groups
Film + discussion	2 groups	2 groups

After the film or film discussion, and again a month later, all groups were tested to see what changes in attitude had occurred. In the low-E groups, the viewing was followed by a reduction in prejudice and the film discussion by even more reduction. In the high-E groups, the viewing was followed by a reduction in prejudice, from very high to less high, whereas the film discussion was followed by less of a reduction. Study of transcripts of the discussions showed that in the low-E groups discussion reinforced the effects of the film whereas in the high-E groups the members 'devoted most of the discussion period to expression of their antipathies towards Negroes' and this tended to counteract the effects of the film.

In general, we may suggest that group effects manifested in discussion would tend to shift the attitudes of members in a direction congruent with the initial attitudes; that is, discussion strengthens existing views. Interestingly, a recent report tells of greater prejudice among a group of technical college students, following a discussion on prejudice, and this underlines the folly of believing that discussion is always for the 'good'.

Proceeding farther along the continuum towards greater activity or participation, we can look next at some early studies by Lewin and his associates (1947). During the second world war, as part of an American campaign to persuade housewives to use more offal, he compared the effects of lectures with the effects of 'group decision'. A follow-up showed that in a given period only 3 per cent of the women who heard the lectures served one of the meats never served before, whereas the comparable figure after group decision was 32 per cent.

What was meant by 'group decision' here was that after a discussion about 'housewives like themselves' the women were asked to indicate, by a show of hands, who was willing to try one of these meats in the next week. These were, in fact, individual decisions in a group setting rather than group consensus. Among the questions raised by this result were these: to what extent were the changes due to clearer awareness of the arguments, clearer perception of the way others in the group were moving, the committing of oneself publicly, or the lowering of ego defences by the direction of the earlier part of the discussion of possible changes at *other* housewives rather than at members themselves? To answer these questions, Bennett conducted further experiments and suggested that the more important factors were the process of making a decision and the degree to which group consensus is obtained and perceived (see Pelz, 1958).

Role play methods

Many different things can be going on in a lecture, as in a group discussion, but one difference we would accept is that the discussion involves more overt activity by more people. People are able to 'put themselves' into a discussion, to become more 'organismically involved' in it than they are in listening to a lecture. What if we were able to go farther and involve people more fully in role playing?

A series of experiments by Janis, King and Mann explored the possibilities (Janis and King, 1954; King and Janis, 1956; Mann, 1967). In the first experiment, subjects were given three minutes to read a prepared outline of arguments. They were then put into groups of three in which one was to persuade the others in line with the arguments; the other two merely listened. It was found that 'the active participants tended to be more influenced than were the passive controls'. But was this due to greater cognitive self-persuasion during improvization or to a greater sense of satisfaction from achievement? The next experiment suggested that it was the amount of improvization which was the potent factor. However, (and this should not surprise us in a young science) another experimenter, Scott (1957), engineered a series of debates with rigged winners and losers and found that the 'winners', more than the 'losers', changed their opinion in the direction of the position they had advocated in the debate. It seems that both improvization and the perception of social approval can have some effect in attitude change.

In a more recent role play experiment, Mann and Janis (1968) attempted to involve the affective component more fully in an attempt to change behaviour. They chose a tough problem, smoking. Many large-scale attempts to change smoking habits had been made by various bodies, but all had failed. For instance, a U.S. government report in 1964 produced the usual drop in smoking but in twelve months the rate was back to normal. In the summer of 1963, Mann and Janis involved twelve female students in 'emotional role play' for one hour. Each student played the part of a patient and was told she had lung cancer. Thereupon, she enacted several scenes which guaranteed that she focused attention on the threat of painful illness, hospitalization and early death. An equated control group heard a recording of one of these sessions. Two weeks later, the active subjects were smoking less than the others and this was being maintained eighteen months later. As one student said; 'He [a professor] was the one that scared me, not the report (Jan. 1964). . . . I got to thinking, what if it were really true and I had to go home and tell everyone that I had cancer'.

Naturally, one must take the results of such experiments as suggestive rather than conclusive. For one thing, the numbers used are very small; experimenting with humans is difficult. For another, one must note that the subjects were American female students and bear in mind that other groups might have reacted differently.

2. The functional approach

The basis of this approach lies in the observation that the same attitude may be held by different people for different reasons and in the realization that if we wish to change a person's attitude we do it most effectively by first finding out which need or function is served for that person by that attitude. We can consider the example of an anti-immigrant attitude in the context of the functional categories set out by Katz and his associates (1954; see also Katz, 1960).

(*a*) An instrumental function, such as where it is intended as a defence of the value of one's property.

(*b*) An ego-defensive function, as where it is more a symptom of one's inner or psychological needs. An example would be the 'authoritarian personality' discussed in chapter 11 (pp. 187-8).

(*c*) A value-expressive function, such as where being anti-immigrant allows one to be in a group where one can express one's personality or skills and be valued and accepted, perhaps as a leader.

(*d*) A knowledge function, as where having an unfavourable stereotype of immigrants helps to structure and simplify one part of a complex environment; seeing things more simply in terms of black or white.

Suppose we were considering an attempt to reduce anti-immigrant attitudes by disseminating more information: 'Let them learn the true facts about immigrants'. Would this work? It might work in case (*a*) if you could produce evidence that property prices would not be adversely affected by an immigrant influx. It might work in case (*d*) if the attitude holder was cognitively capable of coping with more complex ideas such as 'there are immigrants and immigrants as there are natives and natives'. In the case of (*b*) there could be a blanket rejection of the change attempt since acceptance of the information might disrupt the process by which the individual resolves his inner conflicts; he may need his prejudice. It might also be rejected in (*c*) since to accept might mean a rupturing of that group membership which is contributing to one's identity and satisfying one's wants. In fact, in the case of (*b*) and (*c*) there could well be a 'boomerang' effect, a strengthening of the attitude in the face of what is perceived to be an attack on the ego. The answer in case (*b*) could be to reduce an ego-defensive prejudice by giving the subject more self-insight. In case (*c*), one might change a value-expressive attitude by replacing the original group by another group which may have a different attitude but gives the same opportunities for belonging, leadership, self-esteem and so on (e.g. change the gang leader into a team leader).

3. Assimilation – contrast theory

This approach to attitude-changing, which is also called the social judgment–ego involvement approach, has developed from the intertwining of two strands, (*a*) the research on 'communication' carried out at Yale, in particular by Hovland (1953); (*b*) ego involvement theory, associated especially with Muzafer Sherif (1965, 1967). The Yale researches, concerned with such topics as persuader characteristics, how to present an issue, audience characteristics and the persistence of change, are well worth studying but beyond our present scope. One of the questions explored was that of how large a change in attitude a persuader can successfully advocate. Ego involvement theory suggests an answer in terms of the subject's initial position and the degree of his involvement in or commitment to that position; in other words, it considers the centrality of the attitude to the person.

One of the basic limitations of much previous research was that it described an attitude by giving it no more than a single score on a dimension, such as +2 or —3.

Hovland and Sherif realized the possibility that where three people might have the same score, e.g. +2, representing a favourable attitude, the same communication (information, argument, etc.) might be accepted by one, be received indifferently by another, and be rejected by the third.

As an example of their approach, we can take a study of attitudes towards Negroes, made in 1953. They collected a pool of 114 statements ranging over the whole dimension of attitudes towards Negroes. Subjects were asked to sort the statements into piles of similar-value statements, using their own categorization. They were then asked to label the piles to indicate which they would accept or endorse as representing their own views or position, which piles they would reject and which were the ones toward which they were noncommittal. In this way, one could determine each subject's preferred (or 'own') position on the dimension, plus his range of acceptance, rejection and noncommittment. A simple diagrammatic and hypothetical example may help.

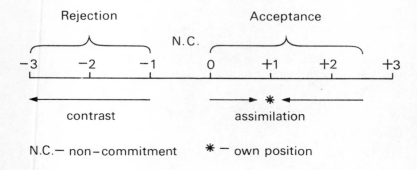

Fig. 10.1

In such a case, a communication pitched at level 0 or +2 would be likely to be within the range acceptable to the subject whereas one which was moderately against the issue, say at —1, or perhaps extremely favourable, at +3, would be rejected.

What Sherif and Hovland found was that if a communication fell within a subject's latitude of acceptance he was likely to perceive it as being nearer his own position than it really was, the 'assimilation effect'. If, on the other hand, it fell into his latitude of rejection he was likely to perceive it as being farther from his own position than it really was, the 'contrast effect'. Thus the greatest amount of change to be hoped for by a persuader is gained by pitching his argument near the limits of acceptance (e.g. —0·5 or +2·5 in our illustration). Any communication arguing for a position beyond —1 is likely to be seen as an argument for the 'other side' and to be repelled.

Sherif argued that the 'own position' was a position to which the subject anchored himself and in terms of which he categorized incoming communications as acceptable, non-acceptable or neutral. The amount of commitment to this anchor point would depend upon the issue. If the issue was a central or ego-involving one for that person then the commitment would be stronger and, so Sherif found, the latitude of acceptance would be narrower and the latitude of rejection wider. With such issues, only small changes of position could be advocated with much hope of assimilation, whereas advocacy of even a moderate degree of change from the subject's own position might result in an entrenchment of that position or, even, a 'boomerang' effect. The Kelley and Volkart experiment described in the next chapter is an illustration of this last point.

Conclusion

Schools are vitally concerned with the promotion of favourable attitudes to school, work, teachers, subjects, other pupils, and so on. Whether, through a more conscious and expert use of our knowledge of attitude change techniques, we come to be regarded as super-Machiavellian salesmen is a matter for discussion. Increased knowledge and skills can subserve many different ends, as the following examples may illustrate.

If we are in a situation where, as teachers, we are aiming to get a particular message across, that is, we are in a convergent or closed-end situation, then it could help us to bear in mind what has been said about organismic involvement. Thus, we know that we are more likely to pierce the ego defences and get the pupils behind the work if we move farther along the continuum from listening to a lecture → reading aloud someone else's arguments → improvizing their own arguments → improvizing and then attempting to persuade others, especially in a context of social approval → role play. We may also be more effective if we use our knowledge of the effects of public commitment and perception of group consensus. Most teachers know the value of saying to a class, 'Now, come on, put up your hands those of you who think you will really try this time'. But, like so much in teaching, it works *for* you only if done with the appropriate class at the appropriate juncture.

On the other hand, there are occasions in school when the stress is very much on 'getting them to think' in an open-ended or divergent way, where we want them to explore as many avenues as possible before coming to their own conclusions. In such cases, we would use the same basic principles as in the previous paragraph, but in different ways. For instance, we would resist the majority pressure which tends to move discussions in congruent directions only; we would try to restrain pupils from committing themselves publicly to one side or another until the ground has been thoroughly turned over and the moment is ripe for decision and action. In the 1971 build-up to the campaigns for and against the entry of Britain into the Common Market one leading politician expressed his relief that a major party had at last 'nailed its flag to the mast; now the discussion can begin'. It might have been nearer the truth had he said that discussion had now ended.

What we have discussed in this chapter suggests that we should gain from being more sensitive and flexible in our dealings with our pupils. We should be more aware of how much or how little change a person can take, of how we may be meeting resistance to our arguments because acceptance would mean a chain of changes in interconnected issues and, possibly, in group affiliations. We should be more wary of ridiculing a pupil's self-image directly, or of doing this indirectly through caustic remarks about the speech or customs of his reference groups, such as his family or social class: it is in such ways that the pupil and the teacher may end up on opposite sides in a 'them and us' situation marked more by contrast than assimilation.

The phrase 'them and us' serves as an apt reminder to us that we must ask ourselves, more directly than hitherto, to what extent we are, when seeming to deal with an individual's attitude, dealing with what is to be more accurately perceived as a group pheno-menon. How much truth is there in Lewin's assertion that it is easier to change the attitude of a group than that of an individual? In the next chapter we shall be looking more closely at the group's part in the formation and changing of attitudes.

Discussion and further study

1. Identify some attitudes which you might meet among pupils (e.g. towards the school, a subject or activity, a teacher, other pupils or school rules). For each attitude separately, consider which one or ones of the following concepts may assist our understanding of how the attitude was formed and how it might be changed if considered undesirable. (Try to consider desirable as well as undesirable attitudes.) (*a*) interconnectedness; (*b*) self-concept; (*c*) dissonance theory; (*d*) the functional approach (*e*) social judgment–involvement; (*f*) group allegiance.

2. Would you agree that a teacher's central concern is to promote change in his pupils' values, attitudes and behaviour patterns? Can or should a teacher avoid trying to persuade pupils to adopt his values? Is good teaching anything more than effective sales technique?

3. Following the format from question 1, discuss some attitudes which you might find among teachers (e.g. toward pupils, classes, activities, rules, colleges, curriculum innovation). Are some attitudes more central and others more peripheral? Do some seem to represent shallow compliance while others seem to be expressions of deeply held views?

4. How may the work of Sherif and Hovland on assimilation-contrast link with ideas on conforming as set out in chapter 4 (especially Asch, Kelman and Jahoda)?

5. Consider the view that individuals may have varying reasons for belonging to the same group or sharing a common attitude, e.g. joining the National Union of School Students.

6. Do you think it likely that, with people as well as with things, we tend to form a like or dislike first and find supporting reasons later? In what way might behaviourist learning theories help to at least partially explain our initial feelings?

7. In what sorts of issues or conditions is the presentation of information more likely/unlikely to bring about changes in attitude?

8. Why is attitude change more likely to follow improvization of an argument than the reading of someone else's argument?

9. There is some evidence that emotional role play is more effective than informational propaganda in changing attitudes. What

176

arguments might support this view?

10. Bennett suggested that (*a*) making a decision, and (*b*) obtaining and perceiving group consensus, could encourage attitude change. Why should this be?

11. 'You might as well say – – –' added the March Hare, 'that "I like what I get" is the same as "I get what I like" '. Reduction of dissonance?

Further reading

Four useful general books are Zimbardo and Ebbesen (1969), Karlins and Abelson (1970), J. A. C. Brown (1963), and Evans (1965). Two more advanced books are Insko (1967) and Thomas (1971). Also worth reading are the articles by Lewin (1947), Mann and Janis (1968), Hovland (1953), Sherif and Sherif (1967). Katz (1960) and Rokeach (1968).

11

Group and individual prejudice

The intention in this chapter is twofold. First, the hope is to bring into clearer focus something which has been implicit in much of what we have said previously: that in order to understand an individual's attitudes one needs to study both the individual and his affiliations, past and present. Secondly, we hope to illustrate the presence and function of individual and group factors by looking at an issue of current and, indeed, perennial interest, namely, ethnic prejudice.

Achieving a better understanding of an individual's attitudes involves us in finding out something about the values and norms of his group or groups, particularly his reference groups, and also in finding out something of his 'individual' psychology. This latter usually means, in any case, assessing certain characteristics, such as intelligence or personality factors, in terms of how far and in what direction he departs from population or group norms. Useful as it undoubtedly is for analytical and descriptive purposes, this isolation of the individual from his groups is difficult and introduces an element of unreality into the situation. After studying him in separation, we need to put him back into that context of social interaction apart from which his most human characteristics would not have arisen or existed. Of course, his attitudes and behaviour may then change. The truly penitent criminal tends to revert to his old attitudes and behaviour when returned to his old environment. The truly penitent schoolboy tends to revert similarly when he returns from his one-to-one confrontation with the teacher to the well-greased interactional grooves of his peer group. If it is true that, as chapter 10 suggested, the individual seeks to steer a consistent and identity-conferring course toward those material, ego-defensive, value-expressive and other goals in which he is most ego-involved, it is also true that his identity or ego and the goals to which his attitudes are functional are to a high degree socially derived. Let us look more closely at the individual's relationship to the group.

This relationship between the individual and the group is a reciprocal one, as we tried to emphasize in Part 1 of this book. In chapter 1, and again in chapter 6, we saw that it is from groups such as the family that he gets satisfaction of his most basic wants for physiological comfort, psychological security, identity, self-esteem and self-actualization. This, however, is only one side of the transaction and we saw in chapter 4 how, for these benefits of group membership, he must pay the price of conformity. These benefits would be denied to him were he not to be adequately socialized by internalization of the central values and aspirations of his culture or subculture, by identification with those who represent these values, or, at the least, by compliance with his group's norms as regards overt attitudes and behaviour. As we saw in Part 2, and particularly in chapter 7, when we looked in more detail at the inner workings of groups, the individual's room for manoeuvre, his ability to influence events or to translate his attitudes into deeds is to some considerable extent circumscribed by his conforming to the positions and roles he occupies in the affective (sociometric), power and communication structures of his groups.

Thus to be able to place an individual in a social category or stereotype will tell us a good deal about him, though by no means all. Knowing his reference groups, we know something of his values and attitudes: knowing his positions and roles, we know something of the social pressures and tensions which either constrain or encourage the expression of these attitudes.

We can include two illustrations of the effects of group membership on attitudes. The first of these, illustrating the way in which individual ego involvement is tied in with group membership, comes from an experiment by Kelley and Volkart (1952). They used twelve Boy Scout troops and began by measuring (*a*) the degree to which the boys valued membership of their troops and (*b*) their attitudes towards camping and forest activities, both of which are central to a scouting way of life. Then a visiting speaker addressed the boys and in the course of his address criticized the boy scout emphasis on these two activities. After the speech, the boys' attitudes to camping and woodcraft were measured again. It was found that those who showed the greater change in the direction advocated by the speaker were those who least valued their membership. Among those who placed high value on membership, there was a 'boomerang' effect in that they moved farther away from the advocated position. Thus, the more ego-involved members showed contrast rather than assimilation; they closed ranks to repel boarders.

Our second illustration of the effects of groups on attitudes concerns what has come to be known in social psychology as the 'risky-shift' phenomenon. Some of the argument for its existence comes from the study of crowd behaviour where, it seems, the individual's usual reactions tend to be amplified. One suggested explanation is that in a crowd there occurs a process of 'de-individuation' in which the individual, sheltered by anonymity, loses some of his restraint. Other evidence comes from experiments. For instance, Kogan and Wallach (1967) placed individual subjects in hypothetical risk-taking situations. An example situation might require the subject to put himself in the shoes of an employee faced with a choice between staying in his present job at a modest but adequate salary or taking a new job with more salary but no long-term security. Subjects were put into many such risk-taking situations and asked to indicate the lowest probability of success they would accept (e.g. 3 to 1, 5 to 1, etc.) before being persuaded to take the riskier but potentially more rewarding alternative. They were then put into groups to discuss each case for five minutes before reaching an agreed group decision. What was found was that group decisions tended to be riskier than individual decisions: the risky-shift phenomenon.

As in so many experiments involving humans, the interpretation of this result is not simple. The effect may be due, or partly due, to the de-individuation process referred to earlier. On the other hand, it may be due to the greater persuasive power of advocates of extreme points of view. Yet another possibility, discussed by Roger Brown (1965), is that in groups we become more aware of the cultural values of our society and one of these, particularly for the male, is for boldness. Evidence for this comes from the finding that those who merely listened to group discussions, without participating in the decision, were similarly riskier in their individual decisions. Others, however, have produced evidence that what the group does in discussion is demonstrate and reinforce the value which happens to predominate in the group on that particular occasion; at times this may be a value for risk, at others it may be a value for caution (Rabow *et al*, 1966). This conforms with the generalization we made in chapter 10 about the way in which group discussion accentuates attitude change in a congruent direction.

Having, in this section, emphasized that the direction and strength of the individual's attitudes are interwoven with his membership of groups, we now turn to a consideration of some sociopsychological viewpoints on that highly intractable human problem of unfavourable attitudes which we label prejudice.

Ethnic prejudice

In chapter 5, we defined prejudice as a negative stereotype and attitude toward a certain category or group. However, as we pointed out in chapter 10, not all attitudes are expressed in action; when they are, we use the word discrimination. The La Piere study (p. 163) was an illustration of how there are many situational and other factors which may prevent a prejudiced person from engaging in acts of discrimination. In this section we shall be dealing with the cognitive and feeling components of attitude rather than with acts of discrimination.

One of the earlier attempts to measure the attitude of ethnic prejudice was by use of the Bogardus (1925) social distance scale. The respondent would be given the name of a group, e.g. Turks, Negroes or Tiranians and then asked to indicate to which of the following classifications he would admit a member of that group:

1. to close kinship by marriage
2. to my club as personal chums
3. to my street as neighbours
4. to employment in my occupation

5. to citizenship in my country
6. as visitors only in my country
7. would exclude from my country.

In practice it was found that a respondent would almost always tick without omission up to a certain point (e.g. would accept into country, citizenship and employment) and then 'draw the line'. Reduction of prejudice would be indicated by a willingness to go higher up this scale, to admit the outsider to a more intimate, more comprehensive and less role-restricted relationship.

Prejudice may be found to exist between individuals, small groups, social classes, national groups or racial groups (whatever this last term means). In this country the term is most frequently used in reference to attitudes toward coloured immigrants but, in fact, colour need not enter into it. For instance, religious beliefs and practices may in some cases be a more critical factor, as illustrated by the history of the Jews, who have been the classic target group for Europeans. In the tenth and eleventh centuries, because Christians were forbidden to lend money at a profit, the Jews were cast in the role of moneylenders to European princelings who needed money for the building of their cities. Put into this role, they came to be perceived as 'naturally' cunning and grasping. Where colour *is* involved, prejudice and discrimination are not the prerogative of the white man, a fact that is illustrated in those countries of Asia and Africa where communities of white farmers and businessmen have been at the receiving end. As Professor Seton-Watson wrote in the mid-1960s, 'the doctrine of "neo-colonialism" deliberately concentrates hatred against these ready-made scapegoats. All that is wrong in these new states can be attributed to them'.

The point that we are making is that what social psychologists study under the heading of prejudice is a universal phenomenon found in Gentile and Jew, Protestant and Catholic, men and women, supporters of Manchester City and Manchester United, members of the N.U.T. and the N.A.S., teenagers and adults. It will be noted that all these references are to categories or groups of people and it is with this aspect of prejudice, the group aspect, that we begin, before turning to individual factors.

The prejudiced group

Social psychologists often refer to our membership groups as 'in-groups' and to other groups as 'out-groups'. The in-group is the group with which we identify and, as discussed in chapter 1, from which we get a good measure of what we call our personal identity. We internalize the values and norms of our in-group and share in its changing fortunes. This is obviously more true the more 'primary' in character the group is, but it also applies at the broader level of society or culture.

Where another culture impinges on ours, the other one, the out-group, threatens the values and norms of our group or culture and, thus, our identity. Usually such a perceived threat results in the closing of ranks and an increase in cohesion. There are probably many instances in modern politics, as in history, of trouble being deliberately fomented on the physical or psychological frontiers with the aim of diverting attention outward, away from internal dissensions which are threatening the break-up of the group. The common enemy becomes the outside target for the projection of frustrations and hostilities with which the group itself cannot cope. As in the case of Sherif's boy-campers (p. 154), members of the out-group are stereotyped (ch. 5); that is to say, a common attitude is developed towards individuals who are members of that out-group, an attitude which includes the components of cognition, feeling and action tendency. What happens thenceforward is that any individual who is perceived as being a Jew, Negro, Yorkshireman, school-teacher or whatever is ascribed all the characteristics which the perceiver has boxed together under that particular label. While it is not necessary that all these characteristics are falsely ascribed. many of them are likely to be, since the strong element of projection which permeates prejudice is an irrational mechanism of ego defence.

We said earlier that difference in colour *need* not be a precondition of prejudice, but we should add that any physical characteristic such as of skin colour or physiognomy may serve as a cue which helps the prejudiced to identify the target group. It may thus speed up the labelling and the application of a stereotype and help concert the in-group's attack on the target group. A further point to make, one which links with what we said in chapter 5 about the perceiver's part and the importance of personal constructs, is that different groups will pick out different critical and identifying factors, according to what matters significantly to them.

An illustration of this comes from a series of studies by Triandis and Triandis (1960). They used a social distance scale which had sixteen stimulus-person constructs. Each of the sixteen persons combined one of two characteristics of race (Negro or white), occupation (high or low prestige), religion (same as or different from subject's) and nationality (high or low status according to previous studies by Bogardus). An example stimulus would be: 'a Portuguese Negro physician of the same religion as you'. When American college students were used as respondents, about 77 per cent of the variance in the social distance scores was accounted for by race, about 17 per cent by occupation, 5 per cent by religion and 1 per cent by nationality. When their studies were extended to other countries, Triandis and Triandis found considerable differences, summarized as follows:

Rank importance for social distance

	Race	Occupation	Religion	Nationality
Americans	1	2	3	4
Germans	3	1	2	4
Japanese	2	1	4	3
Greeks	2	3	1	4

As is the case with construct theory itself, there is a school of thought which argues that it might be more meaningful to *elicit* constructs and target groups from the subject rather than ask for forced choices between groups and constructs which may have more meaning and significance for the researcher who provides them than for the subject. However, it would probably still hold that different groups may judge according to different criteria.

Up to this point we have been concerned with the perceptions, categorizations and stereotypes of any in-group for any out-group, but often the two groups first impinge on one another in conditions of unequal status. For instance, *if* material or technological advancement is taken as the central criterion for status, then where white and coloured groups have come into contact it has almost always been as unequals. This first impression of inequality generalizes and sticks. It is soon cemented into society's system of complementary roles where one leads and one is led, where one supplies the brain and the other, unwillingly, the brawn.

These roles exercise constraint upon attitudes, self-concepts, aspirations and behaviours, so that the first impressions and first relationships tend to be self-fulfilling prophecies. The black boy is destined to become a cotton-picker; a cotton-picker does not need a fancy education, it would merely unsettle him, so it would be pointless to spend as much money on his schools. In any case, he cannot be bright enough to profit from expensive education, as can be seen from his low academic attainment and his inability to use his chances to rise above cotton-picking. Furthermore, he would only waste his chances, since he works for me only when I stand over him; he has no aspirations and fortunately (for him, for me and the system) is quite happy as he is. The interwar Hollywood film portrayal of the white man being paternalistically kind to his faithful but simple old Negro retainer or nanny, who in turn beamed contentment, was probably very comforting to many whites, while many Negroes played their part in maintaining this stereotype. A Negro dean of an American college once admitted (Jencks and Riesman, 1967) that his head still itched when he talked to a white man because as a child he had habitually assumed the 'darky' pose of scratching his head and saying 'Yassir!'

The prejudiced individual

What we have said so far is that societies or groups tend to form stereotyped attitudes with regard to out-groups even where they inhabit the same territory geographically. In some societies this leads to discrimination which is built into legal and other institutional frameworks; in other societies it may exist in much more subtle forms. What we now need to look at more closely is the way in which individuals within any one group vary in the degree to which they espouse and express the prejudice which may be their society's norm.

One reason for some individuals being more prejudiced than the average in their society is that they are more than average conformist to whatever their group norms are. One study (Martin and Westie, 1959) in the southern U.S.A. showed that the more prejudiced whites were from the sections which, on other grounds, we would expect to be more likely to conform with cultural norms; i.e. females, churchgoers, the upwardly mobile and the less educated. Another study (Pettigrew, 1958), this time in South Africa, showed that the most prejudiced of white students were the children of manual workers, in line with the idea (p. 107) that those who conform most to a group's norms are those who are trying to get in or farther in.

In other cases, economic or other frustrations may lead individuals or groups to find scapegoats for failure rather than accept that failure may be due to themselves or to natural causes. For instance, one American study (Krech *et al.*, p. 183) showed that in 1947 only 10 per cent of an economically satisfied sample were anti-Jewish, whereas in an economically dissatisfied sample the figure was 38 per cent. Where relatively poor or unskilled immigrants are concerned, it is much more likely to be the poor whites who are most threatened economically by competition for jobs and the depressing of wages, but frustration and prejudice have been shown to occur at any income level, it being the subjective feeling of dissatisfaction in relation to one's own aspirations that matters.

What is perhaps more significant is the fact that a small proportion of individuals seem to be almost constantly prejudiced against someone. For this person, 'if there wasn't a nigger we'd have to invent one'. This is the sort of person we referred to in chapter 10, on attitudes, as the one who holds the attitude to satisfy inner needs: for him, the attitude serves an ego-defensive function. This personality type has been widely studied since Adorno and his associates produced their book *The Authoritarian Personality* in 1950.

Adorno developed an attitude scale, the F or Fascist scale, which seemed to distinguish well between known members of fascistic organizations and known non-members. Rather similar are the various tests for ethnocentrism (E-scale) and dogmatism (see Warr, ed., 1970). In fact, the authoritarian personality is as likely to be found in an extreme left-wing as in an extreme right-wing political group. The Communist and the Fascist may have more basic similarity than a casual consideration of political affiliation might suggest.

The underlying general theory for Adorno's study came from psychoanalysis and was to the effect that rigid and punitive ways of rearing a child would result in a personality which was fearful, prejudiced and authoritarian. In particular, any expression of hostility toward parents would be firmly repressed. In such a situation, the person would become unwilling to recognize and try to cope with hostilities which he felt toward his parents and others and would, as a form of ego defence, project these feelings outward on to some convenient scapegoat. 'For the anti-Semite, the Jew is a living Rorschach blot'. An authoritarian person would be very ethnocentric, revealing a great sense of unity with his in-group, believing to an unusual degree that his group's values were always best. He would emphasize status, being submissive to his superiors but dominating to his subordinates. His world would tend to reflect the clearcut and hierarchical environment in which he was reared, with a wide gap between adult and child, 'them and us' and black and white. His prejudice would have a very strong emotional and irrational component which would be very difficult to shift. He is the one most likely to distort or deny contrary information. The creation of greater self-insight has been found to bring some amelioration, but not easily.

Reduction of prejudice

What we have said so far is that groups often develop prejudices against other groups and that some individuals within groups are likely, for various reasons, to be more prejudiced than the average. These are the individuals who are likely to form the extremist fringe and to take the lead in any intensification of prejudice, i.e. movement in a congruent direction. We now turn to a few tentative guidelines on how such prejudice may be reduced, the much more difficult problem of inducing change in an incongruent direction, from minus towards plus. Our examples will be from the area of racial prejudice.

Man is often fearful of the unknown and feels threatened by the stranger. When that about which he knows little is a group of people, there is a strong chance that into the void or vacuum of ignorance he will project his own fears so that negative stereotypes, attitudes and myths are established which may not be in accord with the facts about the out-group. From this starting point many have argued that the obvious answer to prejudice is the reduction of ignorance, the presentation of the 'true facts'. Governments and others have spent fortunes on information campaigns, but the evidence is that such campaigns have but limited success. As one leading expert in consumer motivation study put it: 'Since attitudes affect the way a product is seen, affect the very perception of facts, facts alone cannot combat hostile attitudes' (Dichter, 1964, p. 396).

Of course, one could argue that the problem can be solved by bringing the two parties into contact and keeping them that way long enough for dissonance to do its work, for them to see each other as they really are. One difficulty is that all too often the two groups meet on a basis of inequality, an inequality that, as we said earlier, may be built into a system of complementary and mutually defined roles in which, for example, whites are dominant. In the narrow ranges of interaction that ensue, stereotypes may persist unchanged or reinforced.

What, then, of reducing prejudice by encouraging equal status contact in which there will be a broadfronted exchange of information about the other? After all, social psychologists such as Homans and Newcomb have postulated that, in general, interaction is rewarding and produces liking (p. 101), although there is evidence that this may not happen where initial dislike is very strong. In the latter case sores may be continually irritated by friction. Let us therefore look briefly at the idea of enforced contact in the fields of work, housing and schooling. If it be thought a point of criticism that most of our examples come from the U.S.A., we should also remember that that 'melting-pot of nations' has seen and studied for a long time the sorts of problems we in Britain may have to face in the next decades.

In 1952 Minard published a study of Negro and white miners in the Pocahontas coalfield. He found integration at the coal-face, with whites and Negroes working side by side, but beyond the locker-room a colour line became immediately visible. Another study, by Harding and Hogrefe (1952), found that in department stores where whites and Negroes worked together in equal status, attitudes were favourable on job-related items but not, even after four years, with respect to public transport, restaurant facilities, housing or friendship. The difficulty of getting oneself accepted into the first three categories of the Bogardus social distance scale is well known to New York Jews, who have become accustomed to what they term the 'five o'clock shadow'.

An interesting study of enforced residential contact is the one by Deutsch and Collins (1951). They studied two housing schemes in New York and Newark. In the former, Negro and white families were assigned to apartment buildings without regard to colour. In the latter, Negro and white families were housed in segregated units. In each case the proportion of white and Negro families was similar. The researchers found that prejudice was sharply reduced in the integrated projects and explained this in terms of the numerous and inescapable equal-status contacts which were made, especially the informal ones in the shops, in the laundry or on the benches outside. The group norm in this integrated project, and the associated social rewards, were for inter-race neighbourliness, whereas on the segregated project a housewife expected to be socially ostracized by the other white women if she befriended a Negress. Of even greater importance was the fact that, although children in both projects went to desegregated schools, it was only in the integrated-housing project that children's friendships crossed the colour line. In Britain, a survey carried out in 1966-67, in five towns and covering a random sample of 2,500 people, compared the prejudice scores of those people living within ten minutes walk of the nearest coloured neighbour with those of people living at more than that distance and found the scores to be significantly lower among the former, more proximate, group (Bagley, 1969).

With regard to these and similar studies, we have to stress caution about generalizing. Many such studies have, like the Deutsch and Collins one, been focused on groups of poor people, and it may be that satisfaction of their desperate need for a house outweighed any relatively minor quibbles about their neighbour's colour. Where people have more choice there seems to be, in America and in Britain, a stronger tendency to opt for self-segregation than the opposite.

Similar self-segregation has been observed in schools. Zimbardo, in a 1953 study of a college in the northern U.S.A. which admitted Negro and white students on an equal footing, found that 'there was a distinct pattern of self-segregation by black students (which was encouraged by the whites) (Zimbardo and Ebbesen, 1969, p. 102). Furthermore, a follow-up study showed that the pattern was still there ten years later, after a decade of civil rights legislation and presumed changes in prejudiced attitudes'. Certainly, it is reasonable to expect that attitudes should improve to some extent in schools where pupils from different ethnic groups interact frequently over a wide range of activities and in an official ethos of tolerance. But how far into the informal systems of school life does this permeate? Rose (1969), quoting a British study by Kawwa, says that 'it has been observed, both in primary schools and secondary schools with children of different nationalities, that the children are apt to choose their friends from within their own group and reject members of other groups, and that they show this in-group preference whether they are English or immigrant children'. Furthermore, he states that 'friendships formed between white and coloured children are seldom continued beyond school', and that the Youth Service found the situation far from encouraging. What happens, of course, is that these youngsters, like criminals or student-teachers (no disrespect intended), adopt, by and large, the norms and attitudes of the culture into which they are moving or returning. In the case of adolescents, the norms in question are those of their adult reference groups. The biggest problem lies not in producing changed verbal responses on attitude questionnaires, nor even in inducing changes in behaviour, but in maintaining such changes in a different social situation.

In looking thus briefly at work, home and school, we have seen that it is possible for legislators and administrators to arrange for enforced contact during which attitudes seem to improve but that there may be little carryover from these formally arranged situations to informal situations where people have free choice. This has led many people to agree with the old saying that 'stateways cannot make folkways'. However, others disagree and one of these is Allport (1958), who considers that legislation *can* create new folkways; that most people do not become converts in advance but, rather, are converted by the *fait accompli;* that people need their consciences bolstered by law; that laws will help deter those who are deterable; that remedial legislation can break into vicious circles. In particular, remembering what we said earlier about the numbers of prejudiced individuals who are so because they are conforming to the norms of their group, we must agree that state action and intervention would seem justified on the issue of discrimination.

What of individuals who resist change because their attitudes function as ego defences? Lecturing, or otherwise presenting them with the facts, is unlikely to have much success because of selective perception, distortion and denial. With authoritarians, such presentations may even cause a boomerang into greater prejudice unless the source of the information or viewpoints is seen as being highly prestigious when, in fact, authoritarians may be more swayed towards it. The presentation, for discussion, of case studies of prejudice has been found to produce more self-insight and reduction of prejudice than has rational argument, and the change has been more permanent. Role play, putting oneself into the shoes of the other, has also been found useful, as illustrated in an experiment by Culbertson (1957). After measuring the attitudes of her subjects toward Negro/white housing integration, she divided them into groups of six. Three of each had to compose arguments for integration while the other three watched one role player each. When the attitude scales were readministered, it was shown that the attitudes of the role players had improved more than those of the passive observers and in both categories the improvement was much greater than it was in a group of control subjects. It is interesting that the control group itself showed some positive change; this supports other evidence in suggesting that the mere answering of a questionnaire can often produce change.

In summary, we could say that our brief survey of the possibilities for the reduction of ethnic prejudice leads us to what Rose has called a position of 'qualified pessimism'. There are many approaches which produce some results with some people but whereas it is relatively easy to produce shallow, short-term reductions in prejudice where the social situation is controlled, it is another thing to sustain these changes in the face of the multiplicity of forces operating in informal society. Progress in integration beyond level four of the Bogardus scale is likely to be slow. The five o'clock shadow might be reinforced by the sixteen-plus shadow for some time to come.

The next decade

Some of those who view the future of race relations with qualified pessimism do so because they see things as possibly becoming worse before they become better. Implicit in this view are three elements at which we should look briefly. They are (*a*) the 'denial of identity' among the Negro population, (*b*) their rapidly changing aspirations; (*c*) the 'marginal-man' predicament which may face many second-generation immigrants, whether of West Indian or Asian origin.

What is the effect of prolonged prejudice on a target group of inferior status? Among black people, in the U.S.A. and in Britain, several writers have recognized what they call a 'denial of identity', where coloured people tend to deprecate themselves and to associate aspirations with the out-group. A number of studies have shown how this begins quite young, with Negro children tending to identify with or wanting to play with white dolls and puppets rather than coloured ones. In Britain, Milner (1969) found that in his sample of children aged five to eight only 10 per cent of the English children chose an out-group doll to play with whereas the figures were 50 per cent for Asian children and 65 per cent for West Indian children. He claimed that 'the mutilation of identity through prejudice and discrimination is not very much less severe in Britain than in the U.S.' In an effort to counter this deadening effect of low self-esteem, a section of the black population has reacted by launching such campaigns as 'Black is Beautiful'.

Campaigns such as these undoubtedly have their fair share of

193

unpleasant excesses by extremists, but they may also be seen as a hopeful symptom of the eventual disruption by the coloured population of the vicious circle of unfavourable stereotype—low self-esteem—denial of identity—confirmation of stereotype. To date, Negro children have suffered from all the well-documented disabilities which adversely affect the self-concepts, achievement motivation and level of attainment of working-class and lower-stream children. On top of this, they are more easily identified and labelled. Often their aspirations are high, but they lack the skills which enable them to profit from the educational system. Whether this inability to profit is the result of a poor start in a background which does not give them the best preparation for success in school learning, or whether it is the outcome of innate handicaps, is a question which cannot be adequately answered one way or the other until both groups have been given the same early 'life-chances'. The fact seems to be that for most Negro children, as for many white working-class children, school becomes an increasingly unrewarding experience in which they join the worse who become bad rather than the better who become good.

Interesting in this context are some American studies (Gurin *et al.*, 1969) which have applied the concept of 'internal/external fate control' to samples of black and white students. It seems that, in general, Negro youth have come to believe in the 'Protestant ethic' about the importance of personal responsibility and work as a means of attaining desired goals. That is, they agree with the *idea* of internal control over one's fate. However, they also seem to believe that although this applies at a general social level it does not apply to them personally; they believe that their own fate is controlled by external agencies irrespective of their own personal efforts. Their experiences have so often been of effort unrewarded that effort comes to be seen as pointless.

Nevertheless, changes are apparent and they may be coming at an increasing pace. Many people have expressed surprise at the fact that as the American Negro gains more equality so he agitates more, not less, vehemently. What is happening is that as those with inferior status move closer to the higher status groups so their 'comparison levels' change (Thibaut and Kelley, 1959). The goals they have achieved are forgotten as new expectations take over; it comes to be seen that perhaps effort and agitation pay off after all.

The difficulties which are likely to accompany this transition from a period of stable social inequality into (hopefully) a period of stable social equality are well illustrated by a consideration of the problems of the second generation immigrant. The parents may have been very pleased to have established any sort of footing in our society and to have the chance of getting their children into English schools, but the son and daughter are more likely to say 'If I can go to the same school and do just as well there, why can't I get the same job?' Truly, 'man lives by bread alone—when there is no bread'. It was estimated that in Nottingham, in 1967, only 7 per cent of the coloured children in secondary schools were born in this country, whereas in the primary schools the comparable figure was 61 per cent (Rose *et al.,* 1969). This means that the problems associated with large numbers of second generation immigrants moving from school into adult society are likely to increase rapidly in the later 1970s.

The danger is that at one moment we shall be expecting them to 'be British' and the next moment indicating to them that they are 'not British'. In this, they will, like adolescents, the 'nouveau riche', the foreman, the prefect or the deputy headmaster, be in what social psychologists have come to call the 'marginal man' position (Stonequist, 1937). This 'marginal man' is the one condemned by society to live with one foot in one culture and group and the other foot in a different and, perhaps, antagonistic culture and group. He may feel rejected as he moves toward one group but rejected or rejecting as he moves back toward the other group. In the face of the ambivalent attitudes and expectations of others, the marginal man will react ambivalently, showing, for example, the instability and swings of emotion which often typify the adolescent. To illustrate; a sample of Eurasians showed this in a study by Kawwa (1968): they had a strong desire to identify with the higher status Europeans but usually felt rejected by these; they consequently retaliated by rejecting the Europeans. How many of those second generation immigrant children who pass through our schools will end up in a similar limbo?

Discussion and further study

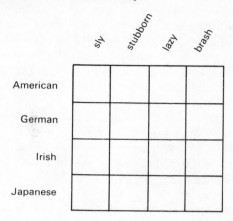

1. (*a*) Working individually, pair each national group with a different adjective, in the way that you think the 'man-in-the-street' would do. i.e. Enter four ticks so that there is one in each column and one in each row.

(*b*) Now pool the results from the group, or from a number of groups, by writing in the number of ticks for each of the sixteen cells. The more of you doing this, the better.

(*c*) Discuss the results. Do they reflect common stereotypes? If so, suggest reasons why these stereotypes may have arisen and why they might be inaccurate. Would you, personally, have the same stereotypes as you say the man-in-the-street has? Consider what the effects were of giving you a limited and forced choice; does this invalidate the point of the exercise?

(*d*) Now try it again with different groups and adjectives, e.g. if you are American, get your own back on the British; if you are Irish, remind each other that 'Taffy was a thief'.

2. How would you define and distinguish between these terms: racial group, ethnic group, cultural group, national group?

3. In an article entitled 'The stranger: an essay in social psychology', Schutz (1964) describes the basic assumptions which maintain one's 'thinking-as-usual'. He goes on 'The stranger . . . does not share the

above-mentioned basic assumptions. He becomes essentially the man who has to place in question nearly everything that seems to be unquestionable to the members of the approached group'.

(*a*) What sorts of basic assumptions might an immigrant not share?

(*b*) How might the in-group react to the immigrant's explicit or implied questioning of their assumptions?

4. Eighty college students following an optional course on 'Immigrant Education' completed the Bogardus social distance scale. About 95 per cent ticked as far as level one, the remainder as far as levels two or three. Why *might* this result be unrepresentative of the general situation in Britain?

5. 'When I was teaching seventeen-year-olds in a College of Further Education, I was so shocked by what I heard my students saying in a classroom debate on colour prejudice—a subject they had chosen to discuss—that I took the first opportunity to tell them how much they had horrified me. I was shocked even further when my reasoned arguments had no effect. But, in retrospect, I do believe I did influence them. I forced them to retreat to rather more entrenched positions in our confrontation and achieved the very opposite effect from that which I had intended' (quoted *Games and Simulation*, BBC, 1972).

(*a*) Analyse this situation in terms of the theories presented in chapter 10.

(*b*) Discuss possible alternatives to the teacher's action.

6. Can 'stateways make folkways'?

7. Suggest why the mere reading or answering of an attitude questionnaire might produce attitude change.

8. 'There is an enormous amount of hostility against parents . . .' (Ottaway, 1966). Do you agree that this is so? Does the psychoanalytic explanation of the 'authoritarian personality' seem credible to you?

9. Consider how many characters, themes and situations in Graham Greene's novels reflect what may have been his own 'marginal man' position at school. 'Was my father not the headmaster? I was like the son of a quisling in a country under occupation. My elder brother was a school prefect and head of the house—in other

words one of Quisling's collaborators. I was surrounded by the forces of the resistance, and yet I couldn't join them without betraying my father and my brother' (*A Sort Of Life*, 1971).

Further reading

Three useful books are Bloom (1971); Ehrlich (1973)—thorough and advanced; and Rose *et al.* (1969). Proshansky and Seidenberg (1965) has a number of useful articles, including Deutsch and Collins on integrated housing, Frenkel-Brunswik *et al.* on 'The authoritarian personality', Stouffer *et al.* on integration in the U.S. army, and Bettelheim and Janowitz on ethnic tolerance. See also Pettigrew (Hollander and Hunt, 1967, 1971), and articles on rigidity and dogmatism in Warr (1970).

12

Teachers, pupils and interaction

Whereas the other chapters in this book took aspects of social-psychological theorizing as themes, and indicated, usually briefly, their relevance to educational issues, this chapter reverses the process. It takes four aspects of school and classroom interaction as focal points and attempts to show how social psychology can bring some illumination to each. The four sections are as follows:

1. The teacher's attitude towards change
2. Pupil perception of teacher expectations
3. Classroom climate and interaction analysis
4. Bridging some gaps

1. The teacher's attitude towards change

The pace of change seems to be quickening in schools as elsewhere in society and it therefore seems all the more important that we should find room to suggest some of the contributions that a sociopsychological viewpoint may make in this area. Our purpose is not to discuss change in curriculum and method as a means of making education more relevant, nor is it to discuss the merits or demerits of particular schemes which are being continually advocated; these are the special concerns of sociologists and curriculum experts. Our concern is to highlight some of those sociopsychological factors which may be contributing to the acceptance or rejection of new ideas by individuals or groups. These factors are often neglected in discussions on change, but their implications are recognized by Taba (1962) in her statement that 'changing the curriculum also involves changing individuals'.

Most of the existing literature on curriculum change seems to fall into two categories. First, there are descriptions of 'new' methods and materials, written usually by persons near the coal-face: secondly, there are analyses of institutions in terms of their susceptibility to change, written usually by sociologists. By and large, however, 'sociologists have been more successful in carrying out static analyses of social institutions, focusing upon the "functional" contributions which the parts make to the whole, than in analysing their dynamic aspects' (Hoyle, 1969). In indicating the relevance of such dynamic aspects as the 'self', attitude-changing, conforming, group processes and leadership, all subjects dealt with in previous chapters, we hope to throw useful light on the failure of many attempts at change, whether from the top or from the grass-roots, to do more than induce a shallow compliance or a frustration which may lead to generalized and harmful cynicism. That these latter situations do exist is evidenced in the schools by the amount of dust-covered apparatus which clutters so many stockrooms, or by the half-hearted acceptance of a new organizational superstructure which lies uncomfortably on an unchanged basic way of thinking and operating.

In looking at the teacher's attitude towards change, we shall follow the convenient plan of looking at individual factors separately from group factors, but we should bear in mind, as argued in the previous chapter, that such a division carries a strong element of unreality.

The individual

As we saw in chapter 1, roles, with their implications for status relationships, dependency or dominance, habits and consistency, are an important part of one's identity. If changing the curriculum means upsetting the existing roles, it may be seen as a threat to identity and may be resisted with all the considerable skill which conscious or unconscious ego defence can muster. For instance, the introduction of team teaching may change relationships between teacher and teacher, and between teacher and pupils, in such a way as to be perceived as a threat to one's status, independence and power to influence people and events. When a new idea is seen as threatening in an area which is central to the self, the latitude of acceptance, as we saw in chapter 10, may shrink and the possibility of a 'boomerang' effect may increase. On the other hand, change that offers opportunities for enhancement of the self is more likely to be accepted.

To circumvent resistant attitudes the first essential may be to determine the function or functions which they serve. Applying Katz's terminology (p. 171) to the example of team teaching, we may see that a teacher's attitude of resistance may serve

1. an instrumental function, as where he thinks his promotion prospects will be harmed;
2. an ego-defensive function, as where he thinks he will be more exposed to criticism or be unable to cope with the changed inter-personal relationships;
3. a value-expressive function, as where in an autonomous situation he is 'boss' or can in other ways be 'himself';
4. a knowledge function, as where he suspects that an ordered and manageable world will become unmanageably complex.

Individuals vary not only in the needs which are being served by their attitudes for or against change; they also vary in their power to influence change. Thus a headmaster who has fulfilled his career aspirations may have no needs which can be served by the acceptance of change and yet he has great power to encourage change should he so wish. On the other hand, a young headmaster of a small school may see the adoption of new ideas as a means of attracting favourable attention from those who can promote his ambitions. The same may be said of heads of departments; their susceptibility to change may depend on their degree of self-satisfaction. New entrants to the profession could, it might be thought, be potent agents of change since they come fresh and pliable from an exposure to many of the newest ideas; alternatively, they may be confused and ready to seek salvation in any suggested scheme. There are two snags. Firstly, entrants find that in order to gain acceptance into their new reference group, the 'staff', they must pay the price by conforming to the staffroom norms. According to one's point of view, their ticket of admission may have to be a display of either cynicism or practical, commonsense realism in the face of fancy ideas. Secondly, these entrants lack power and, like the gunner in Torrance's study (p. 145), their ideas are unlikely to be accepted, even if right. So often, rejection is not of what is said but of who said it! (See Finlayson and Cohen, 1967; Hoy, 1968; Shipman, 1967.)

Thus, in general, although not without many exceptions, as we ascend the career pyramid so the need and the willingness to change may decrease while the power to effect change increases. It might therefore be argued that the most appropriate level at which to introduce new ideas is the middle level, such as in the case of a head of department who has some experience and power but still has some energy and unsatisfied ambition. At the base and at the apex, more of our effort might run into the sand.

The group

If we now change the focus to the group's place in curriculum change, it would be well to take note of the view of Lewin (1947) and others that the basic unit of change *is* the group rather than the individual. Trying to effect a change in an individual which moves him away from the norms of his important reference-groups is to cause an uncomfortable straining at the anchor. Thus at a weekend course a group may support a teacher's acceptance of new ideas, but his enthusiasm may wither soon after he returns on Monday morning to his more vital reference group in the staffroom. This parallels the phenomenon of recidivism in which the criminal relapses when returned to his old mates.

What is wanted is an understanding of the need to give social support to the teacher with new ideas. Harking back to Asch's point about the vital difference between being alone and having a minimum of social support, we see how a small group of two or three others might be sufficient to support an individual in his deviance from the majority by giving him that sense of belongingness and assurance of sanity we all need. Perhaps the best chance of innovation comes before a new staff has attained cohesion and made alignments. Otherwise, a headmaster faced by his inability to pierce the defence-in-depth of the 'old guard' may have to resort to the bringing in of non-aligned young teachers who are given to understand that their careers and his pet schemes prosper together.

Going back to Lewin's point, we may believe that we shall be able to induce more change if we form individuals into groups, perhaps labelling them 'working-parties'. Certainly this might work, since a small group offers more chance for involvement and self-fulfilment, but much depends on how this small group is viewed by the larger group which may have the final say in acceptance or rejection. Furthermore, much depends on the characteristics of the individual members of any small groups. Where members are heterogeneous in personality they may stimulate each other but may, by the same token, find it harder to reach agreement. Where members are more homogeneous in personality or needs or aspirations or interests, then we are more likely to witness the so-called 'risky-shift' phenomenon at work (p. 181). However, as we have already discussed, a group's effect is usually to move attitudes in a direction congruent with that of existing attitudes and this may as easily be a cautious shift as a risky shift. Thus forming individuals into groups is of itself no more a guarantee of greater acceptance of change than it is of greater effectiveness in the stifling of new ideas.

In the proliferation of groups which we are witnessing in the field of curriculum development and innovation, what should be our guidelines as to the sort of group leadership which is most desirable? A general principle is that what is needed is the smallest group which contains all the skills necessary to do the job in hand. This suggests heterogeneity of membership so that the pooling of different viewpoints can be obtained with the avoidance of duplication. However, as we suggested above, heterogeneity, like largeness, can increase the problems of communication and make participation and the meshing of personalities more difficult. This is where the leader can be very important in coordinating effort and preventing personal clashes over status. The ideal leader would combine task and socio-emotional roles but would see his main function as an enabling one, encouraging the identification of all members with the broad task by allowing participation in goal-setting and ongoing evaluation, and maintaining momentum towards the goal by appropriate switches from group to subgroup and individual work. His influence may be greater if the others can see that they are not puppets dancing on the strings of his ego alone; they also should be ego-involved. The leadership could, for instance, rotate informally, to match changes in task emphasis, or formally, by prior agreement.

One thing that has made a number of teachers cynical about change is the fashionable overemphasis on group work, on the notion that group work is *always* to be preferred to individual effort. As we argued in chapter 9, what we need to aim at is a finer discrimination between those situations in which a group may be superior or preferable and those in which individual efforts are more ego-involving and productive. As an instance, one would wish for a much more discriminating view of team teaching than that which stresses nothing but the advantages which come from social support and the pooling of resources and which is blind to the possibility of a frustrating loss of autonomy and flexibility. Flexibility, for example, is often mentioned as a potential strength of team teaching and there is much truth in this when the team teaching is done whole-heartedly. In favourable conditions, where members are committed and have or make the time to be in continual debate with each other, it is possible to adapt plans and materials from week to week. All too often, however, the reality is that harassed teachers may agree on a team project before term begins, get the details made sacrosanct by the duplicator and by intricate dovetailing of individual time-tables and materials, and fail to find the energy or time to modify the scheme until the next holiday. In this way they may end up being less flexible than the individual teacher who is sensitive to the needs of his classes and is required to consult only himself and them.

Another reason why too many teachers become unduly cynical about change in general is that they are too often bombarded with exhortations to adopt changes that other particular groups have found to be successful in particular situations. In this context, we must digress a moment to look at what social-psychologists call the 'Hawthorne Effect' (Homans, 1941; Olmsted, 1961). This term was coined from the extensive studies carried out at the Hawthorne plant of the Western Electric Company in Chicago during the late 1920s and early 1930s. One thing these studies demonstrated was the way in which a small work group can develop its own informal organization, with norms that may increase, maintain or restrict the level of production through sanctions against deviants such as 'chisellers' and 'rate-busters'. More important for our present discussion, however, was one of the accidental or unhypothesised discoveries, labelled the 'Hawthorne Effect'. The experimenters found that whatever the manipulation of financial incentives or environmental factors, such as the improvement of lighting or, alternatively, its reduction to the level of bright moonlight, the productivity of the experimental group kept on rising. Eventually they realized that the group members were responding to the greater attention being paid to them: they came to perceive themselves as a special group and this boosted morale and productivity.

In schools, better-than-average results may be produced by teachers and children who realize that they are the focus of some special attention. Perhaps they are responding to the special expectations communicated by a group of experimenters who are committed to the experiment and who would get an extra 'kick' out of special results. When the new methods are more widely adopted they may lose their special appeal and results may be little better or worse than those produced by earlier methods. However, this argument that change or novelty can of itself produce beneficial but perhaps shortlived and non-generalizable results should not be taken as an argument that all advocated changes are equally unlikely to produce widespread and long-term advantages. What it might lead us to consider is that each teacher should find his own ways of making his pupils feel they are 'special', but this, of course, might always have been one of the secrets of the good teacher.

It is not difficult to agree with those, particularly sociologists, who maintain that a good deal of change is needed in some of our curricula and methods and if in this brief section we seem to have given a disproportionate weight to resistance and cynicism among teachers it is only because this represents the situation as seen by the author to exist in many staffrooms. It is not enough to moan at such resistance when it is met: an attempt must be made to analyse the sociopsychological factors which encourage it and then to alter things so that as many teachers as possible may see change as self-enhancing rather than self-deflating. If, for instance, teachers were to be encouraged to analyse and experiment with their own teaching we might have less of either that compliant conformity or that blanket rejection with which expert authority has too often been met in the past.

2. Pupil perception of teacher expectation

Much has been said and written about the self-fulfilling prophecy and the effect of expectation on behaviour, especially in relation to the categorization of pupils into different schools and different ability groupings. Most of this literature is written from the sociologist's angle. The argument is along the lines that if you give a dog a bad name you hang him. Social psychologists have now begun to add to the literature on this subject, a notable example being Hargreaves's (1967) study, Social Relations in a Secondary School', where he describes the ways in which pupils' behaviours come to match their differential categorization into ability streams.

Topics already dealt with in this book which have relevance to this subject include 'the self', 'the significant other', 'interperson perception', 'behaviour in the presence of others' and 'attitude formation and changing'. We now propose to look briefly at examples of work by some social psychologists who have begun the study of the more detailed processes by which the expectations of one person for another can affect the behaviour of that other.

Categorizations into ability groupings, or into selective and non-selective schools, represent a very obvious communication of one's expectations to another, but communication of expectations can be very much more subtle than this. Let us look at an example which although not from the classroom, as I think you will guess, bears some interesting resemblances to what often goes on there. It concerns a horse called Clever Hans which amazed people by counting out with its hoof the answers to a variety of questions. In fact, it was common belief that the horse could count, subtract, read, spell and so on, until some controlled experiments proved otherwise. It appears that whenever people asked Hans a question, unbeknown to themselves they leaned forward very slightly and this was the signal at which Hans began to tap his hoof. Then, as Hans approached the correct number, the questioner would make a very slight head movement in anticipation and this would be Hans's cue to stop. Subtle and often unconscious cues such as these are, presumably, also communicated from one person to another and they may be non-verbal, verbal or paralinguistic. These last refer to how a thing is said rather than what is said.

On the effects of teacher expectations in the classroom, some interesting work has been done by Rosenthal. In a number of laboratory studies in the 1960s, where he used assistants to run experiments where subjects were engaged in such jobs as the training of rats or the rating of faces in photographs, he demonstrated that he could bring forth particular results merely by leading his assistants to expect such results (Rosenthal, 1966). His work must make us wonder how often this phenomenon has affected results in 'objective' experimenting with humans.

Rosenthal and Jacobson were then led to conduct an experiment in the school situation, reported in their book, *Pygmalion in the Classroom*, (1968). The subjects were in the first six grades of a Californian elementary school, each grade having three classes which were differentiated by speed of reading. All pupils were given a test which the teachers were led to believe could be used to predict which children were about to 'bloom', i.e. make an intellectual spurt. A few months later, each teacher was given, casually, a list of the 'bloomers' in his class. In fact, these were the 20 per cent who had been selected at random by the experimenters. When the same tests were repeated the following year and the year after that, it was found that the 'bloomers' had indeed made significant gains in I.Q. over the control group. Additionally, the experimental pupils were the ones most often picked out by teachers as being happy, more curious and more interesting.

This experiment has since been subjected to criticism. For instance, Thorndike (1968) suggested that the data did not support the conclusions although there were, he admitted, other grounds for believing in the 'general reasonableness of the self-fulfilling prophecy effect'. Other replications of the experiment have produced somewhat conflicting results, but most writers agree that expectations *can* be transmitted by subtle cues to produce matching behaviour. In demonstrating the existence of this 'Pygmalion' phenomenon,

Rosenthal and Jacobson also suggested that this might arise more from the quality than from the quantity of the teacher-pupil interaction. Let us, then, look at two experiments which throw some light on the more detailed processes involved. The first is by Beez (1970) and the second by Rubovitz and Maehr (1971).

In the Beez (1970) experiment, sixty teachers were each given one child aged five or six years. The teacher first spent ten minutes attempting to teach up to twenty words from cards. He then gave the child five jigsaw puzzles to complete; all but one of the children completed all five puzzles within the allotted time. Before the teaching episode, the sixty children had been allotted randomly into a 'high ability' or 'low ability' group, and each teacher had been presented with one of two folders containing some fake evidence to suggest which group his pupil was in. After the lesson, each child was tested by an experimenter to determine how many words he had learned, while the teacher completed a questionnaire. Here are some of the main findings.

	Highs	Lows
Mean number of words teachers tried to teach	10·43	5·66
Mean number of words learned by children	5·9	3·1
Mean teacher rating of intellectual ability on 5-point scale	3·43	1·93
Mean teacher rating of social competency on 5-point scale	3·33	2·57
Proportion of teachers rating word tasks as too difficult	3·3%	63%

Bearing in mind that the contact of teacher and pupil was a very short one, but also bearing in mind the one-to-one ratio and the tendency of first impressions to stick, it is worth recording Beez's comment that 'even in the face of successful performance on the puzzle tasks, (the teacher's) expectation is not changed'.

In the Rubovitz and Maehr (1971) experiment, a number of microteaching situations were set up in which twenty-six teachers (actually students) conducted discussion lessons, each teacher having four twelve-year-old pupils. The topic was 'television'.

Beforehand, each teacher had been given fake I.Q. scores which led him to identify two pupils as being from the 'regular' stream and two from the 'gifted' stream. An observer sat behind the pupils and categorized the teacher's behaviour for forty minutes; this observer did not know which of the pupils were the 'gifted' ones. Results showed two significant differences in two aspects of teacher-initiated interaction. First, teachers requested more statements from 'gifted' pupils. Secondly, they gave more praise to statements from these pupils. Furthermore, when the teachers were asked, later, to give their own personal evaluations of the pupils, they expressed marked agreement with the labels which had been randomly assigned. If, as seems entirely reasonable, praise from teachers and verbalizations from pupils are important for motivation and learning, then it also seems that the existence of a link between perception, expectation and academic performance is being spelled out gradually and convincingly.

3. Classroom climate and interaction analysis

In the late 1930s, two seminal research projects were separately undertaken which between them resulted in establishing new ways of analysing classroom behaviour. First, there was the work of Anderson and Brewer (1945–6) on the categorization of inter-personal behaviour. Among the many things to which this was a precursor was Bales's 'Interaction process analysis' which we described in chapter 7 (see p. 111), and which has proved a useful tool for analysing interaction patterns within groups. Secondly, there was the work of Lewin, Lippitt and White (1939) on social climates, which we described in chapter 8. Put simply, the ideas that have emerged from these two lines of research are: (a) that learning can be importantly influenced by the socio-emotional climate of the classroom; (b) that the individual most influential in creating this climate is the teacher; (c) that we can identify certain dimensions of the teacher's interaction with his pupils and relate measurements on these dimensions to the classroom climate and the learning that occurs.

'Classroom climate' refers particularly to generalized or shared attitudes or expectations which the pupils have about the teacher, about other pupils and about the work. Expectations, as we have stressed elsewhere in this book, influence a large part of behaviour. One example of different social climates generating different behaviours was in the Lewin, Lippitt and White studies, where the main distinction was between authoritarian and democratic styles of leadership. Anderson used the labels dominative/integrative to describe a similar dimension, while one of the key figures in the development of interaction analysis in the 1950s and 60s, Ned Flanders, used the terminology 'direct influence/indirect influence'.

Flanders (1967, 1970) suggested that, in the long run, indirect influence produced the more favourable attitudes, and the superior work, although direct influence was appropriate in certain circumstances, at certain stages or with certain classes (cf. Fiedler's work, see ch. 8). In laboratory experiments, Flanders had found that a sustained dominative pattern reduced the ability of subjects to recall work which had been studied, and produced disruptive anxiety as indicated in galvanic skin response tests and by changes in heart-beat rate. He argued that direct influence, or teacher domination, if very marked and persistent, could produce in the pupils a state of dependency on the teacher in which the pupil's concern over his relationship with the teacher could divert attention from the learning task. Other writers (e.g. Hargreaves, 1972) have also stressed that too much concern with pleasing the teacher can divert attention from the task and reduce understanding.

Flanders assumed, although acknowledging a certain amount of variability in teacher behaviour, that one could sample the verbal interaction between a teacher and his pupils to obtain a fairly accurate picture of the socio-emotional climate in that classroom. To obtain such samples, he devised a ten-category system to cover direct and indirect teacher influence, student talk, silence or confusion. These categories are set out on p. 211, in summary form.

The observer first memorizes the categories and then may practise their use with tape-recorded samples of verbal behaviour. He records a category number every time the category of behaviour changes, and every three seconds for any category that persists. The category numbers are recorded in a column so as to preserve the

Flanders's categories for interaction analysis

Teacher talk	Indirect influence	1.	Accepts feelings
		2.	Praises or encourages
		3.	Accepts or uses ideas of student
		4.	Asks questions
	Direct influence	5.	Lectures
		6.	Gives directions
		7.	Criticises, or justifies authority
Student talk		8.	Student talk in response to teacher
		9.	Student talk initiated by student
		10.	Silence or confusion

Fig. 12.1

sequence, and the results are then transferred to a matrix. Let us consider a hypothetical sequence of verbal interaction involving a teacher (T) and pupils (P), marking the categories in brackets.

P. Is dew another example, Sir? (9)

T. Yes; that's a good example. (2) In fact, it forms in a similar way (3) following a fall in the air temperature (3). So, when is one likely to find dew on the ground? (4)

P. In the morning, after a clear night, Sir? (8)

T. Quite right (2). Now, I want you all to write me a paragraph (6) explaining the connection between a clear night sky (6) and the occurrence of morning dew. Get on with it (6) (Silence, hopefully (10) or confusion (10)).

Such a sequence would be recorded in a column, as fig. 12.2, and then each pair of figures would be transferred to the matrix.

This brief illustration may be just sufficient to indicate how the type, sequence and ratio of teacher and pupil verbal behaviour can be recorded. Other category systems may use rather different terminology and may include interesting refinements. For example, the VICS categories used by Amidon and Hunter (see Amidon and Hough, 1967) have major categories of teacher-initiated talk, teacher response, pupil response, pupil-initiated talk, and they also distinguish between pupil-teacher and pupil-pupil responses as well

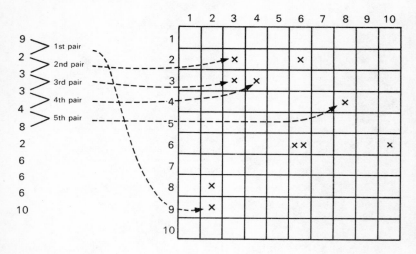

Fig. 12.2

as between 'broad' and 'narrow' questions.

The chief attraction of interaction analysis lies in its greater objectivity, so that 'the inferences reached are based on events which can be said to have occurred with a greater degree of certainty than is usually true of classroom observations' (Flanders, 1970). Teachers can now analyse their classroom interaction in such a way as to identify chains of events and the part played in these sequences by their own behaviour. Researchers can ask if there are certain of these observable patterns which are more likely to produce positive attitudes and better learning. If the more promising patterns can be identified, student teachers may be encouraged to practise them, not so much in the hope that they should all be teachers in the same mould as in the hope that they would have a wider repertoire of interaction skills to deploy as the situation warranted.

Interaction analysis has been criticized by some (e.g. Hargreaves, 1972) who say that it fails to capture the essential flavour of class-room interaction and fossilizes a process that is too complex, subtle and dynamic to be pinned down in this way. However, others may agree that, like sociometry, it represents one of the more hopeful developments through which sociopsychological theorizing can be translated into skills that deal more directly and precisely with the problems of teaching. One thing we should not forget is that inter-action analysis is only a tool; we are still left to argue about what the desirable balance is, educationally, between direct and indirect teacher influence or between teacher and pupil initiation and response. Flanders himself admits to a bias towards the nurturing of independence and self-direction among learners; for him, the 'democratic' social or classroom climate would be the more desir-able one. A further point to bear in mind is the danger of coming to believe that the little we are now managing to measure fairly objectively and reliably is the whole of what we would like to evaluate. Just as measures of height, weight, I.Q. and sociometric status would be a very incomplete basis for our evaluation of a person as a person, so measures on the initiation response dimension, useful as they are, are probably very far from being measures of good or bad teaching.

4. Bridging some gaps

More than once in this book (e.g. ch. 1, 2 and 5) we have described how man brings some order, consistency, meaning and predict-ability into the infinite complexity of his physical and social en-vironment by categorizing it. So long as the framework of categories which he erects can cope with new events, he is likely to maintain it, but if too many new experiences are not properly assimilated (to use Piagetian terms) then man will accommodate by restructuring this framework or model, making new categories which will assimilate new information and ideas more comfortably, and which will be better aligned to deal with what he sees as his current problems. One set of categories which man has erected to cope with much of his experience is that of academic disciplines and if we look at two of these, social psychology and sociology, we may detect a move to close the gap which appeared to have widened between them since the days of Cooley, Dewey and Mead. What seems to be blurring the line between them is a common focus on the phenomenon of interaction, interaction between man and society, between one sub-cultural group and another and between teachers and pupils.

Social psychology and sociology

In chapter 1 we stressed Mead's insistence that man and society are interacting and interdependent. This perspective seems to have been resuscitated lately as a germinating point for what has been called an 'interpretive paradigm' in sociology, as opposed to the more traditional 'normative paradigm' (Gorbutt, 1972). Instead of regarding socialization, including education, as a one-way process of moulding the individual to the norms of a society which exists 'out there', the interpretive paradigm sees the relationship of man and society as a dynamic, dialectic, reciprocal process in which, for example, teachers and pupils socialize each other as they engage in a continuous 'social construction of reality'. A modern writer on sociology, Peter Berger (1969), sees this reciprocal process in terms of three steps which he calls externalization, objectivation and internalization.

Externalisation is the ongoing outpouring of human being into the world, both in the physical and mental ability of men. Objectivation is the attainment by the products of this activity (again both physical and mental) of a reality that confronts its original producers as a facticity external to and other than themselves. Internalization is the reappropriation by man of this same reality, transforming it once again from structures of the objective world into structures of the subjective consciousness. It is through externalization that society is a human product. It is through objectivation that society becomes a reality 'sui generis'. It is through internalization that man is a product of society (pp. 3-4).

One of the things objectivized in society is a framework of categories which its members may use to perceive, define, interpret and evaluate situations, people or events. Such socially shared perspectives are embodied in a society's institutions ('human activity perpetuating itself': O.U. 7, 1971 E.282) and in its language. Those social psychologists and sociologists who follow the 'symbolic interaction' approach of Mead (O.U. 1971, D.283) see language, the possession of a constructed and shared system of symbols and meanings, as crucial to a person's ability to stand outside his 'self' and to take the role of the other, thus making much of the other's perspectives and behaviour understandable and predictable.

Yet there are also important subjective differences in the meanings that individuals or subgroups may attach to the 'same' experience and this, also, is becoming a shared focus for many psychologists and sociologists. As an example of the former, we can refer to Kelly's work on personal constructs (p. 83), where he explored the individual's idiosyncratic frames of reference for evaluating things and people. Among sociologists, we have the instance of Bernstein's consideration of the effects upon a child from working-class contexts of entering the middle-class contexts of the typical school:

> All that informs the child, that gives meaning and purpose to him outside of the school, ceases to be valid or accorded significance and opportunity for enhancement within the school. He has to orient towards a different structure of meaning, whether it is in the form of reading-books (Janet and John), in the form of language use and dialect, or in the patterns of social relationships. . . . A wedge is progressively driven between the child as a member of the family and community and the child as a member of the school (Bernstein, 1970).

Whereas, in past decades, educational sociologists have been busiest mapping the incidence of educational inequality, 'head-counting' the proportions from each social class who jump each successive hurdle, some are now moving from the macro-level towards a micro-level in an effort to find out how these inequalities arise and are perpetuated. In particular, the 'social phenomenologists' are exploring the effects on classroom interaction and achievement of disjunctions in the ways that teachers and pupils define, interpret or gain meaning from what is going on. Where disjunctions are marked, where 'teachers and pupils occupy different social worlds' (O.U. 1971, E.282) there occurs a lack of communication, a lack of shared meanings, so that what is relevant and significant to one makes no mark upon the other. These sociologists are overlapping more and more with social psychologists in considering the effects upon interaction and learning of such phenomena as these: personal constructs and subjective frames of reference, language codes, impression formation, stereotyping, labelling, positions and

215

roles, expectations, self-concepts and attitudes. In fact, these sociologists are also helping to blur some of the disciplinary dividing lines between themselves and philosophers in that they are questioning the basic assumptions about authority, leadership and educational success and failure upon which much of our schooling rests. If reality is socially constructed then, they ask, what group has the authority to erect its own ideology, its own values and perspectives, its own version of what constitutes worthwhile knowledge, as standards towards which others are led with varying degrees of success or failure. Whereas social psychologists have considered leadership mainly from the angle of the effects of varying styles on learning, sciologists are now adding their weight to the more philosophical question of who has the right to lead whom and to where?

This increasing concern of social psychologists and sociologists with the disjunction between various individuals or groups within the school may be consonant with current trends in schools, for one could argue that the school is more and more likely to become an arena in which different versions of reality meet. Greater ranges of ability, of social background and even of ethnic background are likely to be encountered more frequently within one school and even, despite the effects of streaming, within one classroom. All this points to the need for the teacher to become more sensitive to the varying perspectives affecting interaction and learning in his classroom. In psychological terms, he needs to develop more empathy, more ability to take the role of the other, to see how the social or group context of the individual is affecting that individual's behaviour. In broader sociological terms, we can say that 'if the culture of the teacher is to become part of the consciousness of the child, then the culture of the child must first be in the consciousness of the teacher' (Bernstein, 1970). The problem is that of withdrawing the wedge and building, in its place, two-way bridges of understanding.

Training for sensitivity

If, as both social psychology and sociology are leading us to believe, a prime need in teachers is for increased sensitivity to the phenomenological worlds of others, how is this to be cultivated? Perhaps we should look on this problem as one of the acquisition of a changed attitude towards other people and the self, an attitude of openness in which we can resist the fossilization of early impressions and stereotypes and remain receptive to continuing feedback from and about the other. The hope should be that our categorizing may become as subtle and flexible as is consonant with our ability to cope and the demands upon us to act.

If increased sensitivity is a matter of attitude as well as of knowledge, we could consider increasing it through each or all of the three attitude components: cognitive, affective and behavioural. Our discussions in chapter 10 would suggest that listening to lectures or merely reading a book such as this one would have but limited effect. Such approaches at the cognitive informational level may produce shallow-rooted changes which might be reflected in intellectual stances and verbal compliances in pen-and-paper tests or examination answers but, unless the dissonance they create is soon followed up, the cracks they produce in existing attitudes are soon cemented over by our stronger affective, behavioural or habitual processes. If, however, lectures or reading are followed or accompanied by discussion, the impressions made may be deeper and longer-lasting.

What, then, of an approach through the affective component? We have a rather extreme example of this sort of approach in the T (training)-group technique which has been more widely used in training for other helping professions than for teaching (Ottaway, 1966). There are numerous variations of this technique, but an illustrative situation would involve about a dozen members who meet with a 'consultant' for a number of sessions amounting altogether to, perhaps, between ten and forty hours. There would be no external task to employ their energies and to focus their feelings. The consultant would give little or no help apart from occasional interpretations. In this frustrating vacuum, with no clear task or rigid group structure to give them support, members would become uncomfortable and, sooner or later, expressions of interpersonal feeling would emerge which would be reverberated and amplified between the walls of this introverted group like the proverbial wind in a bottle. In this situation, members come face-to-face with latent feelings of interpersonal hostility, frustration and the like. To give an instance of its potential relevance to teachers, members may realize clearly for the first time what effects their 'jokes', sarcasm or indifference may have been having on other individuals. Hard objective evidence on the effects of T-groups is difficult to obtain, but it is likely that the experience and analysis of such overted feelings may help many members to make significant discoveries about themselves, others and group dynamics which may help to make them more sensitive interactors in other situations. However, there are snags. First, much depends on the personality of the member and the degree of his anxiety and ego-defensiveness. Some authoritarians (see p. 187) and highly anxious persons may reveal 'contrast' effects and reject the whole situation; a few may even suffer nervous breakdown. (Some advocates of T-groups might say: 'Better now than later!'.) Secondly, such exercises are difficult and costly to mount and require a very skilled and experienced form of non-directive leadership, usually by an outsider who is seen to have no connection with course assessment. If the techniques were modified so as to avoid the danger of extreme emotional tension then, some would argue, the sting which stimulates learning would be removed. All in all, these snags make it look as though this approach to attitude change through extreme affective channels is unlikely to spread widely or quickly in teacher training.

Are there any training situations which are analogous to an approach to attitude changing via the behavioural channel? Probably many jobs and attitudes have been learned by repetitious performance modelled on another's behaviour, sitting at 'Nelly's elbow' and 'becoming what you do'. At the extreme, the danger with this is that one picks up a style or habit which, although it works, may not be the best or the most suited for you. Nevertheless, one may go on working with it until it becomes increasingly fluent and stereotyped, but without asking, or being asked, enough questions. In this way, one may copy a technique (e.g. of stereotyped interaction with a class of pupils) which is applicable only in the narrow range of situations in which it was learned, which is less flexible and transferable and which, because it works, may make sensitivity to alternatives seem unnecessary. Much, however, depends on how narrowly we define 'training'; if combined with tutorial help leading to continuous critical self-appraisal, it has much more to commend it.

Probably the most hopeful techniques for promoting attitudes conducive to social sensitivity are those which employ a mixture of cognitive, affective and behavioural elements and which emphasize contact, activity and ego-involvement. Looking first at contact, it may be said that a number of years spent in a residential college, in contact with what is inevitably a rather homogeneous company, is not the best preparation for coping with the varied social perspectives which meet in the school classroom. Contacts with children during school practices may make up a little for this but the contrasting status and role of teacher and pupil too often means that they see each other as if peering from opposing ends of a long and narrow tube. It is often the teacher of craft subjects who is good at understanding the pupil as a person, and one reason for this is that his work is often organized on an individual or small group basis which allows opportunity for the occasional informal and relaxed chat. Teachers of English also appear to have better than average opportunities for the building of such two-way bridges. It is probable that colleges could do more to assist students to set up similar situations which, while being controlled and purposeful, allow for a more broadly based two-way flow of information. Perhaps, as happens in youth work training, students should be given more guidance in setting up situations in which they talk less and listen more. A study of youth work training, where there are some well-articulated training schemes (e.g. Button, 1971), might also stimulate us to extend our 'field study' gathering of data as a basis for analysis and discussion (e.g. friendship studies). True, the conditions and emphases may differ, but ideas can often be adapted and emphases may change.

Organizing live contacts of the right sort is often difficult, but there are a number of alternatives being explored which might help improve our understanding of others. These alternatives, which emphasize activity and ego-involvement, include simulation techniques (BBC, 1972) such as case studies and role play. Case studies usually include the description of real or hypothetical cases in vivid detail. Role play goes farther in the direction of 'organismic involvement' and may, for instance, use case study as an information-gathering preliminary to the assuming of roles. There are many forms which role play may take. As an example, it may take the form of a planning exercise to do with the layout and common use of a proposed park. Various members present the cases for, or play the roles of, an old age pensioner, the mother of young toddlers, a dog owner, secretary of a youth football team, council official and so on. The possible conflict of perspectives needs no elaboration. In another case, a 'critical incident' or problem situation between two people might be made the basis for two persons playing opposed parts and then playing the roles in reverse. Many of these methods are based upon earlier attitude change experiments and, although some are designed primarily to give experience in decision-making, they are probably effective in penetrating the ego defences and increasing one's sensitivity to the other's perspectives.

So far, we have considered the cultivation of sensitivity to others in a rather undifferentiated way, but there is an increasing amount of experimental work being done on training along relatively narrow fronts such as sensitivity to pupil satisfaction, to pupils' perceptions of teachers, to pupil comprehension and boredom. A few brief examples must suffice. Jackson found that 'in general, satisfaction seems to be more visible to teachers than is dissatisfaction, satisfied girls and dissatisfied boys tend to be particularly salient, and students whose I.Q. scores are average or above manage in someway to communicate their attitudes more clearly to teachers than do students with low I.Q.s'. Gage and co-workers found that feedback to a teacher of her pupils' perception of her produced significant changes in her behaviour and improved her accuracy in perceiving the attitudes of her pupils. Jecker used videotaped lessons in a training programme for students and found that as little as six to eight hours of training on analysis and discussion of non-verbal cues to comprehension in pupils, cues such as chin-rubbing and brow-furrowing, produced a significant though small gain in accuracy of perception among his experimental group.

Conclusion

What we have been indicating in this section is that social psychologists and sociologists have more and more combined to underline the importance of a teacher's ability to empathize with the variety of others for whom the school and classroom are meeting places. Each individual is enmeshed in his own system of overlapping social webs, his membership and reference groups, and we need to understand how these influence his loyalties, his expectations and his perspectives. We need, also, to experiment further with training techniques which may help to broaden the range of our perceptual and interactional skills with different groups and individuals. We are not arguing that understanding is enough on its own to guarantee good teaching. 'Predictive empathy'–the 'ability to identify another person's feelings and problems from *their* point of view'–needs to be supplemented by 'interactive empathy' in which this understanding is communicated to the other. Then, on this basis, the teacher must act to arrange a better match between himself, the pupil and the content and difficulty of the work. As a start, no doubt we should do well to emulate that Irish village idiot who, when asked how he found the long-lost donkey when everyone else had failed, said, 'Well, I just thought,–now, if that was me, where would I go?' Yet, I can't help going on to ask myself what it was that the donkey ran away from and was probably returned to. If it wasn't the donkey-work and it wasn't the carrots . . . ?

Discussion and further study

1. 'The significant people for a school teacher are other school teachers' (Waller, 1932, p. 389). Discuss. What are the implications regarding the attitudes of probationer teachers? (See Shipman 1967, Hoy 1968, Finlayson and Cohen 1967.)
2. Observe a teacher's attitudes towards teaching, children, ideas, etc. (*a*) in the staffroom and (*b*) in the classroom. Do they differ? If so, in what ways? Why? To what extent may a teacher, like a restaurant waiter, have an 'on-stage' and an 'off-stage' self? See Goffman (1969) on impression management; also ideas of Jones and Davis etc. as summarized in Lindesmith and Strauss (1968), chapter 12.
3. Debate the possible pros and cons of team-teaching (245) and

then discuss the possible effects and probable limitations of your debate.

4. The 'Hawthorne Effect' was studied in industry (Homans, 1941; Olmsted, 1961). Does it apply in education?

5. Consider Likert's diagram (p. 119). How do the various levels compare as potential inlet points for new ideas?

6. What is the relevance of 'the self', 'the significant other' and 'interperson perception' (chs. 1, 2 and 5) to pupil perception of teacher expectation?

7. 'The Hughie G---- Half Hour'.

Work in a small group, e.g. 5 to 7. Devise a question with four possible answers, e.g. When Sam Smith had an accident, what did he break: (*a*) his foot, (*b*) his neck, (*c*) his finger, (*d*) his shoulder? Now person A records privately his choice of correct answers, e.g. (*d*). He then reads aloud the question, together with the possible answers, trying to suggest the correct solution by non-verbal or paralinguistic cues. Check the number who got the correct answer; discuss. This process is repeated about ten times until person A is reasonably successful in communicating the correct answer in as subtle and economical a way as he can; e.g. without winking or nudging. Then it is person B's turn, and so on. Finish with a general discussion; e.g. does this sort of thing occur in classrooms; would it be a useful skill to develop and control?

8. Why was it important that some of the adult participants in the (*a*) Beez (1970) and (*b*) Rubovitz and Maehr (1971) experiments should not know the category to which the children had been ascribed?

9. How might the work of Kelman (p. 62) relate to what Flanders and Hargreaves have to say about (*a*) dependency on the teacher, and (*b*) pleasing the teacher?

10. Training in classroom interaction analysis takes many hours, but try this to get the flavour. Tape record two brief episodes (e.g. 3 minutes each) of T/P interaction (simulate, if real thing is difficult to obtain). Working independently, categorize according to the Flanders system (p. 211). Compare results. Record on matrixes. Discuss. Note: some of the interest of the result will depend upon the selection of suitable and contrasting episodes.

11. Discuss examples of what Amidon and Hunter (1967) mean by 'broad' and 'narrow' questions.

12. 'Much of the context of our schools is unwittingly drawn from aspects of the symbolic world of the middle class, and so when the child steps into school he is stepping into a symbolic system which does not provide for him a linkage with his life outside. ---It is an accepted educational principle that we should work with what the child can offer; why don't we practise it?' (Bernstein, 1970). Discuss, preferably after reading the article.

13. How appropriate is it to regard sensitivity to others as an attitude?

14. In your experience, what sort of 'joking' references can hurt?

15. 'There is an enormous amount of hostility against parents and teachers. There is an enormous opposition to authority of a dominative or dogmatic kind. The holding under of this aggression is potentially most destructive. It seems to me that when a teacher understands the problems of aggression he is at once a better teacher of any school subject' (Ottaway, 1966, p. 157). Do you agree with all or any of the above points?

16. What sorts of school activities are likely to lead to (*a*) little, (*b*) much increase in the teacher's awareness of pupil perspectives? How far is such awareness desirable?

17. Choose a 'critical incident' relating to, e.g. tutor–student relationships, demands of teaching practice, the marking of homework. Identify the interested parties, prepare arguments and role-play a meeting to discuss the case.

18. 'Kelly's First Principle' was that 'if you don't know what is wrong with the patient, ask him, he may tell you'. (See Bannister and Fransella, 1971.) If we were to substitute 'pupil' for 'patient', could this apply in schools?

Further reading
Referring to the headings listed on p. 199.
1. Taba (1962), and Hoyle (1969); for Hawthorne studies (see Homans (1941 and Olmsted (1961)); risky-shift, Kogan and Wallach (1967), Bem, Wallach and Kogan (1965); probationary teachers, Finlayson and Cohen (1967), Hoy (1968), Shipman (1967).

2. Hargreaves (1972); Pidgeon (1970); article by Rubovitz and Maehr (1971).

3. Flanders (1967, 1970).

4. For some recent developments in sociology, see article by Gorbutt (1972) and O.U. E.282, *Man and Society*, esp. Units 1 and 2 and the Reader. On defining the classroom situation, see Hargreaves (1972), ch. 6. On social sensitivity, see Ottaway (1966) and Richardson (1967). Youth-work training, Button (1971). On 'empathy', see Natale (1972) and articles by Jackson (1968), Jecker (*et al* 1965) and Gage (*et al* 1963).

Bibliography

Abbreviations

Am.J.Psychol.	*American Journal of Psychology*
Am.J.Sociol.	*American Journal of Sociology*
BJEP	*British Journal of Educational Psychology*
Ed.Res.	*Educational Research*
J.Ed.Res.	*Journal of Educational Research*
Hum.Rel.	*Human Relations*
JASP	*Journal of Abnormal and Social Psychology*
JPSP	*Journal of Personality and Social Psychology*
J.Exp.Psychol.	*Journal of Experimental Psychology*
J.Soc.Issues	*Journal of Social Issues*
J.Pers.	*Journal of Personality*
Perc. and MS	*Perceptual and Motor Skills*
Psychol.Bull.	*Psychological Bulletin*

OU	Open University
B-M	Bobbs-Merrill reprints

ADCOCK, C. J. (1964) *Fundamentals of Psychology*, Penguin.

ADLER, A. (1945) *Social Interest: a challenge to mankind*, Faber.

ADORNO, T. W., FRENKEL-BRUNSWICK, E., LEVINSON, D. J. and SANFORD, R. N. (1950) *The Authoritarian Personality*, Harper & Row.

ALBROW, M. (1970) *Bureaucracy*, Macmillan (Papermac).

ALEXANDER, C. N. (1967) 'Ordinal position and sociometric status', *Sociometry* **29**; repr. in Sutton-Smith and Rosenberg (1970).

ALLPORT, F. H. (1920) 'The influence of the group upon association and thought', *J.Exp.Psychol.*, **3**.

ALLPORT, G. W. (1958) *The Nature of Prejudice*, Doubleday Anchor.

ALLPORT, G. W. (1961) *Pattern and Growth in Personality*, Holt, Rinehart & Winston.

ALTMAN, I. and McGINNIES, E. (1960) 'Interpersonal perception and communication in discussion groups of varied attitudinal composition', in *JASP*, **60**, 390–95.

AMIDON, E. J. and HOUGH, J. B. (1967) *Interaction Analysis: theory research and application*, Addison-Wesley, esp. article by E. J. Amidon and E. Hunter (1966) 'Improving Teaching: the analysis of classroom verbal interaction'.

ANDERSON, H. H. and BREWER, H. M. (1945–46) 'Studies of teachers' classroom personalities', *Applied Psychology* Monographs of the American Association for Applied Psychology, nos 6, 8 and 11, Stanford University Press.

ANDERSON, R. C. (1959) 'Learning in discussions: a resumé of the authoritarian-democratic studies', *Harvard Educ.Review*, **29**, 201–15; repr. in Charters and Gage (1963) and Wrightsman (1968).

ARGYLE, M. (1967) *The Psychology of Interpersonal Behaviour*, Penguin, ch. 3.

ARGYLE, M. (1969) *Social Interaction*, Methuen.

ARGYLE, M., ed. (1973) *Social Encounters: readings in social interaction*, Penguin.

ARONSON, E. and LINDER, D. (1965) 'Gain and loss of esteem as det of interpersonal attraction', *Journal of Experimental Social Psychology*, **1**, 156–71.

ASCH, S. (1946) 'Forming impressions of personality', *JASP*, **41**, 258–90.

ASCH, S. (1952) *Social Psychology*, Prentice-Hall.

ASCH, S. (1958) 'Effects of group pressure on modif. and distortion of judgment', in Maccoby *et al*, (1959).

BABLADELIS, G. and ADAMS, S., eds (1967) *The Shaping of Personality*, Prentice-Hall.

BACKMAN, C. W. and SECORD, P. F. (1968) *A Social Psychological View of Education*, Harcourt Brace.

BAGLEY, C. (1969) 'Coloured neighbours', *New Society*, 7 Aug.

BALES, R. F. (1950) 'A set of categories for the analysis of small group interaction', *American Sociological Review*, **15**, no. 2, 257–63; repr. in Hollander and Hunt, 1967–71 and B-M S–5.

BALES, R. F. and SLATER, P. E. (1955) 'Role differentiation in small decision-making groups', in Talcott Parsons, ed., *Family, Socialisation and Interaction Process*, New York, Free Press; repr. in Gibb (1969).

BALES, R. F., STRODTBECK, F. L., MILLS, T. M. and ROSEBOROUGH, M. E. (1951) 'Channels of communication in small groups', *Am.Sociol.Rev.* **16**; repr. in B-M S–6.

BANDURA, A. and WALTERS, R. H. (1963) *Social Learning and Personality Development*, Holt, Rinehart & Winston.

BANNISTER, D. and FRANSELLA, P. (1971) *Inquiring Man: the theory of personal constructs*, Penguin.

BANNISTER, D. and MAIR, J. M. M. (1968) *The Evaluation of Personal Constructs*, Academic Press.

BARKER, R. G. and WRIGHT, H. F. (1954) *The Midwest and its Children*, Harper & Row.

BAVELAS, A. (1960) 'Leadership: man and function', *Administrative Science Quarterly*, **5**, 491–8; repr. in Hollander and Hunt (1967–71) and Gibb (1969).

BAYER, A. E. (1967) 'Birth order and college attendance', *Journal of Marriage and Family Living*, **40**, 480–4; see also Sutton-Smith and Rosenberg (1970) pp. 72–4.

BEEZ, W. V. (1970) 'Influence of biased psychological reports on teacher behaviour and pupil performance', in M. W. Miles and W. W. Charters, eds., *Learning in Social Settings*, Allyn & Bacon; repr. in Morrison and McIntyre (1972).

BEM, D. J., WALLACH, M. A. and KOGAN, N. (1965) 'Group decision making under risk of aversive consequences', *JPSP* **1**, 453–60; repr., in Smith (1970).

BERGER, P. (1969) *The Social Reality of Religion*, Faber.

BERKOWITZ, L. (1956) 'Personality and group position', *Sociometry*, **19**, 210–22.

BERNSTEIN, B. (1970) 'Education cannot compensate for society', *New Society*, Feb; repr. in OU (1971), E282, *School and Society*, Reader.

BERSCHEID, E. and WALSTER, E. (1969) *Interpersonal Attraction*, Addison-Wesley.

BLOCK, J. and THOMAS, H. (1955) 'Is satisfaction with self a measure of adjustment?', *JASP*, **51**, no. 2, repr. in G. Babladelis and S. Adams, eds., *The Shaping of Personality*, Prentice-Hall, 1967.

BLOOM, L. (1971) *The Social Psychology of Race Relations*, Allen & Unwin.

BOGARDUS, E. S. (1925) 'Measuring social distance', *Journal of Applied Sociology*, **9**; repr. in Thomas (1971).

BONARIUS, J. C. J. (1965) 'Research in the personal construct theory of George A. Kelly', in B. A. Maher, ed., *Progress in Experimental Personality Research*, Academic Press, vol. 2.

BOSSARD, J. H. S. (1945) 'Family modes of expression', *American Sociological Review*, **10**, 222–37.

BRITISH BROADCASTING CORPORATION (1972) *Games and Simulations*, BBC Publications.

BRONFENBRENNER, U. and GALLWEY, M. (1968) 'A review of the theoretical framework for the study of interperson perception', in Wrightsman (1968).

BROOKOVER, W. B., THOMAS, S. and PATERSON, A. (1964) 'Self-concept of ability and school achievement', *Sociology of Education*, **37**, 271–8.

BROWN, J. A. C. (1961) *Freud and the Post-Freudians*, Penguin (Pelican); ch. 8 on

Fromm.

BROWN, J. A. C. *Techniques of Persuasion,* Penguin (1963).

BROWN, R. (1954) 'Mass phenomena', in G. Lindzey, ed., *Handbook of Social Psychology,* 3 vols, Addison-Wesley (2nd edn, 1969), vol. 2.

BROWN, R. (1965) *Social Psychology,* Collier-Macmillan.

BRUNER, J. S., SHAPIRO, D. and TAGIURI, R. (1958) 'The meaning of traits in isolation and combination', in R. Tagiuri, and L. Petrullo, eds., *Person Perception and Interpersonal Behavior,* Stanford University Press.

BUTTON, L. (1971) *Discovery and Experience,* Oxford University Press.

CARTER, L. F., HAYTHORN, W. and HOWELL, M. A. (1950) 'A further investigation of criteria of leadership', *JASP* **45**, 350–60.

CATTELL, R. B., SAUNDERS, D. R. and STICE, G. F. (1953) 'Dimensions of syntality in small groups', *Hum.Rel.,* **6**, 331–56.

CHARTERS, W. W. and GAGE, N. L., eds. (1963) *Readings in the Social Psychology of Education,* Allyn & Bacon.

CLINE, M. (1956) 'The influence of social contact on the perception of faces', *Journal of Personality,* **25**, 142–58.

COHEN, A. R. (1961) 'Cognitive tuning as a factor affecting impression formation', in *J.Pers.,* **29**, 235–45.

COOK, M. (1971) *Interpersonal Perception,* Penguin.

COOLEY, C. H. (1902) *Human Nature and the Social Order,* Scribner; repr. New York, Free Press, 1956.

COOLEY, C. H. (1909) *Social Organisation,* Scribner.

COWEN, E. L., HEILIZER, F. and AXELROD, H. S. (1955) 'Self-concept conflict indicators and learning', *JASP,* **51**, 242–5.

CROCKETT, W. H. (1965) 'Cognitive complexity and impression formation', in Maher (1965).

CRUTCHFIELD, R. S. (1955) 'Conformity and character', *American Psychologist,* **10**; repr. in Wrightsman (1968).

CULBERTSON, F. M. (1957) 'Modification of an emotionally-held attitude through role-playing', *JASP,* **54**, 230–3.

DAILEY, C. A. (1952) 'The effects of premature conclusion upon the acquisition of understanding of a person', in *Journal of Psychology,* **33**, 133–52.

DARLEY, J. M. and BERSCHEID, E. (1967) 'Increased liking caused by anticipation of personal contact', *Hum.Rel.* **20**, 29–39.

DASHIELL, J. F. (1930) 'An experimental analysis of some group effects', *JASP* **25**, 190–9.

DAVIS, J. H. (1969) *Group Performance,* Addison-Wesley.

DAVIS, K. E. quoted in Jones and Gerard (1967), p. 280.

DEUTSCH, M. (1949) 'An experimental study of the effects of co-operation and competition upon group process', *Hum.Rel.* **2**; repr. in Wrightsman (1968).

DEUTSCH, M. and COLLINS, M. E. (1951) *Inter-racial housing—a Psychological Evaluation of a Social Experiment*, University of Minnesota Press; described in Bloom (1971), pp. 165–6.

DEUTSCH, M. and KRAUSS, R. M. (1965) *Theories in Social Psychology*, Basic Books.

DICHTER, E. (1964) *Handbook of Consumer Motivation*, McGraw-Hill.

DITTES, J. E. (1959) 'Attractiveness of group as function of self-esteem and acceptance by group', *JASP*, **59**, 77–82.

DORNBUSCH, S. M. and MIYAMOTO, S. F. (1956) 'A test of interactional hypotheses of self-conception', *Am.J.Sociol.* **61**.

DORNBUSCH, S. M., HASTORF, A. H., RICHARDSON, S. A., MUZZY, R. E. and VREELAND, R. S. (1965) 'The perceiver and the perceived', *JPSP* **1**, 434–40.

EDMUNDS, L. F. (1963) *Rudolf Steiner Education*, Steiner.

EDWARDS, A. L. (1959) 'Social desirability and personality test construction', in Semeonoff (1966).

EHRLICH, H. J. (1973) *The Social Psychology of Prejudice*, Wiley.

ELKIN, F. (1960) *The Child and Society*, Random House.

ENTWISTLE, N. J. and CUNNINGHAM, S. (1968) 'Neuroticism and scholastic attainment: a linear relationship', *BJEP*, **38**; repr. in OU E281, unit 5.

ERIKSON, E. H. (1950; 1964) *Childhood and Society*, Hogarth Press; rev. edn. 1964; Penguin, 1965.

EVANS, K. M. (1965) *Attitudes and Interests in Education*, Routledge.

EYSENCK, H. J. (1957) *Sense and Nonsense in Psychology*, Penguin (Pelican).

EYSENCK, H. J. and COOKSON, D. (1970) 'Personality in primary school children, 3: Family background', *BJEP*, June.

FESTINGER, L. (1951) 'Architecture and group membership', *J.Soc.Issues*.

FESTINGER, L. (1954) 'A theory of social comparison processes', *Hum.Rel.*, pp. 117–40; repr. in B-M. P–111.

FESTINGER, L. (1957) *A Theory of Cognitive Dissonance*, Stanford University Press, abridged in Hollander and Hunt (1967, 1971).

FESTINGER, L. and CARLSMITH, J. M. (1959) 'Cognitive consequences of forced compliance', *JASP*, **58**; repr. in Wrightsman (1968).

FESTINGER, L., SCHACHTER, S. and BACK, K. (1950) *Social Pressures in Informal Groups*, Harper.

FIEDLER, F. (1954) 'Assumed similarity measures as predictors of team effectiveness', in *JASP* **49**, 381–8.

FIEDLER, F. (1958) *Leader Attitude and Group Effectiveness*, University of Illinois Press.

FIEDLER, F. (1962) 'Leader attitudes, group climate and group activity', *JASP*,

65; repr. in Wrightsman (1968).

FIEDLER, F. (1965a) 'The contingency model', in Proshansky and Seidenberg (1965); repr. in Smith, 1970.

FIEDLER, F. (1965b) 'Leadership: a new model', repr. in Gibb (1969).

FINLAYSON, P. S. and COHEN, L. (1967) 'Teacher's role: conceptions of students and headteachers', *BJEP,* 37; repr. in Morrison and McIntyre (1972).

FLANDERS, N. A. (1967) 'Teacher influence in the classroom', in Amidon and Hough.

FLANDERS, N. A. (1970) *Analysing Teacher Behaviours,* Addison-Wesley.

FREEDMAN, J. L., CARLSMITH, J. M. and SEARS, D. O. (1970) *Social Psychology,* Prentice-Hall.

FRIEDMAN, I. (1955) 'Phenomenal, ideal and projected conceptions of self', *JASP* **51**, 611–15.

GABRIEL, J. (1968) *Children Growing Up,* University of London Press.

GAGE, N. L., RUNKEL, P. J. and CHATTERJEE, B. B. (1963) 'Changing teacher behaviour through feedback from pupils', in Charters and Gage (1963); repr. in Argyle (1973).

GATES, G. S. (1923) 'An experimental study of the growth of social perception. *Journal of Educational Psychology,* **14**.

GERGEN, K. J. (1969) *The Psychology of Behaviour Exchange,* Addison-Wesley.

GHISELLI, E. E. and LODAHL, T. M. (1958) 'Patterns of managerial traits and group effectiveness', *JASP,* 57.

GIBB, C. A., ed. (1969) *Leadership,* Penguin.

GOFFMAN, E. (1959) *The Presentation of Self in Everyday Life,* Doubleday.

GORBUTT, D. (1972) 'The new sociology of education', *Education for Teaching,* Autumn.

GORDON, K. (1923) 'A study of esthetic judgements', *J.Exp.Psychol.* **6**, 36–43.

GREENSPOON, T. (1955) 'The reinforcing effect of two spoken sounds on the frequency of two responses', *Am.J.Psychol.* **68**.

GRONLUND, N. (1959) *Sociometry in the Classroom,* Harper & Row.

GURIN, P., LAO, R. and BEATTIE, M. (1969) 'Internal-external control in the motivational dynamics of Negro youth', in *J.Soc.Issues,* **25**, no. 3.

GURNEE, H. (1937) 'Maze learning in the collective situation', *J.Psychol.* **3**, 437–43.

HAMID, P. N. (1970) 'Birth order and family schemata', *Perc. and MS,* **31**, 807–10.

HARDING, J. and HOGREFE, R. (1952) 'Attitudes of white department store employees towards Negro co-workers', *J.Soc.Issues,* **8**, no. 1.

HARE, A. P., BORGATTA, E. F. and BALES, R. F., eds (1965) *Small Groups,* Knopf.

HARGREAVES, D. (1967) *Social Relations in a Secondary School,* Routledge.

230

HARGREAVES, D. (1972) *Interpersonal Relations and Education,* Routledge.

HARRIS, IRVING (1964) *The Promised Seed: a comparative study of eminent first and later sons,* New York, Free Press.

HASTORF, A. H., SCHNEIDER, D. J. and POLEFKA, J. (1970) *Person Perception* Addison-Wesley.

HAVIGHURST, R. J., ROBINSON, M. Z. and DORR, M. J. (1946) 'The development of the ideal-self in childhood and adolescence', *Journal of Educational Research,* **40**.

HAYTHORN, W., COUCH, A., HAEFNER, D., LANGHAM, P. and CARTER, L. (1956) 'Effects of varying combinations of authoritarian and equalitarian leaders and followers', *JASP,* **53**; repr. in Maccoby *et al.* (1959).

HEIDER, F. (1958) *The Psychology of Interpersonal Relations,* Wiley.

HEINICKE, C. M. and BALES, R. F. (1953) 'Developmental trends in the structure of small groups', *Sociometry,* **16**.

HILTON, I. (1967) 'Differences in behaviour of mothers towards first and later-born children', *JPSP,* **7**.

HINKLE, D. N. (1965) Unpublished thesis discussed in Bannister and Fransella (1971), p. 73.

HOFSTÄTTER, P. R. (1957) *Gruppendynamik = Kritik der Massenpsychologie,* Hamburg, Rowohit Taschenbuch.

HOLLANDER, E. P. and HUNT, R. G., eds (1967; 1971) *Current Perspectives in Social Psychology,* 2nd edn, 1967; 3rd edn, 1971, Oxford University Press.

HOLLANDER, E. P. and WEBB, W. B. (1955) 'Leadership, followership and friendship', *JASP,* **50**, 163–7.

HOMANS, G. C. (1941) 'Group factors in worker productivity', in Proshansky and Seidenberg (1965).

HOMANS, G. C. (1958) 'Social behavior as exchange', *Am.J.Sociol.* **63**; repr. in Hollander and Hunt (1967; 1971).

HOPPE, R. A., MILTON, G. A. and SIMMEL, E. L. (1970) *Early Experiences and the Processes of Socialisation,* Academic Press.

HOVLAND, C. I. (1953) *Yale Studies of Communication and Persuasion;* repr. in Charters and Gage (1963).

HOY, W. K. (1968) 'Influence of experience on the beginning teacher', *School Review,* **76**; repr. in Morrison and McIntyre (1972).

HOYLE, E. (1969) in *Journal of Curriculum Studies,* **1**, no. 2 May, no. 3, Nov.

HUGUENARD, T., SAGER, E. B. and FERGUSON, L. W. (1970) 'Interview time, set and outcome', *Perc. and MS,* 31.

INSKO, C. A. (1967) *Theories of Attitude Change,* Appleton.

JACKSON, P. W. (1968) 'Teachers' perceptions of pupils' attitudes towards school', in *Life in Classrooms,* Holt, Rinehart & Winston; abridged in

Morrison and McIntyre (1972).

JACOBS, L., BERSCHEID, E. and WALSTER, E. (1971) 'Self-esteem and attraction', *JPSP*, **17**, no. 1, 84–91.

JAHODA, M. (1959) 'Conformity and independence: a psychological analysis', *Hum.Rel.* **12**, 99–120.

JANIS, I. L. and KING, B. T. (1954) 'Influence of role-playing on opinion change', *JASP*, **49**, 211–18; repr. in Maccoby *et al.* (1959); see also King and Janis, 1956; Mann and Janis, 1968.

JECKER, J. D., MACCOBY, N. and BREITROSE, H. S. (1965) 'Improving accuracy in interpersonal non-verbal cues of comprehension', *Psychology in The Schools* extract in Morrison and McIntyre (1972).

JENCKS, C. and RIESMAN, D. (1967) 'The American Negro College', *Harvard Educational Review,* **37**

JONES, E. E. and GERARD, H. B. (1967) *Foundations of Social Psychology* Wiley.

KARLINS, M. and ABELSON, H. I. (1970) *Persuasion,* 2nd edn, Crosby Lockwood.

KATZ, D. (1960) 'The functional approach to the study of attitudes', *Public Opinion Quarterly;* repr. in Hollander and Hunt, (1967; 1971).

KATZ, P. and ZIGLER, E. (1967) 'Self-image disparity', *JPSP* **5**, 186–95.

KATZ, D., SARNOFF, I. and McCLINTOCK, C. (1954) 'The motivational basis of attitude change', *JASP,* **49**; repr. in Proshansky and Seidenberg (1965), and OU D100, *Understanding Society,* Reader.

KELLEY, H. H. (1950) 'Warm-cold variable in first impression of persons', *J.Pers.,* **18**.

KELLEY, H. H. and VOLKART, (1952) 'Resistance to change of group-anchored attitudes', *Am.Soc.Rev.,* **17**.

KELMAN, H. C. (1958) 'Three processes of social influence', in Hollander and Hunt (1967 and 1971) repr. in OU D100, *Understanding Society,* Reader. See also 'Three processes of attitude change' in Proshansky and Seidenberg, 1965.

KELVIN, P. (1969) *The Bases of Social Behavior,* Holt, Rinehart & Winston.

KING, B. T. and JANIS, I. L. (1956) 'Improvised and non-improvised role-playing and opinion changes', *Hum.Rel.,* **9**, 177–85; (see also Janis and King, 1954).

KNIGHT, M. (1950) *William James,* Penguin.

KOCH, H. L. (1956) 'Sibling influence on children's speech', *Journal of Speech Disorders,* **21**.

KOCH, H. L. (1957) 'The relation in young children between characteristics of their playmates and certain attributes of their siblings', *Child Development,* **28**, 175–202.

KOGAN, N. and WALLACH, M. A. (1967) in G. Mandler, ed., *New Directions in Psychology,* vol. 3.

KRECH, D., CRUTCHFIELD, R. S. and BALLACHEY, E. L. (1962) *Individual in Society*, McGraw-Hill.

KUHN, H. H. (1960) 'Self attitudes by age, sex and professional training', *Sociological Quarterly*, **1**.

LASKO, J. K. (1954) 'Parent behaviour toward first and second children', *Genetic Psychology Monographs*, **49**, 97–137.

LANDIS, L. (1929) in *Journal of Comparative Psychology*, **4**, 447–509.

La PIERE, R. T. (1934) 'Attitudes versus actions', *Social Forces*, **13**, 230–7.

LAWRENCE, D. (1971) 'The effects of counselling on retarded readers', *Ed.Res.*, Feb., p. 13.

LEAVITT, H. J. (1951) 'Some effects of certain communication patterns on group performance', *JASP*, **46**; repr. in Vinacke *et al.* (1964).

Le BON, G. (1898) *The Crowd*.

LEES, J. P. and STEWART, A. H. (1957) 'Family and sibship position and scholastic ability', *Sociological Review* (Univ. Coll. North Staffs), **5**, 85–106; 176–89.

LEWIN, K. (1947) 'Group decision and social change', in Proshansky and Seidenberg (1965).

LIKERT, R. (1961) 'An overview of new patterns of management', in Hollander and Hunt (1967, 1971).

LINDESMITH, A. R. and STRAUSS, A. L. (1968) *Social Psychology*, 3rd edn.

LIPPITT, R. and WHITE, R. K. (1959) 'An experimental study of leadership and group life', in Maccoby *et al.*

LUCHINS, A. S. (1957) 'Primacy-recency in impression formation', in C. Hovland, ed, *The Order of Presentation in Persuasion*, Yale University Press.

MᶜARTHUR, C. (1956) 'Personalities of first and second children', *Psychiatry*, **19**, 47–54.

MACCOBY, E. E., NEWCOMB, T. M. and HARTLEY, E. L. (1959) *Readings in Social Psychology*, 3rd edn, New York, Holt; London, Methuen.

McDAVID, J. W. and HARARI, H. (1967) *Social Psychology*, Harper & Row.

McGREGOR, D. (1960) *The Human Side of Enterprise*, McGraw-Hill.

MAHER, B. A., ed. (1965) *Progress in Experimental Personality Research*, Academic Press, vol. 2.

MAIER, N. R. F. and SOLEM, A. R. (1952) 'Contribution of a discussion leader to the quality of group thinking', *Hum.Rel.* **5**.

MANN, R. D. (1959) 'Review of relationships between personality and performance in small groups', *Psychol.Bull.* 56.

MANIS, M. (1955) 'Social interaction and the self-concept', *JASP* **51**, 362–70.

MANN, L. and JANIS, I. L. (1968) 'Long-term effects of emotional role-play', *JPSP*, **8**.

MARTIN, J. G. and WESTIE, F. R. (1959) 'The tolerant personality', *Am.Soc.Rev.* 24.

MASLOW, A. H. (1943) 'A theory of human motivation', *Psychol.Rev.* **50**, repr. in B-M P–509.

MASLOW, A. H. (1968) *Towards a Psychology of Being*, 2nd edn., Van Nostrand.

MATHER, D. R. (1968) 'By process of monomania' and 'Leadership and delegation', *Education*, 9 and 16 Feb.

MERTON, R. K. (1959) *Social Theory and Social Structure*, N.Y., Free Press.

MILGRAM, S. (1961) 'Nationality and conformity', *Scientific American*, **205**, 45–51.

MILLER, G. A. (1966) *Psychology: the science of mental life*, Penguin.

MILLER, H. and BIERI, J. (1965) 'Cognitive complexity as a function of the significance of the stimulus objects being judged', *Psychological Reports* **16**, 1203–4.

MILLER, N. E. and DOLLARD, J. (1941) *Social Learning and Imitation*, Yale University Press.

MILLER, N., CAMPBELL, D., TWEDT, H. and O'CONNELL, E. J. (1966) 'Similarity, contrast and complementarity in friendship choices', *JPSP*, **3**, 3–12.

MILNER, D. (1969) 'Effects of Prejudice', *Race Today*, Aug.

MINARD, R. D. (1952) 'Race relations in the Pocahontas coalfield', *J.Soc. Issues*, **8**, no. 1.

MITNICK, L. and MᶜGINNIES, E. (1958) 'Influencing ethnocentrism in small discussion groups through a film communication', *JASP* **56**, 82–90.

MORENO, J. B. (1934) *Who Shall Survive?*, 2nd edn., Beacon House.

MORRISON, A. and MᶜINTYRE, D., eds (1972) *Social Psychology of Teaching*, Penguin.

MORSE, M. (1967) *The Unattached*, Penguin.

MOULY, G. (1968) *The Psychology of Effective Teaching*, Holt, Rinehart & Winston.

MUSGROVE, F. (1964) *Youth and the Social Order*, Routledge.

MUSSEN, P. H. (1963) *The Psychological Development of the Child*, Prentice-Hall.

NATALE, S. (1972) *An Experiment in Empathy*. National Foundation for Educational Research.

NEWCOMB, T. M. (1961) *The Acquaintance Process*, Holt, Rinehart & Winston.

NEWCOMB, T. (1967) 'The prediction of personal attraction', in Hollander and Hunt (1967, 1971) repr. B-M S–209.

NISBETT, R. E. (1968) 'Birth order and participation in dangerous sports', *JPSP*, **8**, no. 4, 351–3.

OLMSTED, M. (1961) *The Small Group*, Random House.

OPEN UNIVERSITY (1970) D.100, *Understanding Society*, units 5–9 and Reader, Open University Press.

OPEN UNIVERSITY (1971) D.283, *The Sociological Perspective*, Units 5–8 on Social Interaction, Open University Press.

OPEN UNIVERSITY (1971) E.282, Units 1 and 2, *The Construction of Reality*.

OPEN UNIVERSITY (1971) E.282, *School and Society*, Reader, Routledge.

OPEN UNIVERSITY (1972) E.281, Unit 5, *Personality Dimensions and Achievement*, Open University Press.

OTTAWAY, A. K. C. (1966) *Learning Through Group Experience*, Routledge.

PALMER, R. D. (1966) 'Birth order and identification', *J. Consulting Psychology*, **30**, no. 2, 129–35.

PATRICK, J. (1973) *A Glasgow Gang Observed*, Eyre Methuen.

PELZ, E. B. (1958) 'Some factors in group decision', in Maccoby *et al.* (1959).

PESSIN, J. (1933) 'Comparative effects of social and mechanical stimulation on memorising', *Am.J.Psychol.*, 45.

PETTIGREW, T. F. (1958) 'Personality and sociocultural factors in intergroup attitudes', *Journal of Conflict Resolution*, **2**.

PIDGEON, D. A. (1970) *Expectations and Pupil Performance*, National Foundation for Educational Research.

PROSHANSKY, H. and SEIDENBERG, B., eds. (1965) *Basic Studies in Social Psychology* [Readings], Holt, Rinehart & Winston.

PURKEY, W. W. (1968) 'The search for self—evaluating student self-concepts', *Florida Educ. Research and Development Research Bulletin*, 4, no. 2; repr. in Open University E.281, unit 10, 1972.

RABOW, J., FOWLER, F. J., HOFEUER, M. A., BRADFORD, D. L. and SHIBUYA, Y. (1966) 'The role of social norms and leadership in risk-taking', *Sociometry*, **29**, 16–27.

REESE, H. W. (1961) 'Relationships between self-acceptance and sociometric choices', *JASP*, **62**, 472–4.

RHINE, W. R. (1968) 'Birth order differences in conformity and level of achievement arousal', *Child Development*, **39**.

RICHARDSON, E. (1967) *Group Study for Teachers*, Routledge.

RIECKEN, H. W. (1958) 'Effect of talkativeness on group solution of problems', *Sociometry*, **21**.

ROGERS, C. R. (1961) *On Becoming a Person*, Houghton Mifflin.

ROGERS, C. R. (1965) 'The therapeutic relationship', *Australian Journal of Psychology*, **17**, no. 2; repr. in Babladelis and Adams (1967).

ROKEACH, M. (1968) 'The nature of attitudes', *International Encyclopaedia of the Social Science*; repr. in Open University D.100 *Understanding Society*.

ROSE, E. J. B. and associates (1969) *Colour and Citizenship*, O.U. Press.

235

ROSENBERG, M. J. (1960) 'Cognitive reorganisation in response to the hypnotic reversal of attitudinal affect', *J.Pers.* **28**, 39–63.

ROSENBERG, M. (1965) *Society and the Adolescent Self-image,* Princeton University Press.

ROSENTHAL, R. (1966) *Experimental Effects in Behavioral Research,* Appleton.

ROSENTHAL, R. and JACOBSON, L. (1968) *Pygmalion in the Classroom,* Holt, Rinehart & Winston. (See Thorndike, 1968, for review.)

ROSS, E. A. (1908) *Social Psychology: an outline and source book,* New York, Macmillan.

ROTHBART, M. K. (1971) 'Birth order and mother-child interaction in an achievement situation', *JPSP,* **17**, no. 2.

RUBOVITZ, R. C. and MAEHR, M. L. (1971) 'Pygmalion analysed', *JPSP,* **19**, no. 2, 197–203.

SAMPLE, J. A. and WILSON, T. R. (1965) 'Leader behaviour, group productivity and rating of LPC', *JPSP,* **1**, 266–72.

SAMPSON, E. E. and HANCOCK, F. T. (1967) 'Ordinal position, personality and conformity', *JPSP,* **5**, 398–407.

SARBIN, T. R. and JONES, D. S. (1956) 'An experimental analysis of role behaviour', *JASP,* **51**.

SCHACHTER, S. (1951) 'Deviation, rejection and communication', *JASP,* **46**; repr. in Vinacke *et al.* (1964).

SCHACHTER, S. (1959) *The Psychology of Affiliation,* Stanford University Press.

SCHACHTER, S. and SINGER, J. E. (1962) 'Cognitive, social and physiological determinants of emotional states', *Psychol.Rev.* **69**, 379–99.

SARNOFF, S. and ZIMBARDO, P. G. (1961) 'Anxiety, fear and social affiliation', *JASP,* **62**, 356–63.

SCHLOSBERG, H. (1952) 'The description of facial expressions in terms of two dimensions', *J.Exp.Psychol.,* **44**, 229–37.

SCHUTZ, W. C. (1958) *FIRO: a three-dimensional theory of interpersonal behavior,* Holt, Rinehart & Winston.

SCHUTZ, A. (1964) 'The stranger: an essay in social psychology', in A. Brudersen, ed., *Studies in Social Theory,* The Hague; repr. in OU E.282, *School and Society,* Reader.

SCOTT, W. A. (1957) 'Attitude change through reward of verbal behaviour', *JASP,* **55**, 72–5.

SEARS, R. R., MACCOBY, E. E. and LEVIN, H. (1957) *Patterns of Child-rearing,* Row, Peterson.

SEBALD, H. (1962) 'Limitations of communication', *Journal of Communication,* **12**, 142–9.

SECORD, P. F. and BACKMAN, C. W. (1964) *Social Psychology,* McGraw-Hill.

SELLS, S. B. and ROFF, N. (1963) 'Peer acceptance-rejection and birth-order', *American Psychologist,* **18**, 35; see also Sutton-Smith and Rosenberg (1970), p. 117.

SEMEONOFF, S., ed. (1966) *Personality Assessment,* Penguin.

SHAW, M. E. (1964) 'Communication network', in L. Berkowitz, ed., Advances in Experimental Social Psychology, Academic Press, vol. 1; repr. in Smith (1970).

SHERIF, C. W. and SHERIF, M., eds (1967) *Attitudes, Ego-involvement and Change,* Wiley. See also articles in Hollander and Hunt (1967, 1971); and Vinacke *et al.* (1964).

SHERIF, C. W., SHERIF, M. and NEBERGALL, R. (1965) *Attitude and Attitude Change,* Saunders.

SHERIF, M. (1935) 'A study of some social factors in perception', *Arch.Psychol.,* **187**, 12.

SHERIF, M. (1966) *Group Conflict and Co-operation,* Houghton-Mifflin; excerpts in Charters and Gage (1963) and Smith (1970).

SHIPMAN, M. (1967) 'Theory and practice in the education of teachers', *Ed.Res.* **9**, June.

SILVERMAN, I. (1964) 'Self-esteem and differential responsiveness to success and failure', *JASP,* **69**, no. 1; also in Babledelis and Adams (1967).

SLATER, P. E. (1958) 'Contrasting correlates of group size', *Sociometry,* **21**, 129–39.

SMITH, P. S., ed. (1970) *Group Processes,* Penguin (see esp. article by Shaw).

SOLOMON, D. (1965) 'Birth order, family composition and teaching style', *Psychological Reports,* **17**.

SOUCAR, E. (1970) 'Students' perceptions of liked and disliked teachers', *Perc. and MS,* **31**, 19–24.

STEINER, I. D. and JOHNSON, H. H. (1963) 'Authoritarianism and tolerance of trait inconsistency', *JASP,* **67**, 388–91.

STEPHAN, F. F. and MISHLER, E. G. (1952) 'Distribution of participation in small groups', *Am.Soc.Rev.,* **17**.

STONEQUIST, E. V. (1937) *The Marginal Man,* Scribner.

STRAUSS, A. (1964) *G. H. Mead on Social Psychology,* Univ. of Chicago Press.

SULLIVAN, H. S. (1955) *Conceptions of Modern Psychiatry,* Tavistock Press.

SUTTON-SMITH, B. and ROSENBERG, B. G. (1970) *The Sibling,* Holt, Rinehart & Winston.

TABA, H. (1962) *Curriculum Development,* Harcourt Brace.

TAFT, R. (1955) 'The ability to judge people', *Psychological Bulletin,* **52**, 1–23.

TAYLOR, D. W., BERRY, P. C. and BLOCK, C. H. (1958) 'Does group participation when using brainstorming facilitate or inhibit creative thinking?', *Adminis-*

trative Science Quarterly, **3**, 23–47.

THELEN, H. A. (1949) 'Group dynamics in instruction=principle of least group size', *School Review*, **57**, 139–48.

THIBAUT, J. W. and KELLEY, H. H. *The Social Psychology of Groups*, Wiley.

THOMAS, K., ed. (1971) *Attitudes and Behaviour*, Penguin.

THORNDIKE, R. L. (1938) 'On what type of task will a group do well?', *JASP*, **33**, 409–13.

THORNDIKE, R. L. (1968) 'Review of *Pygmalion in the Classroom*, *American Educational Research Journal*, Nov.; for Rosenthal's reply see issue for Nov. 1969.

TOMAN, W. (1970) 'Sibling position of a sample of distinguished persons', *Perc. and MS*, **31**.

TOMAN, W. (1971) 'The duplication theorem of social relationships', *Psychol. Rev*. **78**.

TORRANCE, E. P. (1955) 'Some consequences of power differences on decision-making in permanent and temporary three-man groups', repr. in Hare *et al.* (1965).

TORRANCE, E. P. and ARSAN, K. (1963) 'Experimental study of homogeneous and heterogeneous groups for creative scientific tasks', in Charters and Gage (1963).

TRIANDIS, H. C. and TRIANDIS, L. M. (1962) 'Cross-cultural study of social distance', *Psychological Monographs*, **76**.

TRIANDIS, H. C. and TRIANDIS, L. M. (1960) 'Race, social class, religion, and nationality as determinants of social distance', *JASP*, **61**, 110–18.

TUCKMAN, B. W. (1965) 'Developmental sequence in small groups', *Psychol. Bull*. **63**; repr. in Smith (1970).

VERNON, P. E. (1933) in *Journal of Social Psychology*, **4**, 42–58.

VERNON, P. E. (1963) *Personality Assessment*, Methuen.

VINACKE, W. E., WILSON, W. R. and MEREDITH, G. M., eds. (1964) *Dimensions of Social Psychology* [readings] Scott, Foresman.

WALKER, E. L. (1966) *Conditioning and Instrumental Learning*, Wadsworth.

WALLER, W. (1932) *The Sociology of Teaching;* repr. Wiley, 1965.

WALSTER, E. (1966) 'The assignment of responsibility for an accident', *JPSP*, **5**, 508–16.

WARR, P. B., ed. (1970) *Thought and Personality*, Penguin.

WARWICK, D. (1971) *Team Teaching*, University of London Press.

WARWICK, D. (1973) Article on team teaching, *The Times Educational Supplement*, 30 March.

WAY, L. (1956) *Alfred Adler: an introduction to his psychology*, Penguin.

WHYTE, W. F. (1941) '*A study of clique behaviour: Corner boys*', *Am.J.Sociol.*,

March; repr. B-M.S–311, and OU D.100, *Understanding Society,* Reader.

WILLIS, R. H. (1965) 'Conformity, independence and anticonformity', *Hum. Rel.;* repr. in Hollander and Hunt (1967, 1971); Proshansky and Seidenberg. 1965; and Wrightsman, 1968.

WINCH, R. F., KTSANES, T. and KTSANES, V. (1955) 'Empirical elaboration of the theory of complementary needs in mate-selection', *JASP,* **51**, 508–13.

WISHNER, J. (1960) 'Re-analysis of "Impressions of Personality" ', *Psychological Review,* **67**, no. 2, 96–112.

WOODWORTH, R. S. (1938) *Experimental psychology,* Methuen.

WRIGHT, D. S. *et al.* (1970) *Introducing Psychology: an experimental approach,* Penguin 1970.

WRIGHTSMAN, L. S., ed. (1968) *Contemporary Issues in Social Psychology,* Wadsworth: Prentice-Hall.

WYLIE, R. C. (1961) *The Self Concept: a critical survey of recent literature,* University of Nebraska Press.

ZAJONC, R. B. (1966) *Social Psychology: an experimental approach,* Wadsworth: Prentice-Hall.

ZAJONC, R. B. (1968) 'Attitudinal effects of mere exposure'. *JPSP,* **8**.

ZELDITCH, M. (1955) 'Role differentiation in the nuclear family', in Parsons and Bales, *Family, Socialisation and Interaction Process,* New York, Free Press.

ZIMBARDO, P. G. and EBBESEN, E. B. (1969) *Influencing Attitudes and Changing Behavior,* Addison-Wesley.

ZIMBARDO, P. G. and FORMICA, R. (1963) 'Emotional comparison and self-esteem as determinants of affiliations', *J.Pers.* **31**, 141–62.

References

J.P.S.P.   Journal of Personality and Social Psychology.
J.A.S.P.   Journal of Abnormal and Social Psychology.
B.M.   Bobbs-Merrill Reprints.

ADORNO-FRENKEL-BRUNSWIK, T. W., ELSE, LEVINSON & SANFORD: The Authoritarian Personality, 1950.

ALBROW, M.: Bureaucracy. Papermac, 1970. Discusses concepts of 'bureaucracy'.

ALEXANDER, C. N.: Ordinal Position and Sociometric Status. Sociometry, 1967, **29**.

ALLPORT, F. H.: The infl. of the group upon association and thought. *J.Exp.Psych.*, 1920, **3**.

ALLPORT, G. W.: op. cit. p. 136.

ALLPORT, G. W.: 'Pattern & Growth in Personality', 1961. (*a*) p. 111–117. (*b*) p. 155. (*c*) p. 347–8.

ALLPORT, G. W.: The nature of Prejudice, 1958. Addison-Wesley.

ALTMAN, I. & MCGINNIES, E.: in *JASP*, 1960, **60**, 390–95.

AMIDON, E. J. & HOUGH, J. B.: Interaction Analysis: theory, research and applic., 1967.

ANDERSON, H. H. & BREWER: St. of Teachers' Classroom Personalities. *App. Ps. Mon.*, 1945–6.

ANDERSON, R. C.: Learning in Discussions: a resume of the Auth-Dem studies.

ARGYLE, M. (ed.): 'Social Encounters: Readings in Social Interaction'. Penguin, 1973.

ARGYLE, M.: 'Social Interaction'. 1969, (*a*) 179, (*b*) 332–3, (*c*) 238.

ARGYLE, M.: The Psych. of Interpersonal Behaviour. Pelican, 1967, chap. 3.

ARONSON, E. & LINDER, D.: 'Gain and Loss of Esteem as Det. of Interp. Attrac.' *J.Exp.S.P.*, 1965, **1**, 156–171.

ASCH, S.: Effects of group pressure on modif. and distortion of judg. In (152).

ASCH, S.: 'Forming Impressions of Personality'. *JASP*, 1946, **41**, 258–290.

ASCH, S.: Social Psychology, 1952.

BAGLEY, C.: in *New Society*, 7th Aug., 1969.

BALES R. F. & SLATER: Role differentiation in small decision-making groups.

BANDURA, A. & WALTERS, R. H.: Soc. Learning and Personality Development, 1963.

BANNISTER, D. & FRANSELLA, F.: 'Inquiring Man: The theory of Personal Constructs'. Penguin, 1971, p. 73.

BARKER, R. G. & WRIGHT, H. F.: Midwest and its Children, 1955.

BAVELAS, A.: Leadership: Man and Function.

BEEZ, W. V.: Infl. of biased psych. reports on T. behav. and P. perf. 1970.

BERGER, P.: The Social Reality of Religion, 1969, pp. 3–4.

BERKOWITZ, L.: Personality and Group Position. Sociometry, 1956, **19**, 210–22.

BERNSTEIN, B.: 'Education cannot compensate for society'. *New Society*, Feb., **70**.

BLOCK, J. & THOMAS, H.: Is sat, with self a measure of adjustment? *JASP*, **51**, **2**, 1955.

BLOOM, L.: The Soc. Psychology of Race Relations. George, Allen & Unwin, 1971.

BOGARDUS, E. S.: Measuring Social Distance, *J. App. Soc.*, 1925, **9**.

BOSSARD, J. H. S.: Family modes of expression, *AM. Soc. Rev.*, 1945, **10**, 222–237.

BRONFENBRENNER *et al.*: in (65), part IV.

BROOKOVER, THOMAS & PATERSON: *Sociol. of Educ.*, 1964, **37**, p. 271–8.

BROWN, J. A. C.: Freud and the Post-Freudians, Pelican 1961, chapter 8 is on Fromm.

BROWN, R.: 'Mass Phenomena', 1954, in G. Lindzey (ed.), '*Hdbk. of Soc. Ps.*', Vol. 2.

BROWN, R.: Social Psychology, 1965.

BRUNER, SHAPIRO & TAGIURI: Person Perception and Behaviour, 1958.

BUTTON, L.: Discovery and Experience. *O.U.P.*, 1971.

CARTER, HAYTHORN & HOWELL: The criteria of leadership. *JASP*, 1950, **45**, 350–58.

CATTELL, R. B., SAUNDERS & STICE: Dimensions of Syntality in Small Groups. *Hum Rel.*, 1953, **6**.

CHARTERS & GAGE: Readings in the Social Psychology of Education, 1963.

CLINE, V. B.: Journal of Personality; 1956, **25**, 142–58.

COHEN, A. R.: *J. of Pers.*, 1961, **29**, 235–245.

COOLEY, C. H.: Human Nature and the Social Order, 1902.

(a) R. F. Bales: A set of categories for analysis of small group interaction. In (63) and *BM* S5.

(*b*) Bales *et al.*: Channels of Communic. in small groups. *Am. Soc. Rev.*, 1951, **16** and *BM* S6.

COOLEY, C. H.: Social Organisation, 1909.

COWEN, HEILIZER & AXELROD: Self-concept Conflict Indicators and Learning, *JASP*, 1955, **51**.

CROCKETT, W. H.: 'Cogn. Compl. and Impr. Form.' in Maher (ed.), Prog. Exp. Pers. Res., **2**, 1965.

CRUTCHFIELD, R. S.: Conformity and Character. *Am Psych.*, 1955, **10**.

CULBERTSON, F. M.: Modif. of an emotionally-held att. through role-playing. *JASP*, 1957, **54**.

DAILEY, C. A.: *J. of Psych.*, 1952, **33**, 133–52.

DARLEY & BERSCHEID: Increased liking caused by antic. of personal contact. *Hum. Rel.*, 1967, **20**.

DASHIELL, J. F.: An expt. analysis of some group effects. *JASP*, 1930, **25**, 190–199.

Entwistle & Cunningham: Neuroticism and Schol. Attainment: a linear relat. *BJEP*, **38**, 1968.

DAVIS, J. H.: 'Group Performance', 1969.

DAVIS, K. E.: quoted in Jones and Gerard, 'Foundations of Social Psych.' 1967, p. 280.

DEUTSCH, M. & KRAUSS, R. M.: Theories in Social Psychology, 1965.

DEUTSCH, M.: Effects of co-op. and comp. on group process. *Hum. Rel.* 1949, **2**.

DICHTER, E.: Consumer Motivation, 1964, p. 396.

DITTES, J. E.: in *JASP*, 1959, **59**, 77–82.

DORNBUSCH *et al.*: The Perceiver and the Perceived. *JPSP*, 1965, **1**, 434–40.

EDMUNDS, L. F.: Rudolf Steiner Education.

ERIKSON, E. H.: Childhood and Society, 1950, Penguin, 1965, p. 255.

EYSENCK, H. J. & COOKSON, D.: 'Personality in Prim. Sch. Children, 3, Family Background, *BJEP*, June, 1970.

FESTINGER & CARLSMITH: Cog. conseq. of forced compliance. *JASP*, 1959, **58**.

FESTINGER, L.: A. Theory of Social Comparison Processes. 1954, Bobbs-Merill p. 111.

FESTINGER, SCHACHTER & BACK: Social Pressures in Informal Groups. Harper, 1950, also L. Festinger: Architecture and Group Membership, J. Soc., Issues, 1951.

FIEDLER, F.: (*a*) Leadership–a new model; in (145). (*b*) Leader attitudes, gp. climate and gp. creativity. In (65). (*c*) The Contingency Model–in (132).

FIEDLER, F.: in *JASP* 1954, **49**, 381–8.

FIEDLER, F.: Leader attitude and group effectiveness. 1958.

FLANDERS, N. A.: (*a*) Teacher influence in the classroom, 1967. In (234) and (154). (*b*) Analysing Teacher Behaviours, 1970, p. 7.

FREEDMAN, CARLSMITH & SEARS: Social Psychology, 1970, pp. 72–4.

FRIEDMAN I.: Phenomenal, Ideal and Projected Conceptions of Self. *JASP*, **51**, 1955, p. 611–5.

GAGE, RUNKEL & CHATTERJEO: Changing T. behaviour through feedback from pupils.

'Games and Simulations'–B.B.C. Publications, 1972.

GATES, G. S.: An expt, study of the growth of social perception. *J.ED.Ps.*, 1923, **14**.

GERGEN, K. J.: The psych. of behaviour exchange. Addison-Wesley, 1969, for example.

GHISELLI, E. E. & LODAHL, T. M.: Patterns of manag. traits and gp. eff. *JASP*, 1958, **57**.

GIBB, C. A. (ed.): Leadership. Penguin, 1969.

GOFFMAN, E.: The Presentation of Self in Everyday Life, 1959.

GORDON, K.: A study of aesthetic judgements. *J. of Exp. Ps.*, 1923, **6**, 36–43.

GREENSPOON, T.: Reinf. effect of two spoken sounds on frequency of two responses, *Am.J.Ps.*, 1955, **68**.

GRONLUND N.: Sociometry in the Classroom, 1959.

GURNEE, H.: Maze learning in the collective situation. *J. of Psych.*, 1937, **3**, 437–43.

HAMID, P. N.: Birth Order and Family Schemata. *Perc and Motor Skills*, 1970, **31**, 807–10.

HARDING, J. & HOGREFE, R.: in J. of Soc. Issues, 1952, **8** (1).

HARGREAVES, D.: Interpersonal Relations and Education. *R.K.P.*, 1972. see Gorbutt: 'The New Sociol. of Educ.' in Ed. for Teaching, Autumn, 1972.

HARGREAVES, D.: Social Relations in a Secondary School, *RKP*, 1967.

HAVINGHURST, ROBINSON & DORR: The Dev. of the ideal-self in ch. and adol. *J.Ed.Res.*, 1946, **40**.

HAYTHORN, W.: Effects of varying combinations of auth. and equalit. leaders and followers. *JASP*, 1956.

HEINICKE, C. & BALES: Dev, trends in structures of small groups. *Sociometry*, 1953, **16**.

HILTON, I.: Diffces. in behav. of mothers towards 1st and later-born ch. *JPSP*, 1967, **7**.

HOLLANDER & HUNT (eds.): Current Perspectives in Soc. Psych. 2nd, ed., 1967, 3rd ed., 1971.

HOLLANDER & WEBB: Leadership; Followership and Friendship. *JASP*, 1955, **50**, 163–7.

HOMANS, G. C.: Group factors in worker productivity.

HOMANS, G. C.: Social Behaviour as Exchange. *Am. J. of Soc.*, 1958, **63**.

HOVLAND, C. I.: Yale Studies of Communic. and Persuasion.

(*a*) Sherif, Sherif & Nebergall: The Social-judgement-Involvement Approach, 1965.

(*b*) Sherif & Sherif: Attitudes, ego-involvement and change. 1967.

HOYLE, E.: J. of Curric. Studies, 1, 2 May, 1969; also 1, 3 Nov., 1969.

(*a*) M. Shipman: Theory and Practice in the Ed. of Teachers. Ed. Res. 9 June, 1967.

(*b*) W. K. Hoy: Influence of experience on the beginning teacher. *Sch. Rev.* 1968, **76**.

(*c*) Finlayson & Cohen: Teacher's Role; conceptions of students and head-teachers. *BJEP*, 1967.

HUGUENARD *et al.*: Interview time, set and outcome. *Perc. and Motor Skills*, 1970, **31**.

JACKSON, P. W.: T. perceptions of P. attitudes towards school.

JACOBS, BERSCHEID & WALSTER: *JPSP*, 1971, **17**, 1, 84–91.

JAHODA, M.: Conformity and Independence: a psych. analysis. *Hum. Rel.*, 1959, **12**, 99–120.

JECKER, MACCOBY & BREITROSE: Improving Accur. in Interp. non-verbal cues of comp.

JENCKS & RIESMAN: Harvard Educ., Review, 1967.

(*a*) Martin & Westie: The Tolerant Personality. *Am. Soc. Rev.* 1959, **24**.

(*b*) T. F. Pettigrew: Pers and soc-cult. factors in intergroup atts. J. Conflict Resol., 1958, **2**.

KARLINS, M. & ABELSON, H. I.: 'Persuasion'. 2nd ed., 1970. Crosby Lockwood.

KATZ, D.: The functional approach to the study of attitudes. *Pub. Op. Qtly.*, 1960.

KATZ, P. ZIGLER, E.: 'Self-image Disparity'. *JPSP*, 1967, **5**, p. 186–195.

KATZ, SARNOFF & MCCLINTOCK: Motivational Basis of Att. Change. *JASP*, 1954.

KELLEY, H. H. & VOLKART: Resistance to change of group-anchored atts. *Am. Soc. Rev.*, 1952, **17**.

(*a*) N. Kogan & M. A. Wallach: in G. Mandler, 'New Directions in Psych'. Vol. 3, 1967.

(*b*) Bem, Wallach & Kogan: Gp. decision making under risk of aversive cons.

KELLEY, H. H.: Ward-Cold Variable in first Impressions of Persons. *J. of. Pers.*, 1950, **18**.

KELMAN, H. C.: Three processes of Social Influence, 1958. In (249), (63), (64).

KELVIN, P.: The Bases of Social Behaviour, 1969. (*a*) p. 33–36, (*b*) p. 252, (*c*) p. 233.

KNIGHT, M.: 'William James', Penguin, 1950.

KOCH, H. L.: (*a*) Sibling influence on children's speech. J. of Speech Disorders, 1956, **21**. (*b*) in Child Development, 1957, **28**, 175–202.

KRECH, CRUTCHFIELD & BALLACHEY: Individual in Society, 1962. (*a*) ch. 12, (*b*) 438–9, (*c*) 183, (*d*) 498–50.

KUHN, H. H.: Self attitudes by age, sex and prof. training. *Sociol. Qtly*. 1960, **1**.

LANDIS, L.: J. Comp. Psych., vol. 4, 1929, 447–509.

LAPIERE, R. T.: 'Attitudes versus actions'. Soc. Forces, vol. 13, pp. 230–37, 1934.

LAWRENCE, D.: The effects of Counselling on Retarded Readers, Ed. Res., Feb. 1971, **13**.

LEAVITT, H. J.: Some effects of certain communic. patterns on gp. perf. *JASP*, 1951, **46**.

LEBON, G.: The Crowd, 1898.

LEES, J. P. & STEWART, A. H.: 'Family and Sibship Position and Scholastic Ability– *The Soc. Review*. (U.C.Nth. Staffs.), vol. 5, 1957, pp. 85–106 and 176–189.

LEWIN, K.: Group decision and Social Change.
see E. B. Pelz: Some factors in group decision.

(*a*) Janes & King: Influence of Role-playing on Opinion Change. *JASP*, 1954, 211–18.

(*b*) King & Janis: Improvised and non-impr. role-playing and op.changes. *Hum. Rel.*, 1956, 177–85.

(*c*) Mann & Janis: Long-term effects of Emotional Role-play. *JPSP*, 1968, **8**.

(*d*) L. Mann: in *J. Exp. Soc. Psych*, 1967, **3**, 334–48.

LIKERT, R.: An overview of new patterns of management, 1961.

LINDESMITH & STRAUSS: *Soc. Psych.*, 3rd ed., 1968, Chap. 14, 'Selves and Roles', p. 326.

LIPPITT, R. & WHITE, R. K.: An exptal. study of leadership and group life.

LUCHINS, A. S.: in C. Hovland, 'The Order of Presentation in Persuasion', 1957.

MACCOBY, NEWCOMB & HARTLEY: Readings in Social Psychology. Vol. 3, 1959.

MAIER & SOLEM: Contrib. of disc. leader to quality of group thinking. *Hum. Rel.* 1952, **5**.

MANIS, M.: Soc. Interaction and the Self-concept. *JASP*, **51**, 1955, p. 362–70. Dornbusch & Miyamoto: A test of Interactional Hyp. of Self-conception. *Am.J.Soc.* 1951, 61.

MANN, R. D.: Review of Rel. between Pers. and Perf. in small groups. Ps. Bull., 1959, **56**.

MASLOW, A. H.: 'A Theory of Human Motivation' – *Ps. Rev.*, **50**, July, 1943, B.M. p. 509.

MATHER, D. R.: writing in 'Education', 1968, Feb. 9th and 16th.

MCARTHUR, C.: Personalities of First and Second Children. Psychiatry. 1956, **19**, 47–54.

MCDAVID, J. W. & HARARI, H.: *Social Psychology*, 1967, p. 13.

MCDAVID, J. W. & HARARI, H.: *Social Psychology*, 1967, pp. 417–423.

MCGREGOR, D.: The Human Side of Enterprise, 1960.

MERTON, R. K.: Social Theory and Social Structure, 1959, p. 198.

MILGRAM, S.: Nationality and Conformity. *Scientific American*, 1961, **205**, 45–51.

MILLER & BIERI: Psych. Reports, 1965, **16**, 1203–4.

MILLER, N. *et al.*: Similarity, contrast and complementarity in friendship choices, *JPSP*, 1966, **3**, 3–12.

MILLER, N. E. & DOLLARD, J.: 'Social Learning and Imitation', 1941.

MILNER, D.: 'Effects of Prejudice'. Race Today, Aug., 1969.

e.g. Gurin *et al.*: J. of Soc. Issues, 1969, (XXV, 3).

MINARD, R. D.: Race rel. in the Pocahontas Coalfield. *J. Soc. Issues*, 1952, **8** (1).

MITNICH, L. & MCGINNIES, E.: *FASP*, 1958, **56**, 82–90.

MORENO, J. B.: Who shall survive? 1934.

MORRISON, A. & MCINTYRE, D. (eds.): Social Psychology of Teaching. Penguin, 1972.

MORSE, M.: The Unattached. Pelican, 1967.

MOULY, G. J.: The Psychology of Effective Teaching, 1968, Chap. 4.

NATALE, S.: An experiment in empathy. *NFER*, 1972.

NEWCOMB, T. M.: The Acquaintance Process, 1961.

NEWCOMB, T.: The Prediction of Personal Attraction. In (63) and *BM* S209.
NISBETT, R. E.: B. Order and Participation in Dangerous Sports, *JPSP*, 1968, **8**, 4, 351–353.

OLMSTED, M. S.: The Small Group, 1961, has a few pages on Hawthorne Studies.
OPEN UNIVERSITY: D.283 (1971) The Sociological Perspective. Units 5–8 on soc. inter.
OPEN UNIVERSITY: D.100, Units and Reader.
OPEN UNIVERSITY: E.281, Unit 5.
OPEN UNIVERSITY: E.282, Units 1 and 2, 1971.
OPEN UNIVERSITY: E.282 Reader, 'School and Society', 1971.
OTTAWAY, A. K. C.: Learning through group experience, R.K.P., 1966, p. 157.

PALMER, R. D.: Birth Order and Identification. *J. of Cons. Psych.*, 1966, **30**, 2, 129–135.
PATRICK, J.: A Glasgow Gang Observed. Eyre Methuen, 1973.
PESSIN, J.: Comp. effects of soc. and mech. stim. on memorising, *Am.J.Psych.*, 1933, **45**.
PIDGEON, D. A.: Expectation and Pupil Performance. *NFER*, 1970.
PROSHANSKY & SEIDENBERG: Basic Studies in Soc. Psych. (Readings), 1965.

RABOW *et al.*: *Sociometry*, 1966, **29**, 16–27.
REESE: *JASP*, 1961, **62**, p. 472–4.
RHINE, W. R.: B. Order Diffces. in Conf. and level of Ach, arousal. Ch. Dev., 1968, **39**.
RICHARDSON, E.: Group Study for Teachers. *R.K.P.*, 1967.
RIECKEN, H. W.: Effect of talkativeness on gp. sol. of problems. *Sociometry*, 1958, **21**.
ROGERS, C. R.: The Therapeutic Relationship; in Babladelis and Adams, 'The Shaping of Personality'.
ROKEACH, M.: The nature of attitudes, Int. Encycl. of Soc. Sc. See also (249).
ROSENBERG, M. J.: in *J. of Pers.*, 1960, **28**, 39–63.
ROSENBERG, M.: Society and the Adolescent Self-image, 1965.
ROSENTHAL & JACOBSON: Pygmalion in the Classroom, 1968.
ROSENTHAL, R.: Experimental effects in behavioural research, 1966.
ROSS, E. A.: Social Psychology: an outline and source book, 1908.

ROTHBART, M. K.: B. Order and mother-child interaction in an Ach. sit. *JPSP*, 1971, **17**, 2.

RUBOVITZ, R. C. & MAEHR, M. L.: Pygmalion Analysed. *JPSP*, 1971, **19**, 2. 197–203.

SAMPLE, J. A. & WILSON, T. R.: Leader behav., gp. prod. and rating of LPC, *JPSP*, 1965, **1**.

SAMPSON, E. E. & HANCOCK, F. T.: Ordinal position, personality and conformity, *JPSP*, 1967, **5**.

SARBIN & JONES: An Expt. Analysis of Role Behaviour. *JASP* 1956.

SCHACHTER & SINGER: *Ps. Rev.*, 1962, **69**, 379–99.

SCHACHTER, S. & ZIMBARDO, P. G.: *JASP.*, 1961, **62**, 356–63.

SCHACHTER, S.: Deviation, rejection and communication, *JASP.*, 1951, **46**.

SCHACHTER, S.: The Psychology of Affiliation, 1959, Stanford Univ. Press.

SCHLOSBERG, H.: *J. of Exp. Psych.*, 1952, **44**, 229–237.

SCHUTZ, W. C.: FIRO: A three-dimensional theory of interpersonal behaviour, 1958.

SCOTT, W. A.: Attitude change through reward of verbal behaviour. *JASP*, 1957, **55**, 72–75.

SEBALD, H.: in J. of Communication, 1962, **12**, 142–49.

SECORD & BACKMAN: A. Soc. Ps. View of Education, p. 42–3 gives a summary.

SECORD & BACKMAN: Social Psychology, 1964. See page 67–8.

SEMEONOFF, B. (ed): Personality Assessment, Penguin, 1966. Article 18 by A. L. Edwards on 'Social Desirability and Personality Test Construction'.

SHERIF, M.: A study of some social factors in perception. *Arch. Psych.*, 1935, 187

SHERIF, M.: Group Conflict and Co-operation.

SILVERMAN, I.: Self-esteem and Diff. Resp. to Success and Failure, *JASP*, 1964 **69**, 1.

SLATER, P. E.: Contrasting correlates of group size. *Sociometry*, 1958, **21**, 129–39.

SMITH, P. B. (ed.): Group Processes. Penguin, 1970. Especially article by Shaw.

SOLOMON, D.: Birth order, family composition and teaching style. *Ps. Reports*, 1965, **17**.

SOUCAR, E.: in Perceptual and Motor Skills, 1970, **31**, 19–24.

STEINER, I. D. & JOHNSON, H. H.: in *JASP*, 1963, **67**, 388–391.

STEPHAN, F. F. & MISHLER, E. G.: Distr. of Partic. in Small Groups. *Am. Soc. Rev.*, 1952, **17**.

STONEQUIST, E. V.: The Marginal Man, Scribner, 1937. See also (136d).

SULLIVAN, H. S.: Conceptions of Modern Psychiatry, 1953.
SUTTON-SMITH, B. & ROSENBERG, B. G.: 'The Sibling', 1970 (*a*) 15, (*b*) 110–112, (*c*) 92–3, (*d*) 85, (*e*) 82–3, (*f*) 66–8, (*g*) 75, (*h*) 73–5, (*i*) 137, (*j*) 101–3, (*k*) 34–8.

TABA, H.: Curriculum Development, 1962, chapters 23 and 24 especially.
TAFT, R.: The Ability to Judge People. Ps. Bull, 1955, **52**, 1–23.
TAYLOR, D. W., BERRY & BLOCK: in Admin. Sc. Qtly, 1958, **3**, 23–47.
THELEN, H. A.: in *Sch. Rev.* 1949, **57**, 139–48.
THIBAUT, J. W. & KELLEY, H. H.: The Soc. Psych. of Groups, 1959.
THOMAS, K. (ed): Attitudes and Behaviour. Penguin, 1971.
THORNDIKE, R. L.: 'On what type of task will a group do well?' *JASP*, 1938. **33**, 409–13.
THORNDIKE, R. L.: Review of 'Pygmalion in the Classroom'. *Am. Ed. Res. Jour.*, Nov., 1968, see also the Nov. 1969 issue for Rosenthal's reply.
TOMAN, W.: (*a*) Sibling Pos. of a sample of Distinguished Persons. *Perc. and Motor Skills*, 1970, **31**. (*b*) The duplication theorem of Social Relationships–. *Ps. Review*, 1971, **78**, 5.
TORRANCE, E. P. & ARSAN, K.: Ex. study of hom. and het. gps. for creat. sc. tasks, 1961.
TORRANCE, E. P.: 1955; in Hare, Borgatta and Bales (eds), 'Small Groups'.
TRIANDIS & TRIANDIS: Cross-cultural study of Social Distance. Ps. Monog. vol. 76, no. 540.
TRIANDIS, H. C. & L. M.: Race, Social Class, Religion and Nationality–Soc. Distance. *JASP*, 1960.
TUCKMAN, B. W.: Devel. Sequences in omall Groups. *Ps. Bull*, 1965, **63**.

VERNON, P. E.: *in J. of Soc. Psych.*, 1933, **4**, 42–58.
VERNON, P. E.: Personality Assessment, Methuen, 1963.
VINACKE, WILSON & MEREDITH: Dimensions of Social Psychology. (Readings).

WALLER, W.: The Sociology of Teaching, 1965.
WALSTER, E.: The assignment of responsibility for an accident. *JPSP*, 1966, **5**, 508–16. See also Hastorf, Schneider and Polefka, 'Person Perception', 1970, on attr. theory.
WARR, P. B. (ed.): Thought and Personality, Penguin, 1970, for Leach, Rokeach, Harvey etc.
WARWICK, D.: Tesm. Teaching. *U.L.P.*, 1971.

WAY, L.: 'Alfred Adler – an introd. to his psych.' – Penguin, 1956, p. 72–81.
A. Adler: Social Interest: a challenge to mankind. Faber & Faber, 1945.

WHYTE, W. F.: Corner Boys; a study of clique behaviour, 1941, also in *BM* S311.

WILLIS, R. H.: Conformity, independence and anticonformity. *Hum. Rel.*, 1965. Also (63) (64) (65).

WINCH, R. F. *et al.*: in *JASP*, 1955, **51**, 508–13.

WISHNER, J.: Re-analysis of 'Impressions of Personality', *Ps. Rev.*, 1960, **67**, 2, 96–112.

WOODWORTH, R. S.: Experimental Psychology, 1938.

WRIGHTSMAN, L. S.: Contemporary Issues in Soc. Psych. (Readings), 1968.

WYLIE, R. C.: The Self Concept: a crit. survey of recent lit., 1961, Un. Nebraska Press.

ZAJONC, R. B.: Attitudinal Effects of Mere Exposure, *JPSP*, 1968, **8**.

ZAJONC, R. B.: 'Social Psychology: an experimental approach', 1966, chap. 2.

ZELDITCH, M.: Role differentiation in the nuclear family. In Parsons & Bales, 1955.

ZIMBARDO & EBBESEN: 'Influencing Attitudes and Changing Behaviour'. 1969, (*a*) 123–8, (*b*) 102.

L. Festinger: A Theory of Cognitive Dissonance, 1957, abridged in (63).

ZIMBARDO & FORMICA: *J. of Pers.*, 1963, **31**, 141–62.

Index